The Science of Emotion

◆

Research and Tradition
in the Psychology of Emotions

Randolph R. Cornelius

Vassar College

Prentice Hall, Upper Saddle River, New Jersey 07458

Library of Congress Cataloging-in-Publication Data

CORNELIUS, RANDOLPH R.
   The Science of emotion : research and tradition in the psychology
of emotions / Randolph R. Cornelius.
     p. cm.
   Includes bibliographical references and index.
   ISBN 0–13–300153–9
   1. Emotions. I. Title.
BF531.C595   1996
152.4—dc20   95–37946
                                                 CIP

Acquisitions editor: Heidi Freund
Editorial/production supervision: Merrill Peterson
Buyer: Tricia Kenny
Interior design: Joan Stone
Editorial assistant: Jeff Arkin
Cover photo: "Tears" © Man Ray Trust ADAGP/ARS 1996

© 1996 by Prentice-Hall, Inc.
Simon & Schuster/A Viacom Company
Upper Saddle River, New Jersey 07458

Printed in the United States of America

10 9 8 7 6 5 4 3 2 1

ISBN 0-13-300153-9

PRENTICE-HALL INTERNATIONAL (UK) LIMITED, *London*
PRENTICE-HALL OF AUSTRALIA PTY. LIMITED, *Sydney*
PRENTICE-HALL CANADA INC., *Toronto*
PRENTICE-HALL HISPANOAMERICANA, S.A., *Mexico*
PRENTICE-HALL OF INDIA PRIVATE LIMITED, *New Delhi*
PRENTICE-HALL OF JAPAN, INC., *Tokyo*
SIMON & SCHUSTER ASIA PTE. LTD., *Singapore*
EDITORA PRENTICE-HALL DO BRASIL, LTDA., *Rio de Janeiro*

Contents

___3___

Listening to the Cries and Whispers of the Articulate Body: The Jamesian Perspective

___4___

Feeling is Thinking: The Cognitive Perspective   112

_5_

Emotions and the Politics of Everyday Life: The Social Constructivist Perspective   *149*

_6_

Of Elephants and Blind Men: Comparing the Darwinian, Jamesian, Cognitive, and Social Constructivist Perspectives on Emotion   *184*

___ 7 ___

This book is dedicated

to the memory of my mother,
Arlene Powley Cornelius,

to the memory of my colleague and friend,
Shula Sommers,

and to my love,
Alice Mulder.

Preface

After completing his review of the scientific literature on the psychology of emotions, William James commented that he would rather "read verbal descriptions of the shapes of the rocks on a New Hampshire farm as toil through them again" (James, 1890/1983, p. 1064). Psychologists who write textbooks on emotion love to quote James' comment because the literature on the psychology of emotions is indeed vast and some of it is indeed quite tedious to read. Moreover, like the rocks on a New Hampshire farm in the spring, more and more scientific studies of emotion keep appearing all of the time. After completing *my* review of the scientific literature on emotions, I know just how James felt. However, I don't feel as exhausted as James seems to have felt, primarily because the state of the literature on emotions in psychology and related disciplines is not quite the same as it was in his day.

James' aversion to reading the literature on emotions was linked to his observation that the existent work on emotions had

> nowhere a central point of view, or a deductive or generative principle. They distinguish and refine and specify *in infinitum* without ever getting on to another logical level. Whereas the beauty of all truly scientific work is to get to ever deeper levels. (James, 1890/1983, p. 1064)

To be sure, there are still many scientific studies of emotion published today that merely "distinguish and refine and specify;" this is part of what the everyday work of science is all about—this is Thomas Kuhn's idea of "normal science" (see Kuhn, 1962). Unlike the state of things when James was writing, however, today there *is* a coherence to the literature on emotion. While there doesn't seem to be the "central point of view" that James hoped for, most contemporary scientific research on emotions, it may be argued, exemplifies a relatively small number of points of view, four to be exact. Each of these points of view, or perspectives, has something different to say about emotions and each defines emotion in a somewhat different manner. Further, each could be said to embody a somewhat different "generative principle" or guiding idea of the kind James sought in vain in the scientific literature of his day.

The aim of this book is to introduce you to the science of emotion and to describe the four major theoretical perspectives on emotion in contemporary psychology, presenting you with the central guiding idea of each, as well as the classic and contemporary research associated with each. As a teacher, I'm fond of giving my students lots of examples to illustrate the sometimes arcane concepts of psychology and I also love to tell stories. In writing this book, *my* generative principle has been the idea that you and I are in a classroom together exploring the landscape of contemporary emotion theory and research and how it got to be the way it is today. Thus, I've tried to do in this what I do in the classroom, namely, tell stories and give examples with the aim of getting to the "deeper levels" of contemporary thinking about emotion.

The process of writing this book has involved a number of revelations for me, and not a few changes of opinion. When I talk about the role of theories in scientific research in my laboratory course in social and personality psychology, I have my students read a paper by the political scientist William Connolly on "theoretical self-consciousness" (Connolly, 1974). Connolly argues that theories are responsibly formulated when theorists make a genuine effort to examine closely the moral import of their theories and to confront their favored theories with those that oppose them. For Connolly, this is not only sound ethical practice, it also makes for good science, for examining one's theory from the perspective of opposing theories may reveal weaknesses or shortcomings in one's theory or bring to light new information one has not previously noticed that supports it. The process may also reveal the strengths of theories one has previously rejected.

In writing about the four theoretical traditions in emotion research and theory, I took Connolly's advice to heart and seriously tried to set my own biases aside and to confront the theories within each of the perspectives on their own terms. What I discovered was that I had quite a few biases about what were good and bad theories of emotion. Socialized into the psychology of emotion as a social constructivist, I had always given the more biologically oriented theories of emotion somewhat short shrift. Weighing the evidence in favor of such theories for this book has convinced me that doing this was a mistake. I now think I have a much better sense of the strengths and weaknesses of a set of theories whose validity I once took for granted. If nothing else, writing this book has convinced me of the need to take an ecumenical and integrative approach to the study of emotions considered in all of their contrary complexity.

Every work of science is a collaborative work, if only in the sense that the work unfolds within a community of other scientists who serve as sources of ideas, inspiration, and criticism. Books about science are no exception. Although they have not been collaborators in the formal sense, and so cannot be held accountable for whatever errors there may be in this book, there are many people without whom this book would not have been written. I would first like to thank Dierdre Cavanaugh, who initially suggested the idea of writing a book on emotion to me and kept bugging me until I actually began it. I thank Anne Constantinople, Jannay Morrow, Alice Mulder, Janeen Armm, Jennifer Oken, the students in my social psychology course and advanced social psychology seminar, and several reviewers for their helpful comments on the many draft versions the manuscript for this book went through: Sheila Woody (Yale University), Randy Larson (University of Michigan), Craig Smith (Vanderbilt University), Ross Buck (University of Connecticut), Earl Thomas (Bryn Mawr College), Robert Mauro (University of Oregon), James R. Averill (University of Massachusetts), and Douglas Grimsley (University of North Carolina, Charlotte). I thank Pete Janzow and Heidi Freund for their much-appreciated editorial support, and Lauren Root for her invaluable copyediting. I thank Michele Tugade for her incredible efficiency and good humor as my research assistant. I thank Michael Westerman for the material on social constructivism he suggested to me and our many intellectually stimulating walks around the Vassar campus. I thank Wendy Graham for helping me get a better sense of William James as a person. I thank Eric Amsel, Judi Amsel, Jay Bean, Leon Dreyfus, and Carolyn Palmer for the materials they so kindly lent me. I thank Nancy MacKechnie, Curator of Rare Books and Manuscripts, Shirley Maul, Head of Readers' Services, and the staff of the Interlibrary Loan Office of the Vassar College Library who more than anyone else made this book possible. I thank Sue Ann Tasselmyer and Gail Garrison for their help on too many aspects of this project to enumerate. I thank Ilana Laurence for her help in finding material I needed in the libraries of Paris. I thank Fritz Strack, Robert Plutchik, Joseph LeDoux, Ira Roseman, Paul Ekman, and Richard Lazarus for allowing me to reprint material from their works. I thank Brother Michael Grace, S.J., for his help in tracking down the photograph of Magda Arnold, Wanda Matsubayashi for her help in obtaining the photographs from Paul Ekman's collection, and Fritz Strack for his photographs. I thank Kimberly and Mark from Niles Associates for being there in times of computer crisis. I thank Anne Constantinople, Alice Mulder, Helen and Bill Mulder (my grammar coaches), and my father, Ernest Cornelius, for their enthusiastic and unwavering support of me through the many ups and downs of the researching and writing involved in this book. Finally, I thank my son, Geoffrey Gray-Cornelius, for being such a source of inspiration and a constant reminder of how wonderful life is. Incidentally, the theme music that accompanied my writing was provided by J. S. Bach's *Musical Offering*, the Chills, and the Mekons.

Randy Cornelius

Emotions in Science and Everyday Life

This is a book about emotions. It is about joy, love, anger, fear, happiness, guilt, sadness, embarrassment, hope, and many other emotions as well. It is about the way the muscles in your neck and shoulders tense up and it becomes difficult to control your voice when you have just been insulted. It is about the way the skin around your best friend's eyes crinkles up when she smiles. It is about the hollow feeling in your chest and the constriction you feel at the back of your throat when you realize someone who has died is never coming back. It is about the way you notice your heart beating furiously immediately after the heroine in the movie you're watching has escaped the mortal danger she was in. It is about the way tears begin to form in the corners of your eyes when your child's soccer team wins a difficult game. It is about the way you mutter a curse under your breath and pound your fist lightly on the table when you remember how a teacher treated you unfairly 20 years ago. It is about the way you suddenly realize that your relationship with a new friend has been transformed, perhaps forever, when he expresses his anger over something you said to him. It is about the way you feel your body aglow when you gaze into the eyes of your beloved.

This is also a book about science and scientific traditions. It is about how scientists look for patterns or regularities in nature and then try to explain them. It is about the ways in which scientists formulate and test their ideas about the world. It is about how scientists take their own experiences and, using the methodology of science, check to see if other people experience the world in the same way. It is about the ways in which groups of scientists come to an agreement about the best way to define, study, and explain a phenomenon. And it is about the ways in which scientists sometimes bitterly differ, for sound reasons and in good faith (and sometimes for not-so-sound reasons and in not-so-good faith), with other scientists who don't share their views about how to go about explaining a particular phenomenon.

This is, to be precise, a book about the science of emotion and four of the theoretical traditions that have shaped thinking and research on emotion in psychology for the past 125 years, give or take a decade or two. People have been studying emotions for a lot longer than 125 years, of course. Emotions have been the object of intense interest in both Eastern and Western philosophy since before the time of Lao-Tzu (sixth century B.C.) in the East and of Socrates (470–399 B.C.) in the West, and most contemporary thinking about emotions in psychology can be linked to one Western philosophical tradition or another (see Calhoun & Solomon, 1984). However, the beginning of modern, scientific inquiry into the nature of emotion is thought by many to be Charles Darwin's book on emotional expression in animals and humans, which was published in 1872. Thus, in exploring what I consider to be the four most influential theoretical perspectives in the study of emotion, I begin with the work of Darwin. Besides, psychology has also only been around as a self-consciously scientific discipline for 100 years or so (give or take an argument or two).

Why Study Emotions?

There is a rich tradition in American literature and popular culture of stories about emotional oddballs, people whose emotions are perverse or twisted out of shape, or who have too much or too little emotion. One of my favorite characters in this genre is Jacob Horner, the "hero" of John Barth's novel *The End of the Road*. Horner suffers from an inability to become emotional, to make decisions or commitments. His lack of emotion is disturbing, for to be without emotion is to somehow be less than fully human. James Averill, a contemporary American emotion theorist, points out that people who do not feel emotion are viewed with suspicion, and, at least as it is represented in American popular culture, such suspicion may be justified (see Averill, 1985). The "pod people" in the film *Invasion of the Body Snatchers*, who slowly and insidiously take over Earth by replacing humans with pod-birthed duplicates, are human in every way save one, they do not have emotions—after all, they are vegetables! (There seems to be a particular fascination with such creatures, as there have now been two remakes of the original 1955 film.)

Although it occasionally might be nice to have some respite from the tempests and storms or just dull sloshings of our own and others' emotions, it is difficult to imagine what human life would be like without them. As the philosopher Martin Heidegger (1889–1976) argued (Heidegger, 1927/1962; see Calhoun & Solomon, 1984), our entire consciousness of the world, and this includes our consciousness of ourselves, is suffused with emotion. A recent study by Oatley and Duncan (1994), in which a group of adults was asked to keep a diary of their daily emotional experiences, found that the subjects under study reported they experienced on the average one emotion a day "strongly enough to cause bodily symptoms, thoughts coming involuntarily to mind, or urges to act" (pp. 376–377). The majority of the emotions reported by the subjects, moreover, lasted 5 minutes or longer, with 33% of the emotions lasting 30 minutes or longer. When you add to these relatively intense daily experiences the much less obtrusive moods that continually wax and wane in our consciousness throughout the day, you get a sense of how ubiquitous emotions are. Experience without emotion is like a day without weather. Emotions are the very stuff of what it means to experience the world. It makes sense, then, that the subject matter of thousands of novels, poems, films, newspaper stories, and tabloid headlines is, in one way or another, emotion.

Why I Study Emotion

I became interested in studying emotion after my mother had a serious automobile accident during my first year of college. My mother came through the accident with only a few bruises, but her car was completely destroyed. Quite understandably, she developed a powerful fear of riding in cars that lasted for several years. In addition to showing outright distress when she rode in a car, my mother's fear also manifested itself in her insistence that the family only drive the largest, most tanklike cars available. The fear my mother developed as the result of her accident was not what piqued my interest in emotions, however. Her fear of getting in another accident seemed perfectly reasonable to me and her fear even had the effect of making me a more cautious driver. What got me instead was the aversion she developed to wearing seat belts after the accident.

Her fear developed, I discovered, because a State Trooper at the scene of her accident had casually remarked to her as she was being treated that she probably would not have survived the accident had she been wearing her seat belt. Somehow, the fear my mother had of getting in another accident had generalized to the one bit of real protection she would have if she were to have another accident, namely, her seat belt. No matter how much I tried to explain to her that seat belts in fact save many lives and that the trooper was describing a one-in-a-million occurrence, my mother would have none of it. From the day of her accident until the last time she rode in a car, she never wore a seat belt again.

My experience of trying to convince my mother that she was wrong about seat belts made me curious to learn more about whatever was motivating her to be, as I saw it, so unreasonable. I was already somewhat interested in psychology because I had a fondness for Dada and Surrealist art and had done a bit of reading on the psychology of dreams and psychoanalysis. I actually wanted to be some kind of artist at the time, and I busied myself after my classes building "found object" sculptures modeled on the ambiguous stimuli of the projective psychological tests about which I was reading. After my mother's accident, however, I threw myself into the study of fears and phobias and, although I didn't much like my introductory psychology course, declared my major to be psychology and began what has become a lifelong study of emotions.

My motivation to study emotions has now taken on what the personality psychologist Gordon Allport called *functional autonomy.* I now find the many phenomena associated with emotions to be fascinating in their own right. I still marvel, however, just as I did when I used to argue with my mother about seat belts, at how powerful emotions can be in shaping the course of our lives. (In saying this, it is important to recognize that emotions are not merely disruptive experiences, as the example of my mother's fear would suggest. Almost all contemporary students of emotion agree that emotions serve important adaptive functions in our lives. Occasionally, of course, they do get out of whack, but most of the time they are valuable survival tools. Imagine, after all, what it would be like if we did not have a well-founded fear of heights or fast-moving cars. My guess is that few of us would survive childhood.) Even though I think I know a bit more about them now than I did when I began studying them, emotions nevertheless control my behavior as much as they do anyone else's and, at the level of my own everyday experience, they have lost none of their mystery and power.

Why a "Science" of Emotion?

I want to convince you that emotions are fitting and interesting objects of science. Before I can do that, however, I need to say a few things about the nature of science and how scientists study the world.

Science and method. There are many ways to describe science. Science is sometimes thought of as a body of knowledge about the world, although I think this is misleading. Science is concerned not so much with particular kinds of knowledge about the world, but, rather, with *how* knowledge about the world is produced. Science is really nothing more than a particular way of gathering knowledge about the world. When one speaks of the "scientific method," however, one isn't speaking of a particular set of techniques for studying the world, one is speaking of a set of criteria one's methods must fulfill in order to be considered scientific.

The philosopher Rom Harré defines the scientific method as "a disciplined and orderly way of finding answers" (1981, p. 20). The key to understanding what science and the scientific method are all about is in the words "disciplined and orderly." Science grew out of people's everyday attempts to understand the underlying properties or causes of events in the world, but scientific knowledge about the world is different from our intuitive or unscientific knowledge about it. However richly detailed our intuitive knowledge, it is rarely acquired in a systematic manner, and we rarely subject it to tests of validity. In contrast, the scientific method involves the collection of *systematic observations* of the world, using *reliable measurements* often obtained under *controlled conditions* in which the events one is studying and the methods one uses to study them are *clearly and precisely defined*, most often using *operational definitions* (Shaughnessy & Zechmeister, 1994).[1]

Central to the scientific enterprise is the notion that the hypotheses or questions scientists entertain about the world must be *testable*. In science, it does no good to offer a hypothesis about the world if it is not, at least in principle, testable. Modern science, and this includes psychology, is *empirical*. The empirical approach to the acquisition of knowledge requires *direct observation* as the primary way to answer questions about the world. When a scientist offers a hypothesis—an educated guess based on existing scientific theory and evidence—about the way the world works, she or he must submit that hypothesis to a rigorous test that involves systematically gathering evidence (*data*) relevant to the hypothesis. This is done in such a way as to minimize errors of measurement, hence the need for precise definitions and reliable measurements, and to avoid contamination of the data by any preconceptions or biases the scientist might have about the way the data "should" look (see Agnew & Pyke, 1994, for an excellent introduction to how scientific research is conducted).

Scientists refer to the events they measure as *dependent variables* and to the events they study that influence dependent variables as *independent variables*. *Experiments*, situations in which a researcher manipulates the values of one or more independent variables to assess their effects on one or more de-

---

[1]In *operational definitions*, concepts are defined by reference to observable events or by the methods or "operations" used to produce them. Anxiety, for example, is a purely theoretical concept until we say something like, "Anxiety, for the purposes of this study, is defined as the number of times a person bites her fingernails in a 1-hour period."

pendent variables, are only one of the many methodologies available to scientists and should not be confused with the empirical approach itself. In this book you will encounter many recent examples of both experimental and nonexperimental research on emotions. Although their methods may differ, all of them are empirical studies.

Theories and data. Central to the scientific enterprise are *theories.* Theories are more or less well-organized sets of statements about the way a scientist thinks the world works. Theories organize our knowledge about the world and allow us to understand and explain events in the world, often by reference to unseen or unobservable factors. Darwin's theory of evolution by natural selection, for example, allows us to organize a huge body of information about the anatomical features of different animals, both living and extinct. Darwin's theory allows us to relate the flippers on whales and dolphins to the legs of terrestrial creatures and gives us a pretty good idea of why the flippers of whales and dolphins are the way they are. Theories also allow us to make predictions about the way the world "should" work. Using Darwin's theory, for example, we can predict when a particular species will most likely undergo some kind of change in its morphology (see Weiner, 1994, for a wonderful set of examples of this kind of prediction).

When scientists offer hypotheses about the world, this is done with the aim of testing not only the specific hypotheses involved, but also the larger theory from which they are derived. By means of subjecting hypotheses to empirical tests in this manner, theories, and the descriptions of the world they embody, are refined. In principle, when a hypothesis is not supported by the evidence collected to test it, the theory of which it is a part is modified accordingly. In practice, more often than not, hypotheses are rejected long before theories are modified to any great degree. Recognition of this has led many scientists and philosophers of science to offer "revisionist" accounts of the way science operates (see McGuire, 1983). Part of the revisionist view of science concerns the relationship between theory and data.

People sometimes think that scientific knowledge is built "from the ground up," that scientists simply go out and gather data, compile those data so that empirical regularities of the world are revealed, and then offer theories to account for those regularities. More data are then collected in order to test the theories. This is a very common but misleading way to think about the relationship between theory and data, however. Data about the world do not come to us undefined. Theories themselves define what is to count as data. Data gathering is thus a theoretically driven event (Kuhn, 1962). What one theory considers data, another may consider noise or error. Some psychologists who study emotion, for example, argue that the way people interpret the events they encounter in their environment determines their emotions. For these psychologists, what people say about the events that give rise to their emotions is of vital importance. Psychologists whose focus is on the facial expressions associated with particular emotions may find this kind of information of little theoretical interest or value.

Science and tradition.   In addition to being a particular way of gathering knowledge about the world, science may also be seen as a form of organized social activity. Scientists don't just sit around in their laboratories and experiment on the world; every scientist is part of a community of like-minded scientists within his or her discipline as well as being a member of the community of scientists as a whole. The ideas that scientists have about the world are not based entirely on the results of their own or others empirical investigations of the world either. Every scientist holds a set of assumptions about the way the world works and about the best way to go about exploring and explaining the world that he or she shares with other scientists in his or her discipline. These assumptions influence which kinds of theories scientists find acceptable and which they do not. They also influence what scientific methods they choose to employ in their research and how they analyze their data.

William Connolly uses the term *perspective* to refer to the set of "fundamental *assumptions* or *expectations* [held by scientists] about the 'normal' operation" of the world and the "relatively integrated set of *concepts* within which interpretations of [the world] are constructed "(Connolly, 1974, p. 45).[2] To the extent to which a group of scientists can be said to share the same assumptions about the nature of a particular phenomenon and how to study it, they can be said to share a perspective. To the extent to which the work of a group of scientists who share the same perspective can be related to earlier work by scientists who also shared their perspective, the work can be said to be part of a tradition. Throughout the book, I use the terms *perspective* and *tradition* interchangeably to refer to the broad agreement one can find within certain groups of psychologists about what emotions are all about and how to study them. The four theoretical perspectives on emotion I referred to earlier each embody very different assumptions about the nature of emotion, and because of this, research carried out within the tradition of research each has engendered often looks very different from research carried out within the other traditions.

Before I say any more about what the four perspectives are all about,

---

[2]Connolly uses the term to describe the shared assumptions of groups of social scientists about society, but I think the term may be used meaningfully to talk about the shared assumptions that scientists have about the natural world as well. *Perspective,* used in this manner, is similar to Thomas Kuhn's (1962) use of the term *paradigm.* I prefer *perspective* to *paradigm* in this context, however, because the former is much less global. Psychologists whose work represents different perspectives may nevertheless share many assumptions about the general features of the natural world and the conduct of science.

we need to address the important issue of whether or not emotions can and should be studied by science.

Science and emotions.   Emotions, I hope you agree, are certainly interesting objects of contemplation, but are emotions fitting objects of scientific study? Many have claimed they are not. William Proxmire, the former senator from Wisconsin, gave his first "Golden Fleece Award" for wasting taxpayers' money to Elaine Walster (now Hatfield), a psychologist studying romantic love. Proxmire claimed in the press release that accompanied the award that he objected to Walster receiving $84,000 in grant money from the National Science Foundation because

> no one—not even the NSF—can argue that romantic love lies in the realm of science, but also because I believe firmly that even if they spent $84 million, or even $84 billion, they wouldn't come up with anything the great majority of Americans would profit from. Or believe. Or even want to hear about. (Proxmire, 1980, pp. 6–7)

History seems to have proven Proxmire wrong, as there is a booming business publishing books and magazine articles about what scientists have discovered about love and many other emotions. There seems to be a fascination in American culture not only with emotions such as love, anger, and jealousy, among others, but with what "experts" know about these emotions as well. But can scientists, even with the latest technology and millions of dollars in government grants say anything meaningful about something so, well, fuzzy as emotions?

It is my belief, a belief shared by many psychologists, cognitive scientists, and neuroscientists, that science *can* tell us a great many meaningful and interesting things about emotions, even an emotion as seemingly mysterious as romantic love. Nico Frijda, a Dutch psychologist and contemporary student of emotions, argues that the study of emotions has come far enough to formulate a set of "laws" of emotion. Doing this, he says, "implies not only that the study of emotion has developed sufficiently to do so but also that emotional phenomena are indeed lawful" (Frijda, 1988, p. 349). By "lawful," Frijda means showing "empirical regularities," or that it is possible to show that emotions, far from being ineffable or mysterious or impossible to quantify or study objectively, can be shown to display a relatively small set of recurring features and to be caused by sets of circumstances that can be more or less precisely described. For example, one of Frijda's laws of emotion is the Law of Situational Meaning: *"Emotions arise in response to the meaning structures of given situations; different emotions arise in response to different meaning structures"* (Frijda, 1988, p. 349). This law describes why I become angry and not sad or fearful when I discover that someone has stolen my newspaper for the fifth time this month. Because emotions are lawful events, it can be predicted that you would become angry in the same situation as well. Another of Frijda's laws is the Law of Concern: *"Emotions arise in response to events that are important to the individual's goals, motives, or concerns"* (Frijda, 1988, p. 351). This law describes why I, and almost anyone else, would become angry when something I value has been unjustifiably taken from me.

This is not to say that all scientists who study emotion would agree with the list of laws that Frijda postulates. The study of emotion, as we shall see, is an area of science full of controversy. As perhaps befits the study of emotions, strong feelings about how best to think about emotions abound in this area of science. Most students of emotion, however, would agree with Frijda's claim that emotions are amenable to scientific study and that they do display demonstrable regularities. My purpose in writing this book is to introduce you to the science of emotion and to convince you that emotions are appropriate objects of scientific scrutiny. It is also my purpose to introduce you to some of the different ways in which scientists who study emotion have defined and explained emotions.

What Is an Emotion?

Emotions are complex, multifaceted phenomena that have been defined in many different ways by different psychologists. The answer to the question "What is an emotion?" depends on whom you ask and when you ask him or her. As you will see, psychologists in the last 100 or so years have offered a variety of definitions of emotion, sometimes focusing on this aspect of emotion and sometimes on that. The definition of emotion offered by any one psychologist who studies emotions reflects the particular interests of the psychologist, as well as his or her methodological and theoretical predilections and the theoretical traditions and explanatory paradigms within which he or she works. It will also undoubtedly reflect the influence of whatever "movement" happens to be dominating psychology at the time. Theories of emotion developed during the heyday of behaviorism 30 years ago reflect behaviorist ideas in the same way that current theories of emotion reflect the influence of cognitivism. Surveying some of the many answers to the question of what is an emotion and placing those answers in their historical and theoretical context is what this book is all about, of course, and so I'm not going to jump the gun and offer you a definition of emotion that might prejudice your perceptions of the various definitions of emotion you'll encounter in the following chapters. Before we begin exploring some of the answers offered by the psychologists who study emotion, however, let me offer a few comments about the domain of emotional phenomena in lieu of a more precise definition of emotion.

In everyday language, emotions are often equated with *feelings*, and, indeed, feelings, or particular kinds of subjective experiences or bodily sensations, are included in many psychologists' definition of emotion. Most psychologists, however, think of emotions as being much more than feelings, and some psychologists don't even think feelings are very interesting or important aspects of emotion at all! Emotions may also be characterized by *expressive reactions*, such as smiles, frowns, or clenched teeth, by *physiological reactions* of various kinds, such as increases in heart rate or the production of tears, by instrumental and coping *behavior*, such as running, seeking comfort from one's mother, or rubbing one's hands together, and by *cognitions* of various kinds, such as the thought that one has been unjustifiably wronged by another person. Most psychologists would agree that subjective experiences, expressive reactions, physiological reactions, behavior of various kinds, and particular kinds of cognitions comprise the domain of what they consider to be emotion, but they disagree about which of these components is the most important and which should be used to form a definition.

Beyond acknowledging that emotions are multifaceted phenomena, there is often little agreement among psychologists as to what emotions, fundamentally, are all about. As you will see, some psychologists define emotion primarily in terms of expressive reactions, while others define emotion in terms of cognitions, and others define emotions not in terms of their constituent parts but in terms of their *functions* (see Strongman, 1973). Some psychologists even argue that, although emotions may consist of any or all of these components, none of them in isolation can be used to define emotion. Who is right? At the risk of overusing an already overused metaphor, emotion may be likened to the elephant described by the four blind men in the Sufi tale. "The elephant is broad and flat like a wall," said one, feeling the elephant's side. "The elephant is large and round like a tree trunk," said another, feeling one of the elephant's legs. "The elephant is long and narrow," described the third, feeling the elephant's trunk. "The elephant is small and round and tapers to a point," said the fourth, feeling the elephant's tail. Each of the blind men was correct, of course, but only for that part of the elephant he was feeling.

To a great extent, the way a particular psychologist defines emotion depends on what aspect of emotion he or she is attending to and vice versa. All of the various definitions offered over the years by psychologists may be correct for the particular domain of emotional phenomena to which they apply. But each must be recognized as only a partial definition. Beyond saying that emotions consist of subjective experiences, physiological reactions, cognitions, behavior, and expressive reactions, and that emotions serve important functions having to do with how we get along in the world, I'm not going to offer you my own definition of emotion just yet. I'll let the various scientists you'll meet in the following chapters do that. My hope is that you'll come to the various ways of thinking about emotions with an open mind. What I would like you to see is the internal logic of each of the approaches to studying emotion that I survey and how each definition seems right within the context of the particular assumptions made by the psychologist who offered it. I would also like you to be able to evaluate the various ways in which particular psychologists have thought about emotion in the context of what other psychologists have thought about emotion. By comparing the various ways in which psychologists have thought about emotion, I hope you'll get a sense of the strengths and weaknesses of each approach, of what phenomena are best explained by each approach, and of what phenomena are left unexplained by each.

Four Theoretical Traditions of Research on Emotion in Psychology

In surveying contemporary research on emotion in psychology, one can discern four general perspectives on how to go about defining, studying, and explaining emotion. These are the *Darwinian,* the *Jamesian,* the *cognitive,* and the *social constructivist* perspectives (Plutchik, 1980, includes the first two but not the third and fourth in his list of the "four major traditions in the study of emotions"). Each of these perspectives represents a different way of thinking about emotions. Each has its own set of assumptions about how to define, construct theories about, and conduct research on emotion, and each has associated with it its own tradition of research. Although, as we shall see, there is a fair degree of overlap among the perspectives and some emotion theorists' work crosses two or three of the perspectives (this is especially true of the Darwinian and Jamesian perspectives, for example, in the work of Paul Ekman), each ultimately presents a different picture of what emotions are. Each of the perspectives has its own band of loyal scientists who conduct research, sometimes self-consciously, sometimes unself-consciously, that exemplifies "the way things are understood to be" within the tradition. Table 1.1 presents the key ideas of each of the four traditions along with a classic work and an example of contemporary research from each.

Briefly, the Darwinian perspective, as one might expect, focuses on the function of emotions in the context of evolution by natural selection. Since humans share part of their evolutionary history with other primates as well as other mammals, the emotions of humans and primates should be similar and these should show some similarities, especially in function, with the emotions of other mammals. Psychologists who work within this perspective focus on the emotional displays or expressions of humans and other animals, as did Darwin, although some also examine the adaptive functions

TABLE 1.1.　*Four theoretical traditions of research on emotion in psychology*

Tradition	Key Idea	Classic Work	Contemporary Research
Darwinian	Emotions have adaptive functions, are universal	Darwin (1872/1965)	Ekman et al. (1987)
Jamesian	Emotions = bodily responses	James (1884)	Levenson et al. (1990)
Cognitive	Emotions are based on appraisals	Arnold (1960a)	Smith and Lazarus (1993)
Social Constructivist	Emotions are social constructions, serve social purposes	Averill (1980a)	Smith and Kleinman (1989)

evident in other aspects of emotion. The Jamesian perspective consists of various theories inspired by the enormously influential work of William James. Theories of emotion in the Jamesian tradition echo, in one way or another, James' insistence that the experience of emotion is primarily the experience of bodily changes. The cognitive perspective emphasizes the role of thought in the genesis of emotion and focuses on the way emotions follow from the way individuals appraise events in the environment. Appraisal refers to the process of judging the personal significance for good or ill of an event. The social constructivist perspective rejects many of the assumptions about emotions that are made, implicitly or explicitly, by the theories of emotion cast in the Darwinian and Jamesian molds, most notably, the assumption that emotions are primarily biological phenomena. For social constructivists, emotions are cultural constructions that serve particular social and individual ends and they can only be understood by attending to a social level of analysis.

These four perspectives, and the research traditions that embody them, have had and continue to have a lasting impact on how psychologists think about emotions. Even though the theories of Darwin and James are now more than a 100 years old, theories based on their ideas are still very much in evidence. Indeed, a very dramatic renaissance of Darwinian and Jamesian theories has occurred in contemporary psychology. The cognitive perspective, even though in its explicit form much younger than the Darwinian or Jamesian, has had a tremendous impact on current theorizing about emotion as well. The social constructivist perspective, a comparative upstart, has, in the difficult questions it asks about the nature of emotion and the different kinds of data it has introduced into scientific discourse about emotion, enlivened and enriched both the scientific and lay literatures on emotion considerably.

To these four perspectives one could add a fifth, what Plutchik (1980) terms the *neurological* tradition. This perspective has also had a great influence on the psychology of emotion, and some of the most exciting research in the cognitive and Jamesian traditions in the past few years (see, for example, Davidson, 1993; and LeDoux, 1989) draws upon recent work in neurophysiology and neuroanatomy. However, rather than trying to present the neurophysiology of emotion as a separate tradition of research, I have instead chosen to weave physiological and neurophysiological research, where relevant, into the discussions of the other four traditions. I have also included a brief overview of the neurophysiology of emotion as an appendix. Interested readers who want more detail should consult the excellent review of the neurophysiology of emotion by Joseph LeDoux (1986) or the section on emotion, edited by LeDoux, in Gazzaniga (1995).

The Methodology of Emotion

As you will see, psychologists and other students of the emotions have employed many means in their studies. The methods one chooses depend to a very large extent, of course, on what aspect of emotion one is studying. If one is interested in subjective experience, one typically uses some form of *self-report* methodology. There are many different kinds of self-reports one might obtain from people, depending on one's specific interest. Self-reports of emotion, for example, are widely used in studies in which subjects are placed in an emotion-eliciting situation, say, waiting for an academic examination (e.g., Smith & Ellsworth, 1987) or a "painful injection" (e.g., Schachter, 1959), or are "induced" to experience a particular experience through any of a variety of so-called mood induction techniques (e.g., Morrow & Nolen-Hoeksema, 1990). Studies in which subjects are asked to recall their past emotional experiences are also examples of the use of self-reports. Such reports can range from the very general, as in self-reports of "subjective well-being" (Feist, Bodner, Jacobs, Miles, & Tan, 1995), to the very specific, as in self-reports of episodes of anger (Averill, 1982, see Chapter 5).

Self-reports are also used to obtain information about other aspects of emotional experience. For example, in trying to ascertain the nature of the appraisals involved in fears of spiders, I asked undergraduates who expressed a fear of spiders what it was about spiders that made them fearful (Cornelius & Averill, 1983). In a very different kind of study designed to examine cross-cultural universals in the meaning of emotion (see Chapter 2), Shaver, Wu, and Schwartz (1992) asked groups of subjects in different cultures to sort the names of 135 emotions into categories based on their similarity.

Studies of emotion employing self-report methodologies assume, of course, that people are able and willing to tell researchers what the re-searchers want to know about their emotions. This, it turns out, is a some-what dodgy assumption to make and is one that has occasioned a great deal of controversy in social and personality psychology (Nisbett & Wilson, 1977; Wilson, 1985). First of all, there is the problem of *access* to consider. People may not be able to tell you certain things about their emotions sim-ply because they are things they *can't* tell you about. We would not expect people to have very good access to information about minute changes in the activity of their facial muscles, for example, but we do often expect that peo-ple can describe their emotional experiences of the recent past. As Nisbett and Wilson (1977) have argued, however, the assumption that people can accurately report on even relatively simple aspects of their recent experi-ence is often unfounded.

Apart from whether or not one can be said realistically to have access to certain kinds of information about oneself, is the problem of *memory*. As many psychologists now recognize, memories, even for salient and impor-tant events in our lives, are fragile things. While my memory of how I felt 10 minutes ago may accurately describe how I did indeed feel, my memory of how I felt last week or last year, because of new experiences that I have had or the context of my remembering, may not be accurate at all (Loftus & Lof-tus, 1980). The problems of access and memory are compounded by the problem of *willingness*. The problem here is that people may be all too will-ing to describe their experiences for you, even if they haven't had them and are simply responding to some aspect of the way you are asking them ques-tions about their experience (see Orne, 1962)!

Even though many psychologists are convinced that concerns about the shortcomings of self-report are somewhat overstated, the problem re-mains that self-reports need to be carefully scrutinized for their accuracy, at the very least, and, in the best of circumstances, their use needs to be justi-fied by the theory they are being used to support (see Steinke & Shields, 1992, for an excellent defense of the use of self-reports).

Concerns about the accuracy of self-reports have motivated many stu-dents of emotion to seek out other criteria by which a person's emotional state may be judged. One such set of criteria may be found in the *physiologi-cal changes* that accompany emotions. In *psychophysiology*, the study of the physiological responses that accompany psychological and behavioral events (Wagner, 1988), a combination of self-reports and physiological mea-sures such as heart rate, skin conductance (measurements of the electrical activity of the sweat glands on one's fingers) or electromyographic activity (measurements of the electrical activity produced by muscle movements) are often used as indexes of emotion. For example, Pope and Smith (1994), in a recent study on the differences in the meanings of smiles and frowns, asked subjects to imagine themselves in pleasant or unpleasant scenarios while the electrical activity of the muscles involved in smiling and frowning was monitored. After imagining a pleasant or unpleasant scene, the subjects were also asked to rate their thoughts and feelings on several quantitative scales.

Another set of criteria involves *behavioral indexes* of emotion. Students of emotion interested in behaviors such as facial expressions may directly observe subjects' facial expressions under a variety of conditions, as in Friedman and Miller-Herringer's (1991) study of personality differences in emotional expression in public and private situations. In the facial-expression *judgment* studies of Ekman and his colleagues (for example, Ekman & Friesen, 1971, see Chapter 2), subjects are asked to try to match photographs of facial expressions with the emotions they are supposed to express. Combining behavioral observations with psychophysiological monitoring, Ekman, Davidson, and Friesen (1990) describe how to discriminate true smiles of enjoyment from other types of smiles (see Chapter 3). In facial-expression *manipulation* studies, subjects' faces are manipulated into those characteristic of particular emotions and their self-reported affect is assessed, as in a recent study by Keltner in which the "directed facial action task" was used to produce facial expressions of embarrassment and amusement (Keltner, 1995, see Chapter 3), or the physiological changes induced by the facial manipulation are monitored, as in the studies of Levenson and his colleagues (e.g., Levenson, Ekman, & Friesen, 1990, see Chapter 3).

These few examples in no way exhaust the many different methods used by students of emotion in their research, but they do suggest the range of different methods they use to obtain information about people's emotional experience or evoke emotions in them. With regard to the latter, notice that, in studying emotion, one may actually expose subjects to an emotion-evoking event by, say, showing them a film or video or series of photographs or even a real emotion-eliciting object such as a spider (I confess I did this in graduate school), or have them simply imagine emotion-evoking events. Such mood induction procedures have been found to be surprisingly effective in producing emotion in people, even within the sterile confines of the laboratory (see Gerrards-Hesse, Spies, & Hesse, 1994, for a review of these procedures).

The methods one uses to study emotion, whether they be self-report, psychophysiological, or behavioral, with real or imagined emotion-eliciting stimuli, depend not only on the object of one's study but on the theoretical perspective within which one is working, as these specify what is to be counted as data within the perspective. For example, because emotion words and how they are defined and used are of utmost importance to researchers working within the social constructivist perspective, they are more likely to use self-report methodologies. Jamesians, with their focus on the physiological patterns associated with different emotions, are more likely to use psychophysiological methods. There are exceptions, of course (e.g., see Shaver et al., 1992), but more often than not certain methods tend to cluster within the various theoretical traditions. Much more could be said about the methods used by researchers within the various perspectives, but let's examine them within the context of a full exposition of what the different perspectives are all about.

Plan of the Book

In the chapters that follow, I will introduce you to the Darwinian, Jamesian, cognitive, and social constructivist perspectives, with a chapter being devoted to each perspective. In each chapter, I place each of the perspectives in historical context, describing the major figures associated with each of the perspectives as well as the important works that served to introduce the important ideas of each perspective. Each chapter includes a discussion of the major assumptions of the perspective in question as well as the kinds of questions asked by researchers working within the perspective. Where appropriate, I've included a discussion of some of the major controversies associated with each of the perspectives. Each of the chapters concludes with a description of several examples of current research representative of the perspective under discussion and with suggestions for further reading.

In the next-to-last chapter of the book, I present a comparison of the four perspectives in terms of how each accounts for some of the emotions we all experience in everyday life. By this, I mean your life and my life. One of my strongest beliefs is that science should be able to enlighten us about our everyday experience, and so I've tried to write this book so that I speak to two parts of you, namely, you, the student of psychology, and you, the student of everyday life. The book ends with a brief chapter about the practical implications of the results of some of the research associated with each of the four traditions.

Throughout the book, I present the research associated with each of the perspectives in considerable detail. I've done this because I believe it is important for you to see "up close" what scientific research on emotion looks like but also to give you enough information so that you can make informed decisions about the adequacy of the research yourself. I also want to convince you, of course, that it is possible to conduct valid and meaningful scientific research on the phenomena associated with emotion. Throughout the book, I've also tried to present a little bit of myself. One always reveals something about oneself in one's scientific work in the phenomena one chooses to study and the way one goes about studying and explaining those phenomena, but, in this book, I've tried to be a little more explicitly personal, and, to that end, I've used many examples from my own life. This is not because I think my own experiences necessarily provide better examples than anyone else's, but as a teacher I've always believed that one of the best ways to get students involved in science is to help them see its relevance to their own everyday experience. I've tried to do that both through offering "thought experiments" for you to do that involve your own experience and by describing my experiences in the hope that you'll see your own experiences reflected in mine.

I've also tried to make the book a little more personal for another reason. Socrates said an unexamined life is not worth living. Psychology, and, more generally, science, are, I think, among the most powerful tools one can use to meaningfully examine one's life. As I'm fond of telling my students, an unexamined psychology is not worth doing either. Although it should not and cannot be the final test, I believe that it is useful for people to test the adequacy of the theories psychology offers by trying them out on themselves. In addition to asking, "How valid is this theory or piece of research?," one should also ask, "How well does this account for my own experience?" Research that fails to account for our own experience is not necessarily invalid, of course, but the exercise of sizing up a theory by comparing it with our own experience may point out factors the theory does not take into account. The exercise can then be used to further develop and refine the theory, thus advancing science, or pointing out something we haven't recognized in ourselves, thus advancing our self-knowledge. Either way, we will have learned something. One of my undergraduate teachers, the great humanistic psychologist Sidney Jourard, firmly believed that only good would come out of the confrontation of scientific psychology with personal experience. It is my hope that this book will provide you with some of the tools you will need to think critically about scientific research on emotion in psychology and about emotions in your own life.

Further Reading

AGNEW, N. M., & PYKE, S. W. (1994). *The science game: An introduction to research in the social sciences.* Englewood Cliffs, NJ: Prentice-Hall.

FRIJDA, N. H. (1988). The laws of emotion. *American Psychologist, 43,* 349–358.

LEDOUX, J. E. (1987). Emotion. In F. Plum & V. B. Mountcastle (Eds.), *Handbook of physiology. The nervous system: Vol. 5. Higher function* (pp. 419–459). Washington, DC: American Physiological Society.

Snarling Dogs, Cowering Cats, and Weeping Humans

•

The Darwinian Perspective

> With mankind some expressions, such as the bristling of the hair under the influence of extreme terror, or the uncovering of the teeth under that of furious rage, can hardly be understood, except on the belief that man once existed in a much lower and animal-like condition . . . He who admits on general grounds that the structure and habits of all animals have been gradually evolved, will look at the whole subject of Expression in a new and interesting light.
>
> — Charles Darwin (1872, p. 12)

I teach introductory psychology at least once a year, and I include in the course a fairly in-depth review of contemporary research and thinking about emotion. Almost without exception, every time I begin this section of the course a student will ask how it is that psychologists can scientifically study emotions because emotions are "so personal and private and, anyway, emotions are different for different people." After years of trying to patiently explain the scientific basis for the study of emotion, several semesters ago I decided to try to head this objection off before it happened again.

Now, when I reach the section on emotion the first thing I do—before any student can raise any objections about emotions and science—is to ask for a volunteer to come to the front of the classroom and sit facing the other students. I then tell the student that I am going to show him or her a series of ten cards with the names of emotions on them and that his or her task is to make the appropriate facial expression for each emotion named on the cards. I tell the rest of the class that their task is to guess what emotion the volunteer is trying to express. On my signal, the volunteer then tries to make—one at a time—the facial expressions for anger, sadness, happiness, fear, surprise, disgust, contempt, love, and hope (fear is repeated). After the volunteer has modeled each of the expressions once, I ask the class to tell me what emotion each facial expression was supposed to be. Invariably, I find that there is around 60% to 96% agreement among the students on the facial expressions for anger, fear, happiness, surprise, disgust, and sadness; somewhat lower agreement on the expression for contempt; and very little agreement on the expression for hope. Depending on the student volunteer's ability to come up with an expression for it, there is often also very high agreement for the expression for love. I use these results as a point of departure for a discussion of the ways in which emotions are behavioral phenomena that are very public, and whose form may be very similar for people the world over, making them very amenable to objective, scientific study.

⋅Two aspects of this demonstration of the shared nature of emotional expressions are noteworthy. First, the demonstration represents a very long tradition of thinking about and studying emotions that goes back to Charles Darwin (1809–1882) and, actually, somewhat before him, and, second, not all of my students are convinced by the demonstration that emotions can be studied objectively, the response of those who are not convinced being that emotions are about "feelings" and that feelings can't be studied by science. This chapter is about studying emotions from within the Darwinian tradition and in it you will see the ways in which the ability of my students to identify correctly the emotional expressions of one of their fellow students is an important piece of evidence that supports Darwin's view of emotion. I take up the question of feelings and their place in the study of emotion in the next chapter.

The Darwinian Tradition

What do snarling dogs, cowering cats, and weeping humans have in common? For Darwin and those who have followed him, these emotional displays are part of a great continuum in nature, a continuum of emotional expression from animals to humans that reveals the operation of natural selection on such behaviors. The Darwinian tradition in the study of emotion is associated most often with the research of Paul Ekman and Carroll Izard, although many psychologists share the main tenet of the tradition, namely, the assertion that emotions cannot be understood apart from a consideration of their evolutionary history and their contribution to the survival of both the individual and species. Before describing the current state of research in the Darwinian tradition, we must first go back to Darwin himself and explore his ideas about emotions and where they came from. That means going back to a brief but extraordinarily influential book Darwin wrote toward the end of his life.

Darwin's *The Expression of the Emotions in Man and Animals* (1872)

As he recounts in the autobiography he wrote for his children (F. Darwin, 1904), Darwin's interest in the study of emotion began with the birth of his first child, William, in 1839, and his reading, a year later, of Sir Charles Bell's *The Anatomy and Philosophy of Expression* (Bell, 1840/1877). As soon as William was born, Darwin began to take detailed notes on the infant's development, especially his emotional expressions, for, as he states in his autobiography, "I felt convinced, even at this early period, that the most complex and fine shades of expression must all have a gradual and natural origin" (Darwin, 1904, p. 76). Thus, the study of emotional expression became for Darwin another area in which he could develop his theory of evolution by natural selection. Darwin's keen observations of the emotional expressions of William, his other children, and, seemingly, every human or animal that ever expressed some emotion in his presence, eventually led to the publication in 1872 of *The Expression of the Emotions in Man and Animals*, his last major work.[1]

Originally intended as a single chapter in his *Descent of Man* (1871), Darwin's reflections on the nature and origin of emotional expressions grew into a full-length study that surveyed the available knowledge of expression at the time, offered a simple and comprehensive evolutionary theory of emotional expression, and described in marvelous and painstaking detail the facial expressions and bodily movements that accompany the major emotions in humans and other animals.

Darwin's book is a curious blend of rigorous observation, insightful theorizing, anthropomorphic folk wisdom, and some stories Darwin would have done better to ignore. Darwin had an extraordinary eye for the telling observation but he was also much too credulous in accepting others' reports of animal and human emotional behavior. And so, along with Darwin's accounts of how and why we weep when we are sad, smile when we are happy and knit our brows when we are perplexed, one also finds reports of weeping hippopotamuses and frightened men whose hair turns white

---

[1]Darwin's observations of his son William, begun in 1839, were published as an article in the journal *Mind* in 1877.

FIGURE 2.1. *Charles Darwin and his son William in 1852. (Negatives/Transparencies #326799, Courtesy Department of Library Services, American Museum of Natural History.)*

before the very eyes of onlookers. Darwin, it must be said, also subscribed to the theory, now associated almost exclusively with Jean Baptiste Lamarck (1744–1829), that behavioral traits acquired during one's lifetime could be passed on to one's offspring. This idea, in fact, plays a major role in Darwin's theories about the evolution of various emotional expressions (cf. Fridlund, 1992). But even if we fault Darwin for these mistakes (and it is not at all clear that we should, as there was no theory of genetics in his time), Darwin's influence would remain.

Darwin's legacy to the study of emotion consists of (1) his use of the theory of evolution as a framework for understanding the origin of emotional expressions, (2) the "general principles of expression" that he used to study emotional expressions, and (3) the method he used to test his ideas about the evolution of emotional expression. While some researchers in the

Darwinian tradition question the validity of the general principles of expression Darwin proposed, they are nevertheless firmly committed to the notion that emotional expressions must be understood within the context of evolutionary theory. Moreover, as we shall see, the method Darwin employed to test his ideas has been used by many researchers as a model of how to investigate emotional expression scientifically.

In *Expression of the Emotions* Darwin draws on Bell's treatise for the detailed descriptions Bell offered for various forms of expression (Bell's book was intended to provide artists with anatomically correct depictions of emotional expressions). Darwin, however, strongly disagreed with Bell's claim that the muscles used in emotional expression had been created especially for the expression of emotion only in humans. Bell had argued that, "if we attend to the evidence of anatomical investigation, we shall perceive a remarkable difference between the provision for giving motion to the features in animals, and that for bestowing expression in man" (p. 113). Darwin, of course, believed that nothing could be further from the truth. For, according to Darwin's theory of evolution, there should exist a continuum of emotional expression from animals to humans and the same principles that explain emotional expression in animals should explain emotional expression in humans. How did Darwin explain the emotional expressions of humans and other animals?

For Darwin, perhaps the most important reason emotional expressions take place is because they consist of

> actions [that] are of direct or indirect service under certain states of the mind, in order to relieve or gratify certain sensations desires, &c.; and whenever the same state of mind is induced, however feebly, there is a tendency through the force of habit for the same movements to be performed though they may not be of the least use. (p. 28)

What Darwin means by this can best be illustrated by means of one of his own examples. Anyone who has ever seen a cat alarmed by the approach of a strange dog or the smell of another cat on its owner's clothing will recognize the animal's crouched posture, pulled-back ears and bared teeth (see Figure 2.2). For Darwin, the pulled-back ears that often signal a cat's preparation to pounce or otherwise behave aggressively evolved originally to protect the cat's ears from being bitten during fights with others of its kind. As this action came to be reliably associated with situations involving fighting, it gradually came to be used in *any* situation involving a threat to the animal. Contemporary ethologists (biologists who study behavior) refer to such actions as "intention movements" (Tinbergen, 1952), for they signal an animal's readiness to engage in a more complex pattern of behavior of which the particular movement is a part. Thus, the bared-teeth grimace of an animal, used to threaten an opponent, was originally a part of the action of actu-

Fig. 14. Head of snarling Dog. From life, by Mr. Wood.

Fig. 16. *Cynopithecus niger*, in a placid condition. Drawn from life by Mr. Wolf.

Fig. 15. Cat terrified at a dog. From life, by Mr. Wood.

Fig. 17. The same, when pleased by being caressed.

FIGURE 2.2. *Some of Darwin's illustrations of familiar emotional expressions in animals. (From Darwin, 1872/1965.)*

ally biting another animal. The facial expression that humans make to express disgust was originally associated with the action of actually spitting out some unpleasant food or other foreign substance and is now associated with anything even only metaphorically distasteful (see Rozin & Fallon, 1987). Darwin called the actions upon which our various emotional expressions are based "serviceable associated habits" (Darwin, 1872/1965, p. 28).

To see for yourself the connection between the facial expression for disgust and its "serviceable associated habit," try this little exercise. Go into your bathroom and look in the mirror. First, try to make as neutral or unemotional face as you can. Then, make the best "disgust face" that you can.

Next, go outside and find a nice, fat earthworm, preferably one with some dirt clinging to it. Take the earthworm with you and return to your bathroom mirror. Make a neutral face again and then place the earthworm, dirt and all, into your mouth. Unless you are quite fond of such between-meal snacks, you'll probably feel a very strong urge to spit the worm out of your mouth. As you do, notice carefully the facial expression that you are making; it should resemble very closely the "disgust face" you made earlier. (If you are able to observe your face while you are reading this, it's likely that you are making a disgust face right now.)

Notice that Darwin, by tracing emotional expressions to their presumed underlying action patterns, claimed that emotional expressions evolved not for the purpose of expressing emotion, but for other purposes; it is only because they reliably accompany other actions associated with strong emotion (say, biting an attacker) that we consider them "emotional." In other words, Darwin believed that emotional expressions did not evolve to communicate emotions. In Darwin's words, "Distinct uses, independently of expression, can indeed be assigned with much probability for almost all the facial muscles" (Darwin, 1872/1965, p. 10). As we shall see, many modern students of emotion, while they agree with Darwin that facial expressions have an evolutionary history, disagree with Darwin on this point.

Darwin recognized that his "Principle of serviceable associated Habits" did not explain the origin or function of all emotional expressions and he sought to augment the principle by arguing that

> Certain states of the mind lead to certain habitual actions, which are of service, as under our first principle. Now when a directly opposite state of mind is induced, there is a strong and involuntary tendency to the performance of movements of a directly opposite nature, though these are of no use; and such movements are in some cases highly expressive. (p. 28)

Anyone who has ever had a dog for a pet will immediately understand what Darwin meant by his "principle of Antithesis." When I was a child, my family had an affectionate but not very well-trained German Shepherd named Bridget. Bridget had a wonderful disposition but she also had a very bad habit: she loved to chase motorcycles. We lived on a quiet, dirt road in a semirural part of Florida at the time, and, like our neighbors, we let our dog run free. Whenever a motorcycle would pass by our house, Bridget would run, barking and snarling with vicious abandon, after it. All I had to do, however, was shout her name in my loudest adult voice (loud enough to be heard over the din of the motorcycle) and Bridget would be instantly transformed into a model of docility. She would immediately stop dead in her tracks (well, sometimes) and turn meekly toward me with her back arched, her ears pulled back, and her tail between her legs. To Darwin, her posture and demeanor would represent the antithesis of the aggressive behavior she had displayed just a moment before.

It is interesting to note that, while many of us would interpret Bridget's behavior anthropomorphically as an intentional display of remorse or guilt (my students have argued this point with me many times), Darwin thought that it would be a mistake to link such displays with the attempt by an animal to indicate its changed attitude *voluntarily.* Although Darwin was actually quite fond of attributing human sentiments to dogs, he believed that the relationship between a particular expression and its opposite was purely mechanical and that the two were linked through simple association. "As the performance of ordinary movements of an opposite kind, under opposite impulses of the will, has become habitual in us and in the lower animals, so when actions of one kind have become firmly associated with any sensation or emotion, it appears natural that actions of a directly opposite kind, though of no use, should be unconsciously performed through habit and association, under the influence of a directly opposite sensation or emotion" (Darwin, 1872/1965, p. 65).

Although the principle of serviceable associated habit and the principle of antithesis allowed Darwin to offer explanations for many different emotional expressions, he was not completely satisfied that he had provided explanations for all emotional expressions. For there remained a number of puzzling expressive bodily movements that seemed to him to have little functional value that still required an explanation. These included trembling of the muscles, cries of pain, and screams of rage.

Darwin's explanation for these forms of expression drew upon a very old idea in Western culture, namely, the notion that, whatever it may be, the energy that is produced within our nervous systems in response to various kinds of events in the world, say, for example, being chased by a rabid woodchuck or discovering that your checking account is overdrawn, at certain times simply "overflows." (Suffice it to say that neither Darwin nor anybody else at the time knew very much about the actual workings of the nervous system.) As Darwin put it, "when the cerebro-spinal system is highly excited and nerve-force is liberated in excess, it may be expended in intense sensations, active thought, violent movements, or increased activity of the glands . . . Great pain urges all animals, and has urged them during endless generations to make the most violent and diversified efforts to escape from the cause of suffering" (p. 71). This, in turn, has led to the evolution of a variety of very stereotyped expressive reactions in both animals and humans. According to this notion, the vigorous hand-shaking dance you do after you hit your thumb with a hammer is an effort to almost literally shake free the cause of your pain. The long string of epithets and invectives you utter after bashing your thumb represent the "overflow" of your nervous energy into less "habitual routes," that is, behaviors not directly associated with alleviating pain. (For some of us, such routes become very habitual, something that caused my mother great consternation when I was a teenager).

Before describing the methods he used to test his ideas about emotional expressions, I must say something about Darwin's theory of weeping, for it will serve to nicely summarize his approach to the study of emotions and emotional expressions.

Why Do We Weep? Darwin's Answer

Weeping, for Darwin, was a most curious expression. Associated with great pain and sadness, weeping at first glance seems to serve no purpose; why should the production of tears accompany suffering? Some modern theories of weeping (e.g., William Frey's) assign a literal cleansing action to tears (tears supposedly allow our bodies to drain off some of the toxic byproducts of stress; see Frey and Langseth, 1985). Darwin recognized such a cleansing function, but only in the context of actually washing foreign debris from the surface of the eye. Led by his belief that the origins of most emotional expressions could be traced to some underlying "associated habit," Darwin sought to uncover the nonemotional function of weeping. He found it in the actions of the muscles around the eyes and in the characteristics of respiration during violent activity.

Darwin noticed that, although infants cry and scream quite violently at times, tears do not tend to accompany these actions until the infants are around 6 to 8 months old. Very young infants can produce tears, as Darwin discovered when his coat sleeve accidentally brushed against the eye of one of his own children, presumably William, when the child was 77 days old (p. 152). Nevertheless, Darwin felt that the key to weeping lay in its association with screaming. "[T]here can, I think, be no doubt that the contraction of the muscles around the eyes, during violent expiration or when the expanded chest is forcibly compressed, is, in some manner, intimately connected with the secretion of tears" (p. 167). The most basic and hence original function of tears, Darwin decided, was to protect the eyes during periods of violent screaming. Such behavior leads to an engorging of the blood vessels of the eyes and then to a contraction of the muscles around the eyes to protect them. These both increase the pressure exerted on the eyes by the muscles that surround them. This increase in pressure then stimulates the lachrymal glands to secrete tears. Thus, the secretion of tears evolved to protect the eyes under such circumstances. Weeping came to be an expression of suffering because suffering has long been associated with screaming and other actions that subject the eyes to intense pressure.

Darwin was satisfied that his theory offered an account of weeping (in both humans and other animals) that was in accord with his more general notion that the expressive quality of emotional expressions is essentially an accident. "We must look at weeping as an incidental result, as purposeless as the secretion of tears from a blow outside the eye" (p. 175). The one remaining unanswered question about the experience of weeping, namely, the fact that weeping sometimes results in feelings of emotional release or relief, Darwin dealt with by appealing to the "principle of the direct action of the nervous system." "[B]y as much as the weeping is more violent or hysterical, by so much will the relief be greater,—on the same principle that the writhing of the whole body, the grinding of the teeth, and the uttering of piercing shrieks, all give relief under an agony of pain" (p. 175).

In summary, then, Darwin explained weeping by reference to his principle of "serviceable associated habits." In keeping with his general notion that emotional expressions are remnants of actions that once served some direct purpose for the organism, Darwin saw weeping as a byproduct of the intense pressure put on the eyes during the sometimes intense exertion associated with screaming and crying out. During such episodes, the release of tears serves to protect the eyes. It is through its association with this earlier, direct function that weeping has come to be associated with suffering and sadness. Invoking the principle of "direct action of the nervous system," Darwin further argued that the relief we sometimes feel after weeping is directly related to the level of activity of our nervous system during our suffering. The more intense our agony, the more intense the effort of our nervous system, and hence, the more relieved we feel when this effort has subsided.

Catching Evolution in Progress: Darwin's Method

It is, of course, impossible literally to catch human evolution in progress (although evolutionary research has progressed to the point where it *is* possible to catch the evolution-in-progress of other species, see Weiner, 1994), but Darwin held the belief that one could obtain a glimpse of the evolutionary history of humankind by studying those who he assumed were living examples or exemplars of earlier stages of human development. These included nonhuman animals, especially primates, the "insane," and infants. Darwin also sought to make comparisons between the emotional expressions of Europeans with those of non-Europeans, especially members of less-developed cultures (whom Darwin, like many of his contemporaries, referred to as "savages"), in order to explore the similarities in the emotional expressions of humans regardless of their culture of origin ("for the essence of savagery seems to consist in the retention of a primordial condition," p. 233). To obtain information on the latter, Darwin distributed a questionnaire on emotional expression to a number of missionaries and "protectors of the aborigines" (see Box 2.1). The thirty-six reports Darwin received are sometimes of questionable validity, as are many of the other

---

BOX 2.1

Darwin's Questionnaire on the Emotional
Expressions of Non-Europeans

In an effort to ascertain whether facial expressions of emotion are universal and, hence, innate, Darwin sent a detailed, sixteen-item questionnaire to a number of missionaries, some of whom are identified by name in Darwin's text, who had contact with non-European, aboriginal people in such places as Africa, Borneo, India, Ceylon, New Zealand, the Sandwich Isles, and the United States. These are some of the questions Darwin asked:

- Is astonishment expressed by the eyes and mouth being opened wide, and by the eyebrows being raised?
- Does shame excite a blush when the colour of the skin allows it to be visible? and especially how low down the body does the blush extend?
- When a man is indignant or defiant does he frown, hold his body and head erect, square his shoulders and clench his fists?
- When considering deeply on any subject, or trying to understand any puzzle, does he frown, or wrinkle the skin beneath the lower eyelids?
- When a man sneers or snarls at another, is the corner of the upper lip over the canine or eye tooth raised on the side facing the man whom he addresses?
- Is contempt expressed by a slight protrusion or the lips and by turning up the nose, and with a slight expiration?
- Do children when sulky, pout or greatly protrude the lips?
- Is the head nodded vertically in affirmation, and shaken laterally in negation? (pp. 15–16).

Throughout his book, Darwin faithfully reports many of the responses to his "queries" as he called them. "Mr Washington Matthews states that the conventional sign of astonishment with the wild tribes of the Western parts of the United States, 'is made by placing the half-closed hand over the mouth; in doing this, the head is often bent forwards, and words or low groans are sometimes uttered'" (p. 289).

---

anecdotes he presents as evidence. Darwin, however, employed another method for obtaining evidence of the form and universality of emotional expressions, one that is still in use today.

Inspired by the research of Duchenne de Boulogne (1806–1875) (see Box 2.2), Darwin studied photographs of the insane and ordinary people (many of which he obtained from Duchenne himself) for information about the

---

BOX 2.2

Duchenne de Boulogne and the Anatomy
of Emotional Expression

In 1862, Guillaume-Benjamin Duchenne de Boulogne, a French physician who specialized in the study of neurological disorders, published a
most extraordinary book. Duchenne's *Mécanisme de la Physionomie Hu-*
maine (*The Mechanism of Human Facial Expression*) presented the results
of his "electro-physiological," photographic studies of emotional expression in the human face. In these studies, Duchenne sought to discover the "laws that govern the expressions of the human face"
(Duchenne, 1862/1990, p. 1). He did this by means of electrical stimulation of the individual facial muscles involved in emotional expression.
The Mechanism of Human Facial Expression consists of a remarkable series
of photographs by Duchenne of facial expressions of emotions that *he*
created in a group of human models by means of electrical stimulation.

Duchenne, unlike Darwin and those students of facial expression
who were to follow Darwin, used his own judgment as to what constituted an appropriate expression for a particular emotion. Nevertheless,
it is uncanny how many of his photographs seem to capture, at least
through the illusion of photography, the essential nature of the expressions for many emotions. This is particularly true, I think, for the expressions for fear and sudden fright. Indeed, it is difficult to look at
some of Duchenne's photographs, especially of his principle model, the
"old man," and not feel sympathy for him when he is shown with expressions of anguish, fear, or sadness on his face.[2]

Darwin, in his *Expression of the Emotions,* drew heavily on
Duchenne's photographs and descriptions of the facial muscle patterning of emotional expression. Darwin even asked Duchenne for permission to reproduce some of his photographs in his own book. Duchenne
agreed, apparently sending Darwin his personal copies of the photographs Darwin had requested. It appears as if Darwin, however,
never returned the photographs—reproductions of two of the three
missing plates from Duchenne's own copy of his book (the original edi-
tion was actually a photograph album) are printed in Darwin's book
(Debord, 1990, p. 245).

As much as Darwin, Duchenne was an important pioneer in the
study of emotions and emotional expression and his influence can be
seen in recent studies by Ekman and his colleagues of the so-called
Duchenne smile (Ekman, Davidson, & Friesen, 1990). Duchenne, unlike

---

[2]The "old man" it turns out, suffered from facial anesthesia and so was an ideal subject
for Duchenne's studies, as he could not have felt any of the electrical stimulation that
Duchenne applied to his face. One wonders, however, if he experienced any of the autonomic
nervous system patterns of arousal Paul Ekman and others have found to be associated with
feedback from various facial expressions of emotion (see Chapter 3).

Darwin, however, believed that the patterns of facial muscular activity *had* been created specifically for the purpose of emotional expression. He also believed that, "all human beings [have] the instinctive facility of always expressing their sentiments by contracting the same muscles" (p. 19). This, he argued, "rendered the language [of facial expression] universal and immutable" (p. 19). Modern scientific research on facial expression provides strong support for Duchenne's first conclusion, but only partial support for his second (compare the differences between the conclusions of Ekman et al., 1987, and Fridlund, 1992, in this regard). Perhaps unwittingly, Duchenne, in arguing that facial expressions are immutable, fired the first salvo in a major controversy in the study of facial expressions and emotion, namely, the debate over the role of culture and learning in emotional expressions.

anatomy and cross-cultural generality of various expressions. Significantly, Darwin showed photographs of various expressions (e.g., surprise) to small samples of people (presumably all European) and asked them to judge the expressions they depicted. In asking a group of people to perform what is now called a "judgment task," Darwin set the stage for the research carried out today by Paul Ekman, Carroll Izard, and many others.

"One Hundred Reliable Persons"

One of the first psychologists, if not *the* first to take up Darwin's methods for the study of the facial expressions of emotion was Antoinette Feleky (1875–1950). In 1914 she published a brief paper in which she reported the results of a study in which she presented a set of photographs of a person posing 86 different (!) emotional expressions to "one hundred reliable persons" and asked them to judge what emotion was being posed in each photograph.[3] Several aspects of Feleky's paper are noteworthy. The first is that she used photographs of facial expressions she *herself* posed as stimuli (her article comes complete with a set of reproductions of her photographs). As we shall see, this is a practice in which emotion researchers still engage. The second is the sheer variety and breadth of the "emotions" she posed. These ranged from joy, disgust, wonder, and fear, to religious love, "breathless interest," and hope. One expression was posed to reflect the second line in Gretchen's speech to Faust: "I feel it, you but spare my ignorance / To shame me, sir, you stoop thus low" (p. 35). Another was posed by multiplying 19 by 19, and one photograph was taken just after Feleky had said the word "poison" in Juliet's speech from the poison scene in *Romeo and Juliet*:

---

[3]Making 86 different emotional expressions was nothing for Feleky. In 1924 she published a book on emotions that contained photographs of her making 387 different expressions!

"What if it be a poison, which the friar subtly hath ministered, to have me dead?" Finally, Feleky's results themselves are also of interest.

Even though her procedure was probably not all that reliable a method of obtaining naturally appearing posed expressions (she used her own judgment as to what a particular emotional expression should look like and blamed her subjects if they could not tell what emotion it was), she was able to obtain some agreement as to what her subjects thought some of the expressions were supposed to be.[4] For example, she obtained moderately high agreement for the expressions of *horror* and *terror*. (Thirty-five percent of her subjects identified the former correctly, although just over 16% of them interpreted her expression of horror to be *rage*. Twenty-seven percent of her subjects identified her expression of terror as either *horror* or *fear*.) She also obtained moderately high agreement for her expression of *interest* (60.5% of her subjects identified it as either *attention, interest,* or *interest toward a child*). Feleky seems to have been at her best in portraying the expressions for *disgust* (correctly identified by 36% of her subjects), *contempt*, and "*sneering*" (40.5% of her subjects identified her expression of contempt as either *contempt* or *sneering*, 43.5% identified sneering as either *sneering* or *contempt*). She obtained very low agreement, however, when she asked her subjects to match her expression with emotion terms such as *grief, rapture, romantic love,* and *deep, penetrating thought.*

These results set the stage for more modern studies of emotional expression in the face (and upper torso). Feleky's mistakes, if they can be called that, were (1) to include in her list of "emotions" many terms that should not be considered emotions per se (for example, *sneering* and *laughter* are themselves expressions and not emotions, *modesty* could be considered a personality characteristic, and *devotion* or *antipathy* might best be considered attitudes) and (2) to use her own judgments about what constituted an adequate expression of a particular emotion. These are difficulties to which more recent researchers have paid particular attention.

The Darwinian Tradition in Contemporary Psychology

More than anyone else, research on emotions in the Darwinian tradition is associated with Paul Ekman and Carroll Izard. Although they have their theoretical differences, both Ekman and Izard have a long-standing research interest in demonstrating the cross-cultural universality of facial expressions of emotion as a way of vindicating Darwin's view of emotion (for an explication of Ekman's research program see his *Darwin and Facial Expression* [1973];

[4]However, perhaps because of her method, Feleky was never able to obtain the high levels of agreement that characterize modern studies of facial expression using similar procedures.

for Izard's, see his *Human Emotions* [1977]). The notion that facial expressions of emotion are universal follows directly from the assumption that emotions and the expressions that accompany them are evolved phenomena. If emotional expressions are subject to evolution by natural selection, members of the same species must exhibit the same emotional expressions. Recall that Darwin, in his "queries" to missionaries and in his photographic judgment studies, also sought to provide support for this hypothesis. Darwin, of course, defined expression much more broadly than most modern researchers have done; Ekman and Izard have concerned themselves exclusively with the face. Even though modern researchers might define expression differently than Darwin did, the evidence they have gathered strongly supports the idea that some emotional expressions are universal. In scores of studies over the past 20 years, Ekman and Izard and their colleagues have demonstrated conclusively that the facial expressions for happiness, surprise, sadness, fear, disgust, and anger are correctly identified by people from vastly different cultures. In Ekman's own words, "[t]he evidence now for universality is overwhelming" (Ekman et al., 1987, p. 717). To give you an idea of how this kind of research is conducted and what kinds of things it has discovered, let's turn to one of Ekman and Friesen's most well known and, I think, persuasive studies.

Cross-Cultural Studies of Human Facial Expressions

Ekman and Friesen (1971) sought to provide a particularly strong test of the hypothesis that facial expressions of emotion are universal by first finding a group of people who had very little contact with Western culture and then ascertaining if they could correctly identify the emotional displays of Westerners. Ekman and Friesen found their sample of such people in the Fore, an isolated, preliterate group of people living in the Highlands of New Guinea. At the time that Ekman and Friesen first studied them, the Fore had some contact with missionaries, government workers, and traders but nevertheless still lived in a traditional manner. Even so, the researchers sought out only those members of the group who had had minimal contact with Westerners. The idea was to try to find people who had been, as much as possible, "visually isolated" from Western culture. Those who were selected to participate in the study had never lived in a government town, had never worked for a Caucasian, did not speak English or Pidgin, and had never seen a movie.

The procedure Ekman and Friesen used to test the universality hypothesis was simple. A sample of both adults and children (some 3% of the total Fore population) were shown either two or three photographs of facial expressions of emotion. Each photograph depicted one male or female adult or child spontaneously or voluntarily making the facial expression for happiness, sadness, anger, surprise, disgust, or fear. The photographs used in the study had been previously found to be judged by a high percentage (70%) of subjects in at least two literate cultures as showing a particular emotion. Adult members of the Fore were shown three different photographs at a time and were read a brief "story" involving the emotion depicted in one of the photographs (hence, one was correct and two were incorrect). Children were only shown two of the photographs. The stories given to adults and children, however, were the same. These were

> *Happiness:* His (her) friends have come, and he (she) is happy.
>
> *Sadness:* His (her) child (mother) has died, and he (she) feels very sad.
>
> *Anger:* He (she) is angry; or he (she) is angry, about to fight.
>
> *Surprise:* He (she) is just now looking at something new and unexpected.
>
> *Disgust:* He (she) is looking at something he (she) dislikes; or He (she) is looking at something that smells bad.
>
> *Fear:* He (she) is sitting in his (her) house all alone, and there is no one else in the village. There is no knife, ax, or bow and arrow in the house. A wild pig is standing in the door of the house, and the man (woman) is looking at the pig and is very afraid of it. The pig has been standing in the doorway for a few minutes, and the person is looking at it very afraid, and the pig won't move away from the door, and he (she) is afraid the pig will bite him (her). (p. 126)

In order to be sure that the emotion terms in the stories meant the same things to the Fore as they did to the researchers, Ekman and Friesen first had one person translate the emotion terms into the Fore's language and then had another person translate them back as a check on the original translation. In order to provide for as unbiased a test as possible, Ekman and Friesen, in presenting the correct and incorrect photographs, always paired the correct photograph with one that had been incorrectly identified as the correct one in previous studies. As a result of this procedure, their test was actually biased a bit in the direction of *not* finding cultural similarities in the recognition of emotional expressions. So, what did they find?

For each combination of correct and incorrect facial expressions, for both adults and children, Ekman and Friesen calculated the percentage of subjects who chose the correct expression. These percentages turned out to be extraordinarily high. For all of the emotion stories, except that for fear, the percentage of subjects choosing the correct expression ranged from 64%

to 100%, with most being in the higher end of the range. All of the percentages except three, all of these relative to the fear story, were well beyond what one would expect by chance alone. To show that these results were not just some fluke, Ekman and Friesen performed the same study on the most "Westernized" members of the Fore culture, a group of twenty-three men. The results for these subjects were almost identical to those of their less Westernized kin. Thus, Ekman and Friesen concluded that, with the exception of fear, they had demonstrated that universal facial expressions for at least some emotions did indeed exist.

Why did Ekman and Friesen get such poor results for fear? The small percentage of subjects correctly identifying the fear expression apparently came about because fear was often confused with surprise. One would think that, of all of the emotions, fear would be the best candidate for an emotion with an evolutionary history. Ekman and Friesen argued that this is indeed the case, but among the Fore, events that are likely to elicit fear also tend to be events that are surprising or unexpected. Thus, although the Fore *can* make the distinction between fear and surprise, they typically do not because in their experience the two are closely linked.

At this point you may be wondering whether people in literate cultures can recognize the facial expressions of people from nonliterate cultures. Ekman and Friesen took the opportunity while *they* were in New Guinea to ask members of the Fore culture how they would look in a variety of emotion-producing situations. Ekman and Friesen photographed their expressions and showed them to a sample of college students when they returned to the United States. They found that, with the exception of fear and surprise, most of the students in their sample correctly identified the emotion that was supposed to be depicted (Ekman & Friesen, 1971).

Is There a Universal Facial Expression for Romantic Love?

Recall that when I described the results of my own little in-class, facial-expression judgment studies, I said that my students, in addition to correctly identifying the Big Six, "basic" emotions (anger, fear, sadness, happiness, disgust, surprise), also correctly identified love. Most of the students who have modeled the expression of love for me have tried to come up with an expression for romantic love. Romantic love, you will notice, is not one of the emotions Ekman or anyone else has found to have a universally recognized facial expression associated with it, although several psychologists have argued that some form of love may be a kind of basic emotion (see especially Hazan & Shaver's, 1987, comments on "Romantic Love Conceptualized as an Attachment Process"). Why are my students so good at identifying love?

While it is true that my students are, on average, more sensitive and loving than most people, the real reason, I think, is in the way my student-models attempt to express "love." What they ultimately come up with is a highly conventionalized expression that owes much more to Hollywood than to evolution. Gazing skyward, while holding one's hands over one's heart and sighing deeply are expressions usually not found in other animals. These actions, however, probably are a part of a kind of cultural model or prototype we have of the person-in-love (cf. Fehr, 1994). What my students are revealing when they correctly identify this expression is the extent to which their socialization into Western culture has been successful, and not that one can expect to find vervet monkeys sighing deeply and making goo-goo eyes when they come into heat.

Darwin Was Right

The vindication of Darwin's ideas about the universality of facial expressions of emotion, or, rather, of hypotheses about the universality of facial expressions of emotion derived from Darwin, is now almost complete. In 1987 Ekman and his colleagues published the results of a massive study in which subjects from ten different cultures performed a judgment task similar to that used by Ekman and Friesen in New Guinea. As Table 2.1 illustrates, people from Estonia, Germany, Greece, Hong Kong, Italy, Japan, Sumatra, Turkey, and the United States were all found to interpret the facial expressions of emotion depicted in a set of photographs of Caucasians in much the same way (Ekman et al., 1987). While it is true that all of the subjects used in the study were college students, Ekman argues that, given the number of cultures (this includes all of the above plus another nonliterate culture, the Dani of

TABLE 2.1. *The percentage of Ekman et al.'s subjects in each culture who correctly identified the predicted emotion.*

Nation	Happiness	Surprise	Sadness	Fear	Disgust	Anger
Estonia	90	94	86	91	71	67
Germany	93	87	83	86	61	71
Greece	93	91	80	74	77	77
Hong Kong	92	91	91	84	65	73
Italy	97	92	81	82	89	72
Japan	90	94	87	65	60	67
Scotland	98	88	86	86	79	84
Sumatra	69	78	91	70	70	70
Turkey	87	90	76	76	74	79
United States	95	92	92	84	86	81

Source: Ekman et al., 1987, p. 714. Copyright © 1987 by the American Psychological Association. Reprinted with permission of the author and the publisher.

New Guinea) studied and the consistency of the results, an alternative explanation for the results favoring some form of socialization is not tenable.

FACS About the Face: What Facial Athletes Do for a Living

Ekman and Friesen and their colleagues have not been content simply to
show that people in different cultures interpret the facial expressions of
emotion in similar ways. Following in the footsteps of Duchenne, these researchers have also sought to develop a method of precisely specifying the
muscle movements involved in every human facial expression of emotion.
Developed over many years, Ekman and Friesen call their method the Facial
Action Coding System, or FACS (Ekman & Friesen, 1975; Ekman & Friesen,
1978). (Izard has published his own system for coding facial expressions of
emotion, something he calls Max; see Izard, 1979.) In using FACS, a numerical value is assigned to each muscle of the face corresponding to how much
it is contracted in a particular emotional expression. Each emotional expression thus has its own unique combination of values for the contraction of
each of the muscles of the face. Unlike Feleky, who had to use her own judgment as to what expression went with which emotion, Ekman and Friesen
can specify the exact pattern of muscle contractions for each expression.
They can thus "construct" any emotional expression from scratch by simply
telling a model which muscles to contract. (This has the advantage, by the
way, of allowing them to tell a person to make the expression for a particular emotion without telling him or her what emotion he or she is supposed
to be expressing. We'll explore why they might want to do this in the next
chapter.) Recall that this is quite similar to what Duchenne did with his electrical stimulation. Ekman and Friesen, as far as I know, have never resorted
to direct electrical stimulation of the facial muscles. They (and their students
and colleagues) have, however, developed the ability to contract the individual muscles of their faces to such an extent that they can respond immediately to verbal instructions to contract any of their facial muscles to make
whatever expression is desired. This ability has led Ekman to refer to himself and his colleagues as "facial athletes."

Poker Faces and Secret Smiles: The Influence of "Display Rules" on Emotional Expression

When my son was about 5 years old he used to love playing variants of the
card game Fish. On one particular occasion, when we were playing Di-
nosaur Fish, Geoffrey revealed through his facial expression that he had just

drawn a card he had wanted. I told him that he should be careful not to show too much excitement when that happened because other players would guess what cards he had. I then told him that he should keep a "poker face" while he was looking at his cards. He looked up at me and said, "You mean I should poke you in the face?" As he leapt up to do just that, I told him that what I meant was he shouldn't show that he was happy to have the cards he wanted.

It took me a little while to explain what I meant by keeping a "poker face" to Geoffrey, but you know exactly what I mean. There are certain situations in which it is appropriate to express certain emotions and others in which those expressions would be taboo: we can all bring to mind situations in which we have suppressed or altered the expression of how we are feeling to be in accord with what the situation calls for.

Ekman introduced the term *display rules* to account for the ways in which learning can mask universal facial expressions of emotion (Ekman & Friesen, 1971). This term serves to draw attention to patterns of expression "management" that are part of what one learns when one is socialized into a particular culture. Thus, by positing the existence of such rules of expression management as adjuncts to and modifiers of the set of universal facial expressions, Ekman can explain cultural variability as well as similarity. An excellent demonstration of the operation of display rules may be found in Friesen's doctoral dissertation (Friesen, 1972; see also Ekman, 1972).

Freisen showed a sample of Japanese and a sample of American students either a nonemotional travelogue or a film of a "subincision" ritual in which adolescent boys undergo a particularly gruesome form of bodily mutilation. The faces and physiologies of the two groups of students were identical in their responses to the two films; in particular, both groups displayed clear signs of distress while watching the gruesome film. The responses of the two groups of subjects differed greatly, however, when they were interviewed immediately after seeing the gruesome film. The Japanese students, as predicted, masked their "true" feelings about the film (as determined by their facial expressions and physiological responses during the film) by adopting a neutral expression in the presence of a (Japanese) interviewer. In a recent article, Matsumoto (1990) has extended this finding by obtaining ratings by Japanese and American students of the emotions they would feel it would be appropriate to express in a variety of situations. American students indicated that it is more appropriate to express sadness to one's friends or members of one's family than did Japanese students. Japanese students, on the other hand, indicated that it is more appropriate to express anger to those outside one's circle of close friends and family than did American students. American students also considered happiness in public to be more appropriate than did Japanese students. The last finding is noteworthy because there is a very interesting way in which Friesen's conclusions about display rules must be qualified somewhat given the results of a recent study of individual differences in a personality characteristic associated with emotional expressiveness called *self-monitoring*.

Friedman and Miller-Herringer (1991) secretly videotaped the faces of students engaged in a competitive videogame against two of their fellow students. The students' task was to solve a number of difficult probability problems presented via a computer screen. The students were told that they would be working both in a group and while they were alone. In the group condition, the subject's computer terminal was situated so that he or she sat facing two other subjects, who were actually confederates of the experimenters. In the alone condition, the subject was led to believe that the other two subjects would be working in different rooms. In both conditions, after each of the problems, subjects received feedback as to whether their answer was correct in the form of a numerical score and a verbal message ("Right! Fewer than 10% of college students typically answer this question correctly," p. 768). The subject's cumulative score *and* the scores of the other "subjects" were presented on the computer screens after each problem. The feedback to the subjects about the scores of the other subjects was rigged so that the subjects always seemed to be performing better than the others. Examination of the videotapes of the subjects' faces as they received the feedback about their performance indicated that subjects in the group condition clearly inhibited any overt signs of pleasure or triumph. When subjects were alone, they showed more signs of happiness and "animation" than when they were in a position to be observed by others. So far, this sounds like the kind of behavior that Ekman and Friesen might predict if the students were following a display rule that prohibited taking delight in one's own success in the presence of those who have not succeeded (this is somewhat akin to the German notion of *Schadenfreude*). What's really interesting, however, is what happened when Friedman and Miller-Herringer factored in the subjects' responses to the Self-Monitoring Scale, a personality questionnaire developed by Mark Snyder (1974).

The Self-Monitoring Scale assesses the extent to which a person is responsive to cues about the situational appropriateness of his or her behavior and will alter his or her behavior in response to those cues. Friedman and Miller-Herringer found that, while their subjects in general were less expressive in the presence of others, subjects who scored high on this characteristic modified their behavior the most. Indeed, "high self-monitors" literally bit their lips in an attempt to hide their "true" feelings. Thus, although, as Matsumoto found, American students feel that it is less appropriate to express happiness in public than their Japanese counterparts, they feel that it is more appropriate to express happiness (at least of the kind Friedman and Miller-Herringer induced) in private. This is especially true of those subjects who are sensitive to situational cues of appropriateness. What Friedman and Miller-Herringer seem to have demonstrated is that some people are more affected by display rules than are others. I'll have more to say about display rules (and their cousins, "feeling rules") in Chapter 5 when we explore the social constructivist perspective; for now, let's sit back and briefly review where the Darwinian tradition has taken us. First, however, I must mention the "Dark Ages" of the Darwinian tradition.

The Dark Ages of the Darwinian Tradition

As Ekman never seems to tire of telling us, there was a time in the not-too-distant past (from roughly the 1930s until the late 1960s) when the scientific Zeitgeist regarding facial expressions of emotion was very different from what it is today (for reviews see Ekman, 1973, 1984, 1992a, 1992b; Ekman et al., 1987). In particular, psychology's view of the nature of facial and other expressions of emotion, under the influence of the prevailing behaviorist perspective and the findings of a few well-known cross-cultural studies of emotional expression, was that expression was for the most part culturally-determined. Representative of this Zeitgeist were the ideas of Weston LaBarre, an anthropologist who studied the influence of culture on personality. LaBarre, after reviewing evidence that he and other anthropologists had collected about the cultural relativity of emotional expressions, concluded that, "there is no 'natural' language of emotional gesture" (Labarre, 1947, p. 55). Later, Ray Birdwhistell (1918–1994), in the course of his own study of expressive bodily and facial movements, which he called *kinesics,* argued that

> Insofar as I have been able to determine, just as there are no universal words, no sound complexes, which carry the same meaning the world over, there are no body motions, facial expressions, or gestures which provoke *identical* responses the world over . . . A body can be bowed in grief, in humility, in laughter, or in readiness for aggression. A "smile" in one society portrays friendliness, in another embarrassment, and, in still another may contain a warning that unless tension is reduced, hostility and attack will follow. (Birdwhistell, 1970, p. 34)

Much was made by psychologists and anthropologists influenced by this view of the findings of Otto Klineberg's (1899–1992) studies of emotional expression in Chinese literature (Klineberg, 1938) in which Klineberg concluded that facial expressions of emotion such as smiles could not be trusted for they could accompany many different, indeed, mutually exclusive, emotions. "[T]he smile obviously does not stand for sorrow, even though the occasions [in which it appears] may be unhappy ones. It is rather that . . . an appearance of joy must be maintained" (Klineberg, 1938, p. 195). As Ekman has argued and as the last sentence in the preceding quote from Klineberg illustrates, the many cultural differences in emotional expression described by LaBarre, Klineberg, and Birdwhistell do not indicate that there are no universal expressions of emotion but that cultures differ in the extent to which they modify those expressions by means of display rules. Sometimes this means that a particular expression is completely forbidden, as Klineberg found for expressions of grief among Samurai women, but more often it means that the timing, place, and intensity of the expression are under cultural control.

Ekman has recently argued that the old culturally relative view of emotional expressions is making a comeback in psychological anthropology (Ekman et al., 1987). I doubt if anyone can seriously question the existence of universals for the expression of at least a small number of very basic emotions and so I disagree with Ekman on this point. The new anthropology of emotions does deserve serious consideration, however. This is a topic we'll take up in Chapter 5.

Facing Up to the Evidence: What Does Research Within the Darwinian Tradition Tell Us About Emotions?

As you can see, research in the Darwinian tradition, epitomized by the studies of the universality of facial expressions by Ekman, owes much more to the general evolutionary framework Darwin brought to the study of emotions and emotional expression than to the specific explanations Darwin offered for particular expressions. No one working within the Darwinian tradition doubts the assumption that emotions and the expressions that accompany them are the products of evolution. Once this assumption has been acknowledged, one can begin to ask all sorts of interesting questions about what emotions are for. The answers that today's students of emotion give are certainly different from those offered by Darwin but they nevertheless reveal a profound debt to him. Before addressing the question of what emotions are for, however, we need to consider modern psychology's answer to two related questions.

Are there universal facial expressions of emotion?   The answer to this question, as we have seen, is an unequivocal "Yes." The facial expressions for at least a small set of emotions—happiness, sadness, fear, disgust, anger, and surprise—seem to be recognized by people everywhere. Other factors, such as display rules, do come into play in determining how we are to express our emotions in any particular situation, but the facial expressions for these emotions at least seem to be universal. Notice that this evidence is absolutely necessary if we are to assume that emotions are indeed subject to evolution. Notice also the "leap of faith" that is made by Ekman and others in moving from the finding that there are universals of facial expression to the conclusion that there are universals of emotion (cf. Fridlund, 1992). It is to this question that we must now turn.

Are there "fundamental" emotions?   The existence of a set of universally identified facial expressions of emotion has led a number of modern emotion theorists to claim that the emotions with which these expressions are associated are somehow "basic," "primary" or "fundamental" in the sense that they form the core of our repertoire of emotions. Indeed, Ekman has made the existence of a universally recognized facial expression a necessary component of his definition of emotion (see Ekman, 1984). There are actually two meanings to the term *fundamental* here: one is that the set of "fundamental" emotions represents those patterns of responses to the world that evolution has bequeathed to us by virtue of their being necessary for our survival (think about the importance of fear in this regard); the other is that all of the other emotions that we might possibly experience or express are somehow derived from this small set of simpler emotions.

Emphasizing both of these meanings, Ekman has argued that the six emotions (he now wants to add a seventh, contempt, to his list) that have been found to be recognized universally comprise the set of fundamental emotions, that each of these emotions has a specific function in the survival of both the individual and the species and that all other emotions are more or less complex combinations or modifications of the primary set (Ekman, 1984; Ekman, 1992a). Izard holds a very similar view on the question of basic emotions, arguing, however, that there are *ten* fundamental emotions. Each of these, according to Izard,

> has an inherently adaptive function. They are termed fundamental because each of them has (a) a specific innately determined neural substrate, (b) a characteristic facial expression or neuro-muscular-expressive pattern, and (c) a distinct subjective or phenomenological quality. (Izard, 1977, p. 83; see also Izard, 1992)

The ten fundamental emotions identified by Izard are *interest-excitement, joy, surprise, distress-anguish, anger, disgust, contempt, fear, shame,* and *guilt* (Izard, 1977).

A somewhat different approach to the question of basic or fundamental emotions has been offered by Robert Plutchik. Plutchik also believes that there is a set of basic or primary emotions and each serves a specific "adaptive role in helping organisms deal with key survival issues posed by the environment" (Plutchik, 1980, p. 129). Strongly echoing Darwin, Plutchik also asserts that, "[t]he concept of emotion is applicable to all evolutionary levels and applies to all animals as well as humans" (p. 129) and that, furthermore, even though emotional expression may take somewhat different forms in different species, "there are certain common elements, or prototype patterns, that can be identified [in these different forms of expression]" (p. 129). Plutchik identifies eight primary or "prototype" emotions—*fear/terror, anger/rage, joy/ecstasy, sadness/grief, acceptance/trust, disgust/loathing, expectancy/anticipation,* and *surprise/astonishment*—and maintains that these should be thought of as being pairs of polar opposites, for example, joy versus sadness (Plutchik, 1984). Each member of a pair of opposing emotions and the entire set of pairs can be seen as varying in terms of how much they reflect three basic adaptive reactions to events in the world (see later discussion).

Notice how closely intertwined the question of basic emotions is with the question of what functions are served by emotions. Ekman, Izard, and Plutchik all argue that the emotions on their lists are primary because they serve the adaptive interests of the organism. In their view, what people and dogs and cats and even planaria (well, sometimes) do when they are being "emotional" represent patterns of responses that have persisted precisely because they at one time gave us an edge in our struggles with the environment and each other to survive. Notice, however, that, with the exception of Darwin's claims about the nonemotional origin of emotional expression, we really haven't encountered an explanation for why particular emotional *expressions,* as opposed to the emotions themselves, have evolved they way they have (it is one thing to flee an attacker, it is another to flee an attacker with a particular expression on your face).

What are the functions of the expressive movements that accompany emotions?   Darwin, as we have seen, regarded the origins of the expressive movements that accompany and communicate particular emotions as *epiphenomena,* that is, as not originally serving any necessary purpose *qua* emotions. For Darwin, although facial and other expressive displays currently serve communicative ends, the key to understanding the origin of emotional expression was to be found in the older, primeval, if you will, functions served by the various actions that constitute the expressions. A similar conclusion has been offered much more recently by Robert Zajonc (Zajonc, 1985; Zajonc, Murphy, & Inglehart, 1989; Adelmann & Zajonc, 1989) in his recapitulation of an older theory of emotional experience developed by a French physician named Israel Waynbaum (1871–circa 1944).

Zajonc, following Waynbaum, argues that the patterns of facial muscle activity that accompany various emotions evolved not for the purpose of expression but, rather, to regulate the volume of blood delivered to the brain, especially the hypothalamus (notice how similar this is to Darwin's modus operandi). Zajonc's claim is that muscles of the face, when contracted, act as ligatures on various blood vessels, primarily the external carotid artery and facial veins, either increasing or decreasing cerebral blood flow. These changes in cerebral blood flow, Zajonc asserts, bring about direct changes in subjective experience. Here is what Zajonc says about why we smile:

> Why is the zygomatic muscle involved in smiling and in happiness? The contraction of the major zygomatic muscle . . . has a congestive cerebral circulatory function. The proof is simple. Pull the corners of your mouth

apart by contracting the major zygomatic muscle, as if in intense exaggerated smile. After several seconds, the frontal vein will be gorged with blood. Thus, . . . the zygomatic muscle acts as a ligature on the branches of the external carotid and the slave action of the corrugator blocks the return blood. Cerebral blood is thus momentarily retained . . . which in turn leads to a surge of subjectively felt positive affect. (Zajonc, 1985, p. 17)

As suggested in the above quote, Zajonc's theory has some interesting implications for how we can learn to regulate our own emotions and mood. Whatever the merits of the theory, and it is not without its critics (see, for example, Fridlund & Gilbert, 1985), it does lend itself to an immediate test. Zajonc would suggest that the next time you are feeling a bit mopey and depressed, go sit by yourself in a quiet room and breath slowly but deeply through your nose. This will have the consequence of cooling the blood being carried to your hypothalamus ever so slightly. After a few minutes you should begin to feel much more positive feelings coming over you (Zajonc et al., 1989).

Zajonc's theory is actually a kind of "facial feedback" theory, something we'll explore in much more detail in the next chapter. For now, it's important to note that Zajonc (and Waynbaum) views expressions of emotion on the face as epiphenomenal. A very different, although still very Darwinian, perspective on the function of facial expressions of emotion was offered by R. J. Andrew in a pair of articles published in the early 1960s (Andrew, 1963; Andrew, 1965). While acknowledging, along with Darwin, that many facial expressions of emotion ultimately have their origin in "such sources as responses through which vulnerable areas are protected, responses associated with vigorous respiration, and grooming responses" (Andrew, 1963, p. 1041), Andrew nevertheless argued that, "[f]acial expression has evolved, like other displays, to communicate information about the probable future behavior of the displaying animal" (Andrew, 1963, p. 1034). Thus, Andrew ascribes a specific communicative role to facial expressions of emotion. This view—one might call it the modern Darwinian perspective—is shared by many students of emotion. Izard, in fact, after quoting both Darwin and Andrew on the origin of expressive displays, states that, "[a]t least some facial expressions are derived from responses that served to communicate to other animals" (Izard, 1977, p. 68). A similar position has been advocated more recently by Alan Fridlund (1992).

Unresolved Questions: Recent Criticisms of Facial Expression Research

Even though the "Dark Ages" of the Darwinian tradition are certainly over, and most students of emotion concede that there do seem to be a small number of facial expressions that are universally produced and recognized by humans the world over, Darwinian research, especially about the universality of facial expressions, is not without its critics. Fridlund (Fridlund, 1992, 1994), for example, in the course of a thoroughgoing critique of the research on facial expression by Ekman, Izard, and others, argues that Ekman, Izard, and many other facial expression researchers fail to appreciate sufficiently the fundamentally *social* nature of human and animal expressive displays. From the perspective of behavioral ecology, Fridlund contends, human and animal expressions are *always* communicative and, "are best considered social tools, whether issued by nonhumans or humans" (1992, p. 96). Thus, he argues, it is a mistake to think of facial expressions of emotion as existing solely for the purpose of expressing emotion or of there always being a one-to-one correspondence between facial expressions and emotions.

In support of this position, Fridlund points to studies (e.g., Brightman, Segal;. Werther, & Steiner, 1977; Kraut & Johnson, 1979; Gilbert, Fridlund, & Sabini, 1987) that strongly suggest that at least some human facial expressions of emotion "serve social motives, which themselves may depend little upon emotional state" (p. 101). Kraut and Johnson (1979), for example, found that bowlers more often smile when they are facing others who are watching them bowl, not when they have just scored a strike or spare (when their happiness would presumably be at a peak). Brightman et al. (1977) videotaped subjects eating sweet or salty sandwiches while they were alone or with other subjects. Observers were able to guess what kind of sandwich a subject was eating only when the subject was with others. These findings and others lead Fridlund to argue that Ekman's distinction between natural facial displays of emotion and those tempered or masked by the activity of display rules is misleading and that all facial displays, "signal our social inclinations when we are emotional, and not our emotions themselves" (p. 104). We will explore this perspective in more detail in Chapter 5 but, for now, it is important to recognize that, although Ekman's and Izard's findings on the universality of facial expressions seem to be incontrovertible, there is not universal agreement among psychologists as to what those findings mean (see, for example, Russell & Fehr, 1987; Fridlund, 1991, 1992, 1994).

Perhaps the most vehement critic of contemporary facial expression research in this regard is James Russell. After questioning whether the accurate interpretation of facial expressions of emotion depends more on the context of the expressions than on the expressions themselves (Russell & Fehr, 1987; see also Russell, 1991a), a critique that drew a spirited response from Ekman (Ekman & O'Sullivan, 1987; see also Ekman, O'Sullivan, & Matsumoto, 1991), Russell (1994) published a minutely detailed attack on the methods used by Ekman and his colleagues and other facial expression researchers. Finding fault with the types of subjects used in Ekman's and others' studies of the recognition of facial expressions in Western and non-

Western cultures as well as the ways in which facial expression stimuli were presented in such studies, the facial expression stimuli themselves, and the response format allowed subjects in such studies, Russell concluded that the evidence for the universality of facial expressions of emotions is not all that strong. Ekman (1994), as you might imagine, challenged Russell's criticisms and interpretations of his own and others' studies, and, I think, effectively defused what would have been the most damaging, for example, that the high rates of cross-cultural agreement for the Big Six emotions are an artifact of the way the stimuli are presented (sequentially, with every subject viewing every emotional expression) or the response format given to subjects (in which subjects must choose from a limited list of alternatives).

Nevertheless, even given Ekman's reply, I do think Russell's argument that the *ecological validity* of Ekman's and others' studies of the recognition of emotional expressions has not been demonstrated has some merit. Ecological validity refers to the ability to generalize from the sometimes artificial settings in which research is conducted to the "real-world." The problem is that not enough research has been conducted in real-world settings of spontaneously produced facial expressions. To be sure, some of the research that has been done supports the idea that there are a small number of universally recognized facial expressions, but some of it does not. Recognition rates of spontaneously produced facial expressions, for example, tend to be lower than recognition rates of posed expressions (Motley & Camden, 1988), although observers are very accurate at distinguishing whether a person is in a negative or positive situation, based solely on information from the person's face (Nakamura, Buck, & Kenny, 1990). After reviewing the studies in this area, Russell concludes, "[w]hat little information we have on spontaneous expressions, on unselected expressions . . . and on judgements of the face in context raise the possibility that results from the standard method [used by Ekman and others] may not tell us what happens in natural settings" (Russell, 1994, p. 131). This is a conclusion with which Izard (1994), in his reply to Russell's criticisims, largely agrees (see p. 291).

Thus, even though there is considerable, some might say overwhelming, evidence that some facial expressions of emotion are universally recognized and produced, there is still much to be learned about such phenomena. In particular, we still don't really know the extent to which the facial expressions associated with the Big Six emotions appear in relatively "pure" form in everyday expressions of emotion. (Studies of infants, in whom such expressions might be expected to appear more often, suggest that they don't, see Oster, Hegley, & Nagel, 1992.) Notice that this is a question about the influence of culture on the expression—and some might also say the experience—of emotion. I'll have much more to say about this later.

Other Evolutionary Approaches
to the Study of Emotion

One might justifiably get the impression from the foregoing discussions that psychologists who study emotion from within the Darwinian tradition are only interested in facial expressions. This is not the case, however. There is actually much more to the study of emotion from a Darwinian or evolutionary perspective than the study of facial expressions. Much of the most important research identified with the Darwinian tradition just happens to have been about facial expressions. In order to avoid a kind of conceptual rut, let's briefly examine the work of three other psychologists who adopt an evolutionary perspective on emotion but who do not study facial expression.

Plutchik's "psychoevolutionary" theory of emotions. Plutchik has written extensively on his so-called *structural, psychoevolutionary theory of emotion* (see, e.g., Plutchik, 1984; Plutchik, 1980) that emphasizes the functions of emotional behavior in the survival of both simple and complex organisms. According to Plutchik, in order to make sense out of the confusing array of emotions identified by everyday language, we must find some way to order the emotions into a coherent set. We may first do this, he says, by noting that emotions vary in *intensity,* as in the distinction between anger and rage and fear and panic. Thus, Plutchik thinks of each emotion as a pair of emotions grouped in terms of the least and most intense manifestations of the same emotion, for example, sadness/grief, joy/astonishment. Second, emotions also vary in terms of their similarity to one another. Shame and guilt, he argues, are more similar to one another than are disgust and joy. Third, emotions may be ordered in terms of what he calls *polarity,* that is, some emotions are the *opposite* of others. Sadness, for example, is the opposite of joy. Finally, Plutchik says that "some emotions are fundamental, or primary, and others are derived or secondary, in the same sense that some colors are primary and others are mixed" (Plutchik, 1984, p. 200). These characteristics of emotion begin to make sense when we think about emotions in the context of evolution by natural selection.

According to Plutchik, the concept of emotion ought to apply to all animal life, from amoebae to humans. Emotions, he says, should be most generally thought of as useful adaptations to life's contingencies. Assuming this, "we must look for fundamental patterns of adaptation that can be identified at all phylogenetic levels as clues to the basic emotions" (Plutchik, 1984, p. 201). The key to understanding why emotions have the characteristics they do, for example, variations in intensity, similarity, and so on, lies in

the "functional requirements" created by the environments in which all animals live. "All organisms, in order to survive and maintain their populations, must find and ingest food, avoid injury, and reproduce their kind"
(Plutchik, 1984, p. 201).

Following Scott (1958; see also Scott, 1980), Plutchik proposes that
there are eight basic or prototypical behavior patterns that may be found in
all organisms. These are *incorporation* (ingestion of food or "acceptance of
beneficial stimuli"), *rejection* ("behavior designed to expel something harmful"), *protection* (avoiding danger), *destruction* (destroying barriers to the ful-
fillment of important needs), *reproduction* (which includes "maintenance-of-
contact tendencies" as well as passing on of one's genes), *reintegration*
(reaction to loss), *orientation* (reactions to contact with novel stimuli), and *exploration* (mapping new environments) (Plutchik, 1984, p. 202). Notice that
the eight behavior patterns may be grouped into pairs of polar opposites, *rejection* being the opposite of *incorporation*, and so on. Once this is done,
Plutchik argues, these eight basic behavior patterns may be mapped onto
his short list of the basic emotions found in everyday language (see earlier
discussion). Fear/terror, for example, is associated with the basic behavior
pattern of *protection*, whereas anger/rage is associated with the basic behavior pattern of *destruction*, and so on. The emotions that emerge from this
mapping, fear/terror, anger/rage, joy/ecstasy, sadness/grief, acceptance/
trust, disgust/loathing, expectancy/anticipation, and surprise/astonish-
ment, may then be considered, by definition, to be the basic or fundamental
emotions that all organisms share.

Plutchik models the relationships among the eight basic emotions as
an "emotion solid," similar to the color solid often used to represent the
relationships among colors. Plutchik's emotion solid is presented in Figure
2.3. According to Plutchik, each of the "slices" of the solid represents a different basic emotion and, hence, a prototypical adaptive reaction. The
shape of the model, with its pointed bottom and flat top, indicates that
emotions get more intense and more differentiated as one moves from the
bottom to the top of the solid. Near the bottom of the solid, where emotions are the least intense, there is the least differentiation among them.
Complex emotions, such as love or contempt, may be seen as combinations of basic emotions and may be found at the boundary between two
slices. Love, for example, according to Plutchik, is a combination of joy
and acceptance.

Plutchik has found that when people are asked to rate the similarity of
emotion terms in English, the ordering of the emotion terms that results
looks very much like his proposed emotion solid. Furthermore, after noting
that the mixed emotions in his model resemble familiar personality characteristics, Plutchik (Plutchik, 1980) has used the model heuristically to explore the relationship between emotions and personality.

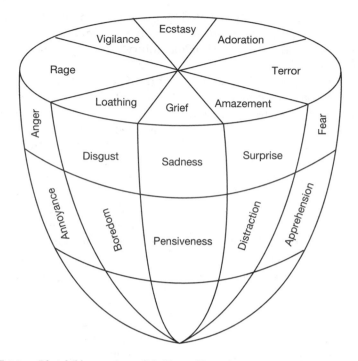

FIGURE 2.3.   *Plutchik's emotion solid. (From "Emotions: A General Psychorevolutionary Theory," by R. Plutchik, in* Approaches to Emotion, *Fig. 8.1, p. 203, eds. K. R. Scherer and P. Ekman, Hillsdale, N.J.: Erlbaum. Copyright 1984 by Lawrence Erlbaum Associates. Reprinted with permission of the publisher and the author.)*

Shaver's evolutionary prototype theory of emotion.   The "prototype" approach to the study of emotion presented by Philip Shaver and his students and colleagues starts with an assumption similar to that adopted by Plutchik, namely, that all human beings share a set of prototypical reactions to certain features of the environments in which they live. Shaver and his colleagues reason that, furthermore, these prototypical reactions should be found in the way emotions are represented in everyday language. "Cross-cultural universality in the representation of emotion strongly suggests a common underlying biology, which cannot be missed despite otherwise notable differences in cultural meaning systems" (Shaver, Wu, & Schwartz, 1992, p. 176). Taking an approach much different from that of Ekman and his colleagues, Shaver's program has been to explore the ways in which emotions are similarly represented in different cultures, thus demonstrating that, "different cultures have independently converged on a single reality" (Shaver et al., 1992, p. 176).

Shaver and his colleagues, following Frijda (see later discussion), think of emotions as "action tendencies" that follow from a person's "appraisal" of the environment in particular ways. The manifestation of such action tendencies may be modified by culture, but, given the similarities in the environments in which all humans live, there should be substantial similarities across cultures in the appraisal patterns and the action patterns associated with them. This assumption leads Shaver and his colleagues to argue that there should be a small number of basic emotions, each associated with a particular pattern of appraisal and action tendency, recognized by all cultures, everywhere.

> [W]hat does it mean to say that certain basic emotions might exist and be recognized cross-culturally? To us it means that in every culture there are at least a few universal patterns of appraisal (evaluations of events in relation to concerns) associated with patterns of action readiness (which often reveal themselves in visible expressions and actions) . . . To the extent that certain emotional syndromes are biologically determined and central to social life, they should be evident to people around the world. This does not mean, however, that knowledge of these syndromes will necessarily take the form of identical emotion taxonomies and prototypes in every culture; they may differ, just as color taxonomies do. (Shaver et al., 1992, p. 179)

Shaver and his colleagues have gathered evidence that people in at least three cultures represent emotions in similar ways using a methodology similar to that used by Plutchik. In one study (Shaver, Schwartz, Kirson, & O'Connor, 1987), a group of American college students sorted 135 emotion names into categories based on their similarity to one another. After subjecting these sortings to a complex statistical technique called *hierarchical cluster analysis*, which yields a picture of the hierarchical relationships among the items submitted to it, Shaver et al. found that six emotions, love, joy, surprise, anger, sadness, and fear, could be described as "basic-level emotion categories." Each of these six emotions were found to "contain" a number of other emotions at a subordinate level. Love, for example, contained the emotion concepts of adoration, affection, fondness, liking, and so on. Anger, on the other hand, contained the concepts of aggravation, irritation, agitation, annoyance, and so on. At a superordinate level, each of the six basic emotions was in turn contained within positive and negative categories.

Shaver and his colleagues repeated this study in Italy and the People's Republic of China and obtained similar results. In particular, they found that the emotion hierarchies derived by subjects' sortings of the similarity of large numbers of emotion terms all contained positive and negative superordinate categories, suggesting that "the distinction between hedonic positivity and negativity is crucial to understanding emotion" (Shaver et al., 1992, pp. 190–191). Second, the hierarchies produced for each culture contained the basic-level emotions of joy/happiness, fear, anger/hate, and sadness/depression. (Notice, that, in order to facilitate comparison across the three cultures, the basic-level categories had to be widened a bit.) Differences among the three cultures were primarily in the subordinate categories, suggesting that there are slight differences in the conceptions of emotions within the basic categories. In addition, in the Chinese hierarchy, love does not appear as a basic-level emotion. Instead, a separate "sad/love" basic-level category appeared. The Chinese hierarchy was also distinguished by a separate, basic-level category for shame.

Shaver and his colleagues conclude from these results that there is substantial overlap in the basic-level emotion concepts and hence basic emotions represented in each of the three cultures, as one would expect if emotions are basic, adaptive responses to the vicissitudes of life that all humans encounter. Further, each of the emotion hierarchies of the three cultures

> deals in some way with attachment-related emotions: love, longing, grief, sympathy, and compassion. But the complex blend of negative and positive emotions associated with attachment gets handled in different ways, in part depending on the number of positive and negative love-related concepts available in a particular culture. (Shaver et al., 1992, p. 196)

Thus, while the representation of emotions in the concepts of the three cultures reveal substantial underlying similarity, there are nevertheless differences among them that reveal each culture's unique qualities. Taken as a whole, however, Shaver and his colleagues assert, these data support the view that evolution has shaped and bequeathed to human nature a set of universal adaptive tendencies that we label emotions.

Frijda's theory of "action tendencies."   In addition to Plutchik's and Shaver's theories, one could also cite Nico Frijda's (1986) work on "action tendencies" as another example of a Darwinian emotion theory not directly concerned with facial expressions. Frijda argues that the action tendencies, or states of readiness to respond associated with emotions—this includes everything from the facial expressions that accompany disgust to the increases in heart rate that accompany extreme fear—should be thought of as adaptive responses to events that have been important to us as a species in our evolutionary past as well as our current environment. Frijda disagrees with Plutchik's notion that the adaptive functions served by emotions can be traced phylogenetically from amoebae to humans—jealousy, for example, is not something a flatworm is likely to experience very often. However, like Plutchik, he thinks that emotions may be thought of as embodying a relatively small set of tendencies to "establish, maintain, or disrupt a relationship with the environment" (Frijda, 1986, p. 71). These are much like Plutchik's prototypical behavior patterns. Frijda's list of ten of the basic rela-

TABLE 2.2.　*Frijda's proposed relational action tendencies and the emotions associated with them*

Action Tendency	Function	Emotion
Approach	Permits consummatory behavior	Desire
Avoidance	Protection	Fear
Being-with	Permits consummatory activity	Enjoyment, Confidence
Attending	Orientation to stimuli	Interest
Rejecting	Protection	Disgust
Nonattending	Selection	Indifference
Agonistic (Attack/Threat)	Regaining control	Anger
Interrupting	Reorientation	Shock, Surprise
Dominating	Generalized control	Arrogance
Submitting	Secondary control	Humility, Resignation

Source: Frijda, 1986, Table 2.1, p. 88. © Maison des Sciences de l'Homme and Cambridge University Press 1986. Reprinted with the permission of Cambridge University Press.

tional action tendencies is presented in Table 2.2. To these Frijda adds a number of what he calls *activation modes,* which are not so much patterns of behavior as they are states of readiness to engage in behavior of a particular kind. "Free activation," for example, the activation mode associated with the emotion of joy, "is in part aimless, unasked for readiness to engage in whatever interaction presents itself and in part readiness to engage in enjoyments" (Frijda, 1986, p. 89).

For Frijda, the action tendencies associated with emotions are so central to what emotions are all about that he says they are, "one and the same thing" (Frijda, 1986, p. 71). The various action tendencies Frijda describes, and hence emotions themselves, have arisen to solve the various problems that humans face in their encounters with the many environments in which they live. Following Magda Arnold, about whom you'll learn more in Chapter 4, Frijda believes that emotions are, at least to some extent, the "awareness of action tendency—of desire to strike or to flee, to investigate or to be with" (Frijda, 1986, p. 71), and that "different action tendencies are what characterize different emotions" (Frijda, Kuipers, & ter Schure, 1989, p. 213).

According to Frijda, the action tendencies associated with the various emotions are closely linked to the way a person perceives or "appraises" the events in his or her environment (see Chapter 4 for full discussion of the concept of appraisal). Readiness to respond to the environment in a particular manner follows directly from certain judgments one has made about the environment. Frijda, Kuipers, and ter Schure (1989) conducted a study to test this notion in which subjects were asked to recall their experiences with a number of emotions and to answer a series of questions about the appraisals and action tendencies associated with the emotions. Frijda et al. found that the states of action readiness associated with a variety of emotions could indeed be predicted from the kinds of appraisals their subjects reported making in the situations in which they experienced the emotions. Moreover, the emotions themselves could be predicted, at levels well above chance, from either the appraisals or the action tendencies. These are precisely the kinds of results one would predict from an analysis of emotions as evolved adaptations to life's little (and big) problems.

I'll have much more to say about action tendencies in the next chapter when I discuss the ways in which contemporary psychologists think about the bodily responses that accompany different emotions, since many Jamesians, as James himself did, think of such responses as having the same kinds of functional significance that Frijda attributes to them. I'll also have more to say about action tendencies in Chapter 4 when I discuss the nature of the appraisal process.

Ever Since Darwin: Representative Research on Emotion from the Darwinian Perspective

Babies do it.   As we have seen, there is compelling evidence that the facial expressions for at least six and possibly seven emotions are universally recognized. Psychologists working within the Darwinian tradition conclude from these data that these expressions and the emotions that accompany them serve important, survival-related functions and reflect innate, genetically programmed processes. If these emotional expressions are, in fact, innately determined, one might expect infants to be able to make the expressions well before they have had the chance to learn them. One might also expect that even very young infants would be able to recognize at least some of the expressions. This is the proposition Tiffany Field and her colleagues set out to test on a sample of newborn babies (Field, Woodson, Greenberg, & Cohen, 1982).

Field et al. obtained a large sample of newborns whose average age was only 36 hours and videotaped their faces while they were held by an adult who made three different kinds of faces at them. Between doing deep knee bends and clicking her tongue to get the infants' attention, the adult made the facial expressions for happiness, sadness, and surprise. Field et al. found that the infants initially spent a lot of time looking at each of the facial expressions but then rather quickly habituated to (became bored by) them and began looking away. Every time the adult would make a new expression, the infants would begin looking at her again. Field et al. took this as evidence that the infants could discriminate among the three expressions. That's pretty nifty for someone who just opened his or her eyes, but that's not all. Field et al. found very strong evidence that the newborns were actually *imitating* the facial expressions of the adult.

Field et al. came to this conclusion by analyzing the data obtained from an observer who watched the infants' faces while they watched the adult. The observer coded the presence of mouth movements and the presence of eye widening and brow furrowing on the part of the infant as well as her guess as to what expression the adult was displaying. Field et al. found that the infants' facial expressions as indicated by mouth, eye, and brow movements closely matched the adults. They also found that the observer's correct guesses as to what expression the adult was modeling were well above what would occur by chance alone. Field et al. concluded that this was an impressive feat, for it involved the ability to not only match the adult's expression but to compare the visual information received about the adult's expression with the "proprioceptive feedback" from the infant's own facial expression.

The results of this study, that babies come into the world not only with the ability to make the facial expressions for three fundamental emotions but that they can discriminate and imitate these expressions as well, have important implications for how we not only think about emotions but how we think about infants as well. If nothing else, these results suggest that newborns have the ability to actively engage the social environment into which they are born.

Raised lips and ruffled feathers: The debate over contempt. One of my favorite things about being a scientist is watching what happens when scientists disagree. Scientists, just like real people, disagree all the time, of course. What's different about scientists is that they often disagree in print. One such disagreement broke out a few years ago between Paul Ekman and Carroll Izard over who had first discovered that the facial expression for contempt was universal and what that expression looks like.

The debate started in 1986 with the publication by Ekman and Friesen of a paper entitled "A New Pan-Cultural Facial Expression of Emotion" (Ekman & Friesen, 1986) in which they report that 75% of the subjects in their study, representing ten different cultures, identified the expression in which the corner of the lip is raised slightly and tightened unilaterally as expressing contempt (that's Ekman himself making the expression in Figure 2.4). Izard and one of his colleagues (Izard & Haynes, 1987) published a paper a short time later in which they challenged Ekman and Friesen's claim to have been the first to demonstrate that there is a universal facial expression for contempt.

Izard and Haynes argued that the credit should go to Darwin, who published the first judgment study of contempt, and to Izard, whose early studies (1971) showed that there were both universal and culturally determined expressions for contempt. In their article, Izard, and Haynes, after reviewing evidence from Darwin, Ekman, and Friesen (Ekman & Friesen,

FIGURE 2.4.   *Ekman's pan-cultural facial expression for contempt. (Figure 1 from Ekman & Friesen, 1986, p. 161. Photograph courtesy of Paul Ekman.)*

1986) and Izard's own studies, conclude that the prototypical or universal facial expression of contempt involves a slight backward tilt of the head and squinting and turning of the eyes toward the object of contempt. "By this logic, the prototypical contempt expression is the human sneer, the homologue of the infrahuman snarl" (Izard & Haynes, 1987, p. 14).

This, of course, did not sit very well with Ekman and Friesen, who published a reply to Izard and Haynes in which they argue that the methodology that Izard (Izard, 1971) used to assess the universality of the facial expressions he claims indicate contempt was flawed. It is their contention that, because Izard offered his subjects *several* words (i.e., *contempt, scorn, disdainful, sneering, derisive,* and *haughty*) with which to identify the various facial expressions he showed them, it is impossible to tell exactly which his subjects were identifying when they chose a particular expression to go with the list of words. Thus, Ekman and Friesen argued that "we do not believe

we were wrong in writing that no one else before us had identified a contempt expression, for no prior study had found high agreement among observers about which expressions showed *just* contempt" (Ekman & Friesen,
1988, p. 18, emphasis added). This may seem like a minor point—that is,
that Izard gave his subjects several terms for each emotion while Ekman
and Friesen gave only one—but important decisions over whether or not
evidence supports or contradicts scientific theories often revolve around the
minute details of research methodology and, in particular, how crucial concepts are "operationalized."

The jury is still out on what constitutes the true universal facial expression of contempt, but Ekman and Friesen published another cross-cultural
judgment study a short time after their reply to Izard and Haynes in which
they present evidence that a high percentage of people from a nonEuropean
culture (this time the Minangkabau of West Sumatra, Indonesia) correctly
identified the Ekman-Friesen contempt expression of members of their own
and other cultures (Ekman & Heider, 1988).

Listen to your mother. Did your mother ever tell you to stop making
a particularly ugly face when you were a kid because, if you didn't, "Your
face will freeze and be like that FOREVER!"? Well, the results of some recent research within the Darwinian tradition suggest that there is some
truth in what your mother had to say. Taking her cue from comments by
Darwin, Tomkins (1975), along with her mentor Carroll Izard, Carol Magai
(Malatesta), and her colleagues (Malatesta, Fiore, & Messina, 1987), designed a study to see if our faces bear permanent witness to the emotions
we habitually express. Malatesta et al. began with the hypothesis that, to the
extent to which a person's personality tends to favor the experience and expression of certain emotions over others, there should be a more or less permanent "record" of those emotions "written" on the person's face. This
record could consist of either the enduring tendency to express a particular
emotion, regardless of the circumstances, or actual changes in the configura-
tion of the face in the form of wrinkles or habitually tense muscles. According to this line of reasoning, a person who is always grouchy should come
to look grouchy or angry no matter what he or she is feeling. Even though
this idea has some intuitive appeal (we all know people who look grouchy
because that's the way they are), how could one study something like this?

Malatesta et al. first assembled a group of older people (whose mean
age was 70 years) and asked them to pose a series of facial expressions for a
photographer. The subjects were asked to make a "neutral" or nonemotional face and then pose the facial expressions for four emotions,
anger, sadness, happiness, and fear. Sound familiar? Before posing for the
photographer, these subjects, who Malatesta et al. called the "encoders,"
were asked to complete a questionnaire, the Differential Emotions Scale
(DES), that assesses the extent to which particular emotions or "emotion

FIGURE 2.5. *Now there is scientific proof that your mother was right! (From Watterson, 1988, p. 133. Calvin and Hobbes © Watterson. Reprinted with permission of Universal Press Syndicate. All rights reserved.)*

traits" dominate their experience. In this way Malatesta et al. could determine what emotions these subjects typically experience. The photographs were then shown to a large group of undergraduates who were asked to judge which of Izard's list of ten fundamental emotions (see earlier discussion) each expression seemed to convey. Malatesta et al. then examined the patterns of errors in the judges' identifications of the facial expressions and found that the errors were not randomly distributed among the photographs of the encoders. Rather, Malatesta et al. found that particular encoders' faces were misjudged in consistent ways. They then examined the correlations between the judges' errors and the emotion traits of the encoders as assessed by the DES. What they found was a pattern of correlations that suggested that the encoders facial expressions of emotion were misjudged in ways that were consistent with the dominant emotions of their personalities.

The moral of this story is that your mother was probably right but there may be more to the story than Malatesta et al.'s results indicate. In particular, although Malatesta favors an interpretation of her results in terms of the lasting consequences for the musculature of the face of a lifetime of expressing particular emotions, the underlying mechanism by which her results were produced is unclear. It could just as easily be that when people are grouchy and angry or fearful or sweet all the time, people respond to them accordingly and this reinforces whatever emotional tendencies the person had to begin with. This gets us into a consideration of the social context of emotions, however, and you'll have to wait for a discussion of that until you get to Chapter 5.

Further Reading

DARWIN, C. (1872/1965). *The expression of the emotions in man and animals.* Chicago: University of Chicago Press.

EKMAN, P., & FRIESEN, W. V. (1971). Constants across cultures in the face and emotion. *Journal of Personality and Social Psychology, 17,* 124–129.

FRIDLUND, A. J. (1994). *Human facial expression. An evolutionary view.* San Diego: Academic Press.

IZARD, C. (1971). *The face of emotion.* New York: Appleton-Century-Crofts.

Listening to the Cries
and Whispers
of the Articulate Body

◆

The Jamesian Perspective

> If we fancy some strong emotion, and then try to abstract from our consciousness of it all the feelings of its characteristic bodily symptoms, we find that we have nothing left behind.
> —William James (1884, p. 193)

In *The Ship Who Sang*, the science-fiction writer Anne McCaffrey imagines a future in which children born with severe birth defects are transplanted into the bodies of ultrasophisticated spacecraft to become their "brains." As such, the bodies of the spacecraft in which they are housed become their own bodies and they are no longer able to hear or see or feel except by mechanical and electronic means. *The Ship Who Sang* tells the story of one such spacecraft, Helva, and her emotional involvement with the men who serve aboard her as "partners." Even though her body is made of metal, the spacecraft that is Helva experiences the emotions that most of us have felt at one time or another—anger, grief, passionate love, and hope—with the same, if not greater, intensity. Indeed, the title of the book refers to the nickname Helva acquires from her habit of singing when she is feeling particularly exhilarated. The American philosopher/psychologist William James (1842–1910), who lived long before it was possible to imagine such a hybrid of human and machine, and yet contemplated what our experience might be like if we were somehow separated from our bodies, would have had a very difficult time accepting the notion that a disembodied brain such as Helva's could experience emotions. After attempting to imagine the possibility himself, James concluded that a "purely disembodied human emotion is a nonentity" (James, 1884, p. 194).

For James and those who have followed him, the body is central to the generation and experience of emotions. The body, for Jamesians, is seen as possessing a complex and articulate language with which it speaks to that

FIGURE 3.1. *William James in the 1890's (Detail, fMS Am 1092. Reprinted by permission of the Houghton Library, Harvard University.)*

part of us that is conscious and experiences the world. Indeed, much of what we experience about the world is the response of our body to it. Without a body, as James imagined in the thought-experiment quoted above, there would be no emotion. It is to James' notion of an articulate body that we now turn. Before we do, however, notice how the way in which we will be thinking about emotions has changed. Whereas Darwin, with his focus on the evolutionary functions of emotions, was concerned primarily with emotional *expression*, James, as we shall see, was concerned primarily with emotional *experience*, even though he too sought to place emotions within the context of evolutionary thinking. This difference in focus has profound consequences for the kinds of phenomena James considered emotional and for the way in which he ultimately defined emotion.

Blood, Sweat, and Tears: Emotions as Bodily Changes

In order to understand James' theory of emotion, we must first have a sense of what he considered to be the *wrong* way to think about emotions. "Common sense says, we lose our fortune, are sorry and weep; we meet a bear, are frightened and run; we are insulted by a rival, are angry and strike" (James, 1884, p. 190). James believed that common sense got the sequence of emotional experience all wrong. We do not, in his view, first perceive some emotion-eliciting stimulus, experience an emotion, and then "express" it in some way. Rather, in order to experience an emotion, we first must experience the bodily changes that have been initiated directly by the perception of the emotion-eliciting stimulus. In James' own words,

> The hypothesis here to be defended says that this order of sequence is incorrect, that the one mental state is not immediately induced by the other, that the bodily manifestations must first be interposed between, and that the more rational statement is that we feel sorry because we cry, angry because we strike, afraid because we tremble, and not that we cry, strike, or tremble, because we are sorry, angry, or fearful, as the case may be. Without the bodily states following on the perception, the latter would be purely cognitive in form, pale, colourless, destitute of emotional warmth. We might then see the bear, and judge it best to run, receive the insult and deem it right to strike, but we could not actually feel afraid or angry. (James, 1884, p. 190)

In what may be the most frequently quoted statement by any psychologist ever, James summarized his view by stating that, "bodily changes follow directly the PERCEPTION of the exciting fact, and . . . our feeling of the same changes as they occur IS the emotion" (James, 1884, pp. 189–190).

In its simplest terms, James' theory states that, in order to have an emotion, one must first have bodily changes of some sort. These "changes" are the more or less automatic responses of our bodies to the perception of something important to us in our environment and it is these bodily changes that we experience as emotions. To see how this works, imagine for a moment that you are walking through the woods on a beautiful spring day. Suddenly, on the path in front of you, you see an obviously rabid woodchuck approaching you, mouth agape, teeth bared, at full gallop. (Don't laugh, this has happened at the college where I teach.) In James' formulation, this perception (combined as it is with your knowledge of the symptoms of rabies in animals, and the fact that rabies is epidemic in your part of the country) results in changes in your nervous system associated with preparing your body to deal with an event that could potentially be life-threatening. These changes are experienced as the emotion fear (see Figure 3.2).

James was convinced that a moment's reflection would be enough to persuade anyone that his theory was correct. James himself, at least, could not imagine that it was possible to experience emotions without experiencing some sort of bodily changes.

> The more closely I scrutinize my states, the more persuaded I become that whatever moods, affections and passions I have, are in very truth constituted by, and made up of, those bodily changes we ordinarily call their expression or consequence; and the more it seems to me that if I were to become corporeally anesthetic, I should be excluded from the life of the affections, harsh and tender alike, and drag out an existence of merely cognitive or intellectual form. (James, 1884, p. 194)

James' theory seems clear enough until one starts thinking about what exactly James meant by "bodily changes." This has been the source of considerable debate among emotion researchers. Indeed, entire scientific careers have been made out of clarifying and criticizing what James meant by this term. James was actually not entirely clear what he meant by the term himself, as he defined bodily changes somewhat differently in each of his three major statements of his theory of emotion (James, 1884, 1890/1983, 1894). What many people thought he said is actually quite different from what he thought (cf. Myers, 1986), although James seemed to be more than willing to give his critics ammunition by often stating his theory in language that was far from unambiguous. Since exactly what constitutes bodily changes in James' theory is such an important issue for students of emotion, let's take a brief tour of what James seems to have meant.

What did James mean by "bodily changes"?   As the "Neo-Jamesian" psychologist James Laird has pointed out, James described three very different kinds of "bodily changes" in his first statement of his theory in 1884, namely, expressive behaviors, instrumental acts, and physiological changes.

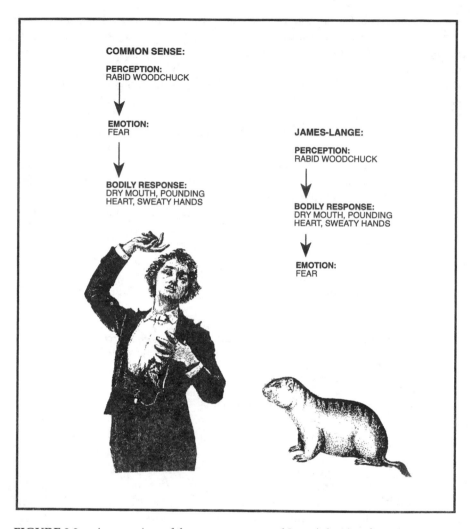

FIGURE 3.2.   *A comparison of the common-sense and James' theories of emotion.*

"Crying is a form of expressive behavior, striking out is an instrumental act, and . . . trembling is a result of physiological changes in . . . arousal level" (Laird & Bresler, 1990, p. 637). Early critics of James' theory focused on his equation of emotion with instrumental acts and attacked what they saw as the absurdity of supposing that we "are afraid because we run" (see James, 1894, for James' replies to his critics). What they missed were the subtleties in James' account of how the myriad responses of our bodies to our environment can provide us with an almost infinite number of possibilities for experience. These responses, for James, included much more than overt behavior. "[T]he various permutations and combinations of which these organic activities are susceptible, make it abstractly possible that no shade of emotion, however slight, should be without a bodily reverberation as unique, when taken in its totality, as is the mental mood itself" (James, 1884, p. 192).

Although James did indeed assert that emotional experience could follow overt behaviors such as running, cowering, or striking a blow, it is also clear that he felt that the generally unseen physiological responses of our bodies to events in our environment are also crucial determinants of emotional experience. James mentioned specifically the heart and circulatory system, but left the way open for almost any physiological response to be included in the list of bodily changes associated with emotion. "Our whole cubic capacity is sensibly alive; and each morsel of it contributes its pulsations of feeling, dim or sharp, pleasant or painful, or dubious" (James, 1884, p. 193).

Most modern interpretations of James take "bodily change" to mean either "visceral" change, that is, increases in sympathetic nervous system[1] activity and the effects of such activity on the heart and stomach and other organs innervated by the sympathetic nervous system (see, for example, Grings & Dawson, 1978; Shields & Shields, 1979), or expressive behavior, that is, changes in posture or facial expression (see, for example, Izard, 1990; Laird & Bresler, 1990). One of the most interesting and counterintuitive predictions James made from his theory—one that must have set his critics' teeth on edge—was that, if one were to adopt the posture, facial expression, or other behavior associated with a particular emotion, one would come to experience that emotion! "If our theory be true, a necessary corollary of it ought to be that any voluntary arousal of the so-called manifestations of a special emotion ought to give us the emotion itself" (James, 1884, p. 197). James felt so strongly about this aspect of his theory that he made it the subject of one of his "Talks to Students on Some of Life's Ideals," a series of lectures on what might be called moral and mental hygiene (James, 1899/1912).

James' "The Gospel of Relaxation," delivered to the Boston Normal School of Gymnastics, expands on the few comments he offered in his original statement of his theory on the effects of what we would now call "feedback" from the face and body on our experience of emotion, and transforms them into a philosophy of life. The idea is really a very simple one. If you are dejected and wish to be happy, don't mope around, act as if you are happy, and you will come to be happy.

---

[1]The *sympathetic nervous system* is a branch of the autonomic nervous system (see Appendix). The autonomic nervous system controls the functions of glands and other internal organs such as the heart and stomach. It is responsible, among other things, for controlling sweating, salivating, secreting digestive juices, changing the motility of the stomach, and shedding tears. In general, the sympathetic nervous system directs activities that prepare the body for vigorous activity. Hence, its close association with emotion.

Thus the sovereign voluntary path to cheerfulness, if our spontaneous cheerfulness be lost, is to sit up cheerfully, to look round cheerfully, and to act and speak as if cheerfulness were already there. If such conduct does not make you soon feel cheerful, nothing else on that occasion can. (James, 1899/1912, p. 201)

In this advice, one can easily see the precedence James gave to feedback from the body. James certainly knew, of course, that when we are sad or angry, we are sad or angry about something. However, he believed that the feedback we receive from our bodies is such a major determinant of our experience of an emotion that it could, in a sense, override the ideational or cognitive component of the emotion. Recent research by Laird and several other Neo-Jamesians suggests that James' advice to "grin and bear it" may very well be correct, as we shall shortly see. It is tempting to wonder if, given the bouts of depression and loss of self-confidence he suffered as a young man (see Lewis, 1991), James ever found it necessary to follow his own advice to students: "[T]o feel brave, act as if we were brave, use all our will to that end, and a courage-fit will very likely replace the fit of fear" (James, 1899/1912, p. 201).

James and Darwin

Although on first glance James' theory might not seem to bear much resemblance to Darwin's, emphasizing as it does feeling rather than expression (see Izard, 1990), James' insistence that an emotion is felt only to the extent to which it is expressed in some way can be seen as a crucial link between his theory and Darwin's. James, indeed, was a strong proponent of Darwin's evolutionary theory in the United States and James' brand of functionalism can be seen as a direct application to psychological phenomena of the idea of adaptation by natural selection.[2]

James almost certainly read Darwin's *Expression of the Emotions* shortly after it was published (see Taylor, 1990) and one can see strong echoes of Darwin's ideas about the usefulness of the various expressions of emotion in animal and human life in James' theory. James, like Darwin, considered the behavior of all animals to be useful adaptations of the animals to their environments. Indeed, James appears to have considered the nervous systems of animals to be simply the means by which animals respond to the

---

[2]*Functionalism,* as it is applied to the school of thought associated with James and the American philosopher John Dewey (1859–1952), refers to the notion that all psychological phenomena in some way contribute to human survival and ought to be studied from an evolutionary perspective. Thus, James, as a proponent of functionalism, was not so much interested in studying the contents of consciousness, as many of his contemporaries were, as he was in discovering what consciousness *did* for those who possessed it.

evolutionarily important events in their environments in appropriate ways. "The neural machinery is but a hyphen between determinate arrangements of matter outside the body and determinate impulses . . . within its organs" (James, 1884, p. 190). All animals, according to James, possess a set of "nervous anticipations" or responses to their environments that are "called forth directly by the perception of certain facts" (p. 191) in those environments. "[T]he nervous system of every living thing is but a bundle of predispositions to react in particular ways upon the contact of particular features of the environment" (p. 190). The bodily responses involved in emotions, for James, consist of just such predispositions to respond to the environment in particular situations. These predispositions, James argued, are part of every organism's evolutionary heritage. A contemporary echo of this idea may be found in Nico Frijda's (1986) conception of emotions as "action tendencies," which were described in Chapter 2. Borrowing the concept from the work of Magda Arnold (Arnold, 1960a), Frijda defines action tendencies, and hence emotions, as "states of readiness to execute a given kind of action" (p. 70), the actions in question being behaviors important to the survival of the organism, for example, calling out for help or defending oneself against a predator.

Thus, like Darwin, James believed that there was a particular evolutionary reason why certain bodily changes like frowning or an accelerated heart beat might accompany an emotion. "The labours of Darwin and his successors are only just beginning to reveal the universal parasitism of each special creature upon other special things, and the way in which each creature brings the signature of its special relations stamped on its nervous system with it upon every scene" (James, 1884, pp. 109–191). This is, I believe, a feature of James' theory that is not really appreciated by many psychologists, and is one that is rarely spoken of in discussions of his theory of emotions. Notwithstanding this, it allows us to see an important connection between the theory of expression of Darwin and the theory of feeling of James. James' contribution, over and above that of Darwin, was to attempt to construct a framework for understanding the place of feelings in an evolutionary theory of emotions. When we meet the Neo-Jamesians below, it should come as no surprise that many of those psychologists who are involved in the renaissance of interest James' theory of emotion are the same psychologists who have spent much of their careers elaborating on Darwin's ideas about emotions.

James and Lange

James' theory of emotion is often presented as the "James-Lange" theory of emotion because shortly after James published his account of his theory, a very similar theory was offered by the Danish physiologist Carl Lange

(1834–1900).[3] Lange (whose name is pronounced "long") began his "psychophysiological study" by asking the question, "What bodily manifestations accompany each of the affections?" (Lange & James, 1922, p. 38) and then detailing the bodily changes that accompany sorrow, joy, fright, anger-rage, and a few less intense emotions. Concluding first that all emotions are accompanied by bodily changes of some sort, à la James, Lange then proposes that common to all of these bodily changes are changes in the circulation of the blood by means of changes in the activity of the muscles that constrict the blood vessels (so-called vasomotor changes) and that these changes account for not only the expressive and behavioral aspects of emotion but for the experience of emotion as well.

> Is it possible that vasomotor disturbances, varied dilation of the blood vessels, and consequent excess of blood, in the separate organs, are the real, primary effects of the affections, whereas the other phenomena,—motor abnormalities, sensation paralysis, subjective sensations, disturbances of secretion, and intelligence—are only secondary disturbances, which have their cause in anomalies of vascular innervation? (Lange, 1885/1922, p. 58)

In two passages that sound as if he must have been listening in to James' thoughts while James was formulating his theory, Lange asserts that, without the circulatory changes he describes, the experience of emotion would be impossible.

> Take away the bodily symptoms from a frightened individual; let his pulse beat calmly, his look be firm, his color normal, his movements quick and sure, his speech strong and his thoughts clear; and what remains of his fear? (Lange, 1885/1922, p. 66)

> We owe all the emotional side of our mental life, our joys and sorrows, our happy and unhappy hours, to our vasomotor system. If the impressions which fall upon our senses did not possess the power of stimulating it, we would wander through life unsympathetic and passionless, all impressions of the outer world would only enrich our knowledge, but would arouse neither joy nor anger, would give us neither care nor fear. (Lange, 1885/1922, p. 80)

Given the almost universal equation of James' and Lange's theories, it is interesting to note that, whereas James acknowledged Lange's contribution to a physiological understanding of emotions (something he failed to

---

[3]Lange's monograph appeared in Danish in 1885 and was published in a German translation, most likely James' source, in 1887. An English translation of the monograph was published, along with James' "What is an emotion?" and his chapter on emotion from *Principles of Psychology,* under both Lange's and James' names in 1922.

do for many others who had proposed similar theories; see Titchener, 1914), James took issue with the specifics of Lange's vasomotor account, arguing that Lange, "simplifies and universalizes the phenomena a little too much" (James, 1890/1983, p. 1062) and places, "far too great stress on the vaso-motor factor in his explanations" (James, 1894, p. 300). Nevertheless, the two theories are strikingly similar in their insistence that, whatever they may be, the bodily concomitants of emotion come first and are followed by the experience of emotion.

Appealing to "All Who Rightly Apprehend This Problem:" James' Evidence for the Validity of His Theory

As mentioned above, James relied primarily on his own introspections to find evidence for his theory. These introspections convinced him that it would be impossible to experience emotions without the body being involved in some way. Again and again, he appealed to his readers to try to imagine what it would be like to experience an emotion without its concomitant bodily changes. For James, the evidence was overwhelming.

> I cannot help thinking that all who rightly apprehend this problem will agree with the proposition above laid down. What kind of emotion of fear would be left, if the feelings neither of quickened heart-beats nor of shallow breathing, neither of trembling lips nor of weakened limbs, neither of goose-flesh nor of visceral stirrings, were present, it is quite impossible to think. (James, 1884, pp. 193–194)

James also felt that the phenomenon of experiencing an emotion that one has merely posed, which he called "a necessary corollary" of his theory, was evidence in favor of his theory. Here too, an appeal was made to introspection: "Everyone knows how panic is increased by flight, and how the giving way to the symptoms of grief or anger increases those passions themselves" (James, 1884, p. 197). As we shall see, experimental findings that posing the expressions for various emotions may lead to the actual experience of the emotions is cited by several Neo-Jamesians as evidence that James' general theory of emotions is for the most part correct. James, however, did not have access to empirical data of this sort and, in spite of his apparent belief that the evidence from everyday introspection offered full support for his theory, he found it necessary ultimately to appeal to a very different kind of evidence, that offered by so-called pathological cases of the experience of emotion.

Scientists love accidents because accidents are often very revealing of nature's design. Ever since the time of Paul Broca, John Hughlings Jackson, and Henry Head, psychologists have found it useful to test their theories of the organization and function of the brain and nervous system by examining the consequences of various accidents and mishaps that result in damage to the brain or nervous system.[4] Such "natural experiments," as unfortunate as they may be for those who have suffered the damage, can serve as invaluable tests of theories that could not otherwise be tested. James considered two kinds of pathologies as being relevant to the evaluation of his theory that feedback from the body is necessary for the experience of emotion.

James first considered cases of "unmotivated" emotion, in which a person suffers from attacks of fear or panic in the absence of any appropriate "cause." To James' mind, the fact that a person could experience all of the feelings and bodily changes associated with anxiety without there being present any apparent instigation for the emotion was evidence in favor of his theory, for what was left to cause the experience of the emotion except for the bodily changes? Moreover, the fact that such attacks of anxiety can sometimes be alleviated by controlling one's breathing and changing one's posture made the case for James' theory even stronger.

> A friend who has had attacks of this most distressing of all maladies, tells me that in his case the whole drama seems to centre about the region of the heart and respiratory apparatus, that his main effort during the attacks is to get control of his inspirations and to slow his heart, and that the moment he attains to breathing deeply and to holding himself erect, the dread . . . seems to depart. (James, 1884, p. 199)

The most conclusive test of his theory, James felt, however, would be found in another set of cases, namely, those in which a person suffered from a complete inability to experience any feelings from his or her body (James, 1884, p. 203). James' prediction was that, if his theory were correct, then a person in such a condition, given that he or she was reasonably intact otherwise, would not experience emotions in any of the ways that "normal" people do.

> A case of complete internal and external corporeal anaesthesia, without motor alteration or alteration of intelligence except emotional apathy, would afford, if not a crucial test, at least a strong presumption, in favor of the truth of the view we have set forth. (James, 1884, p. 203)

In all three of his major statements of his theory, James considered cases of such anaesthesia of either hysterical or organic origin. Even though

---

[4]Paul Broca (1824–1880), French physician and anthropologist, John Hughlings Jackson (1835-1911), the "father" of English neurology, and Henry Head (1861–1940), English physician and neurologist, are considered key figures in the development of modern neurology for their contribution to understanding the functional anatomy of the brain and nervous system.

he ultimately concluded that each of these was either problematic for one reason or another (primarily because the right questions were not put to the subjects) or provided only weak evidence in favor of his theory, James' integrity led him, in each case, to present information from the various cases that could be interpreted as indicating that his theory was wrong. Recognizing that the evidence from this most crucial of sources was not all in his favor, James ended his first statement of his theory with a long postscript in which he argues, essentially, that while the theory may be wrong, it is still a good theory because it frames the question in an interesting way and, moreover, he has convinced *himself* that it is correct!

> We can define the pure psychic emotions far better by starting from such an hypothesis and modifying it in the way of restriction and subtraction, than by having no definite hypothesis at all. Thus will the publication of my article have been justified, even though the theory it advocates, rigorously taken, be erroneous. The best thing I can say for it is, that in writing it, I have almost persuaded myself it may be true. (James, 1884, p. 205)

In his final published statement of his theory, James reviewed the results of studies by a French physician named Sollier of a 44-year old man with nearly complete anesthesia, and the hypnotically induced anesthesia of a sample of women of "hysteric constitution" (Sollier, 1894). Sollier presented the case of the anesthetic man as confirmation of James' theory, for the man seemed to suffer from a complete inability to experience most emotions (although he did report sometimes feeling fear). Sollier's hypnotically induced anesthesiacs also seemed to support James' theory. When anaesthesia of the viscera was induced, Sollier's subjects reported experiencing no emotion whatsoever. Indeed, under these conditions, the subjects reported that they felt as if they were no longer alive.

In spite of the support they seemed to offer for his theory, James was cautious about fully accepting Sollier's findings and even remarked that "M Sollier's experimental results go on the whole farther than 'my theory' ever required" (James, 1894, p. 313). Nevertheless, James concluded that

> if many cases like those of M. Sollier should be found by other observers, I think that Prof. Lange's theory and mine ought no longer be treated as a heresy, but might become the orthodox belief. (James, 1894, p. 314)

While the James-Lange account of emotion is certainly not the "orthodox belief" that James might have wanted it to become, a growing number of emotion researchers have come to believe in its essential soundness. The path to the vindication of the James-Lange theory, however, was long and arduous and it has only been in the past ten years or so that convincing evidence in favor of theory has been presented. Before considering this evidence, however, we must first meet one of James' most vehement critics.

Of Heads and Hearts: Cannon's Critique of the James-Lange Theory

In the standard textbook account of the history of the James-Lange theory, the American physiologist Walter Cannon (1871–1945) plays the role of James' nemesis, the scientist most responsible for widespread abandonment of the theory from the 1930s on. As the story goes, after the publication of Cannon's blistering criticisms of the James-Lange theory, psychologists turned their backs on the theory and psychology went through a kind of dark ages until the theory was "rediscovered" in the 1970s and 1980s. The real story isn't so simple, of course (see Ellsworth, 1994b), but there is some truth to the orthodox view. The credibility of the James-Lange theory did suffer as a result of Cannon's critiques, and the theory is enjoying quite a renaissance, but it is also true that James' ideas about emotions continued to hold the attention of psychologists long after Cannon's attacks had supposedly done them in. Before we turn to some of the modern versions of James' theory, let's see what Cannon had to say, since, however much one might argue that the James-Lange theory never went away, it's important to realize that Cannon's ideas were also very influential, especially for social psychologists. Indeed, they set the stage for what could be considered the first truly social psychological theory of emotion, Stanley Schachter's "cognitive arousal" theory.

On the danger of giving students career advice.   Cannon was a student of James at Harvard and had once considered taking up philosophy as a career. James, however, persuaded him otherwise, reportedly telling the young Cannon, "Don't do it, you will be filling your belly with east wind" (Cannon, 1945, p. 19)! Cannon eventually went on to pursue the study of physiology but not before immersing himself in the then current thinking on emotions by way of a 102-page paper on emotions he wrote in James' undergraduate philosophy course (Benison, Barger, & Wolfe, 1987). Cannon's familiarity with James' theory of emotion led him to include a brief critique of James' theory in the context of a description of the activity of the sympathetic nervous system under various emotional states in a paper he published in 1914.

In the course of detailing the bodily changes that constitute the so-called "fight or flight" response, Cannon noted that the bodily changes that accompany fear, rage, and pain are remarkably similar to one another and that these resemble the bodily changes characteristic of joy, sorrow, and disgust when the latter emotions are "sufficiently intense." Although James sought to distance himself from the idea, many critics (and proponents) of the James-Lange theory, Cannon included, have taken the theory to imply that different emotions must necessarily be preceded by different patterns of bodily change. James himself argued forcefully that variability in the bodily changes of emotion across individuals would render futile any attempt to characterize such changes fully except at a very abstract or "functional" level (see James, 1890/1983; for commentary on this assumption, see Myers, 1986, and Laird & Bresler, 1990). Nevertheless, as it has been interpreted by others, a key feature of the theory was its prediction of what has come to be called "autonomic specificity" (see Levenson, Ekman, & Frieson, 1990). (To avoid confusion, hereafter, I'll refer to this as the "James-Lange theory" to distinguish it from the somewhat more complex and ambiguous ideas of James.) Cannon's research on the physiology of digestion and the disturbances of digestion under strong emotion convinced him that this prediction was wrong.

> [I]n terror and rage and intense elation . . . the responses in the viscera seem too uniform to offer a satisfactory means of distinguishing states which, in man at least are subjectively very different. For this reason, I am inclined to urge that the visceral changes merely contribute to an emotional complex more or less indefinite, but still pertinent, to feelings of disturbance, in organs of which we are not usually aware. (Cannon, 1914, p. 280)

Five reasons why James-Lange was wrong.   In 1927 and 1931, Cannon published two much more detailed attacks on the James-Lange theory. The essence of Cannon's critique was that the body simply does not work in the way James thought it did and therefore the claims of the James-Lange theory about the role of visceral change in the experience of emotion had no validity. Specifically, Cannon presented five different kinds of evidence that suggested that James and Lange were mistaken in believing that changes in visceral activation could account for differences in emotional experience. Keep in mind that this is a claim that James never really made and that it was Lange, much more than James, who posited a central role for feedback from the viscera (Mandler, 1990).

1. Total separation of the viscera from the central nervous system does not alter emotional behavior.
2. The same visceral changes occur in very different emotional states and in nonemotional states.
3. The viscera are relatively insensitive structures.
4. Visceral changes are too slow to be a source of emotional feeling.
5. Artificial induction of the visceral changes typical of strong emotions does not produce them. (Cannon, 1927, pp. 108–113)

From a historical perspective on the development of modern social psychological theories of emotion, the second and third points are the most important. James, of course, believed at least to some extent that his theory would stand or fall depending on evidence of the first type. The evidence that Cannon presented in this regard strongly suggested that emotions could be had without the contribution of the sympathetic nervous system, that is, without feedback from the viscera. Cannon, drawing upon his own investigations as well as extensive research by the English physiologist Charles Sherrington (1857–1952), argued that animals whose sympathetic nervous systems had been surgically separated from their brains still displayed emotional behavior. Notice the catch here, however. Emotional behavior does not necessarily equal emotional experience. Cannon himself admitted that there was no way to know if the animals in question were actually *experiencing* emotions, and remember, for James, experience is what emotions are all about. Thus, the data presented by Cannon in this regard are somewhat beside the point. A more satisfactory evaluation of this question would have to wait for much later investigations of the presence of emotions in humans whose sympathetic nervous systems had been separated from their brains by accidents of various kinds. I'll discuss this evidence shortly.

As mentioned above, James himself apparently did not believe in autonomic specificity. In the decades that followed Cannon's critiques, at least two generations of emotion researchers, however, invested huge amounts of time and energy trying to obtain evidence that different emotions were characterized by different patterns of autonomic response. As early as 1914 Cannon was arguing that no such patterns existed, and in 1927 he reiterated the claim, this time backed by more data, that, "the responses in the viscera seem too uniform to offer a satisfactory means of distinguishing emotions which are very different in subjective quality" (Cannon, 1927, p. 110). Cannon's studies had convinced him that, "the sympathetic system goes into action as a unit" (p. 110) and that only minor variations in the visceral responses for different emotions existed. For James, this information would not have had much importance for, unlike Lange, he saw the differentiation of emotions coming from a variety of sources in the body, not just the viscera.

Can emotions be artificially induced?   Cannon's coup de grâce bypassed the problem of differentiation somewhat and focused on a claim near and dear to James' heart, namely, that emotions—real emotions— could be produced by simulating the bodily movements associated with them. Cannon, maintaining his focus on the viscera, took James' claim to mean that if one could somehow artificially induce some of the visceral changes characteristic of emotion (any emotion would do), the experience of a real emotion should result. Cannon obtained data relevant to this question from a study of the effects of adrenaline injections on the experience of emotion published in 1924 by the Spanish physician Gregorio Marañon (1887–1960) (See Box 3.1). Marañon had given a sample of subjects injections of adrenaline without telling them what the effects of the injection would be and then interviewed them about what they were experiencing. Some of his subjects (about 30%) did report experiencing a genuine emotion, most often anxiety or sadness. However, the majority of his subjects (about 70%) reported feeling merely "as if" they were having an emotion but that the experience was "cold" and not typical of what they felt when they were experiencing a genuine emotion.

> I feel "as if I were afraid," "as if I were experiencing a great delight," "as if I were moved," "as if I were about to cry without knowing why," "as if I had a great fright, except that I am calm." (p. 306)

BOX 3.1

Marañon's Two-Factor Theory of Emotion

It is interesting to note that Marañon himself did not make quite the same inferences about the role of the viscera in the experience of emotion that Cannon did. For Marañon, those subjects who did report experiencing a "real" emotion after the adrenaline injection were the most interesting ones. They, he discovered, all possessed what he called a "motive" for their emotions in that they had been thinking about dead or absent family members or friends or had begun ruminating about the sad events in their lives while under the influence of the injection. For Marañon—and later for Stanley Schachter—this phenomenon revealed the crucial role played by thought in the genesis of emotion. Sympathetic nervous system arousal did appear to be important in the genesis of emotion, but no less important was the existence of some kind of situationally appropriate cognition, what Marañon called a *raison intellectuelle,* that served as a catalyst for the experience of the various bodily changes associated with sympathetic arousal as belonging to a particular emotion. Marañon thus proposed a kind of "two-factor" theory of emotion in which emotions were seen as consisting of sympathetic nervous system arousal (*émotion végétative*) plus a motive, reason or evaluation of the situation (*émotion psychique*) that allowed the symptoms of the arousal to be experienced as emotional (Cornelius, 1991). Some forty years after Marañon, Schachter would offer a very similar two-factor theory of emotion, incorporating James' theory, Cannon's critique of James, and Marañon's findings into a powerful and very influential social psychological theory of emotion, a theory that launched a thousand studies and helped determine the shape of social psychology in the last quarter of the twentieth century (see Reisenzein, 1983).

Cannon concluded from these results that "adrenaline induces in human beings typical bodily changes which are reported as sensations, that in some cases these sensations are reminiscent of previous emotional experiences but do not renew or revive those experiences" (Cannon, 1927, p. 114). In other words, case closed: Artificial induction of the bodily changes characteristic of emotion does not produce emotion. The James-Lange theory is not an adequate account of the genesis of emotion! Cannon went on to propose a countertheory, one that emphasized the role of an area of the brain called the thalamus in giving each emotion its particular experiential quality: "the peculiar quality of the emotions is added to simple sensation when the thalamic processes are roused" (Cannon, 1927, p. 120). Sensations from the organs innervated by the sympathetic nervous system, that is, visceral bodily changes, are the product, not the cause, of processes in the brain that result in the experience of emotion. To be sure, felt bodily changes do add something to the experience of the intensity of emotion, but they are not, as James and Lange argued, part and parcel of what it means to experience emotion. Because of Cannon's focus on the brain, his account of the genesis of emotional experience is often called a "centralist" theory, while the James-Lange account, with its focus on the body, is often called a "peripheralist" theory.

After Cannon

Research on emotion after Cannon developed along two distinct and opposing lines. On one side were those researchers who sought to vindicate the James-Lange theory and who thus collected evidence that there were indeed patterns of visceral or other bodily changes characteristic of each emotion. On the other side were those researchers who, following Cannon, assumed that the visceral changes that accompany emotions were essentially undifferentiated and who thus sought to find other factors that might account for the variety of emotions humans typically experience. Even though researchers in the James camp produced some quite persuasive evidence that there were distinct patterns of physiological responses for at least some emotions (fear, anger, happiness), up until the end of the 1970s the view that emotions were autonomically undifferentiated for the most part prevailed.

High-Voltage Shocks and Abusive Experimenters: The Search for Autonomic Specificity

Some of the best evidence in support of the James-Lange theory was obtained in research carried out in the 1950s by Ax (1953) and Funkenstein, King, and Drolette (1954). It was not, however, the kind of research to which one would point when trying to convince someone that social psychologists from the 1950s might have dressed funny but were essentially harmless. For example, in his attempt to recreate real-life emotions in the laboratory, Ax led subjects to believe that an electric shock generator to which they were attached had dangerously malfunctioned, shooting sparks into the air and greatly alarming the experimenter. As if that weren't enough, after the experimenter had gained control of the situation, subjects in Ax's study were introduced to an obnoxious polygraph operator who proceeded to verbally abuse them for five minutes. These fear- and anger-inducing scenarios apparently worked quite well, as subjects in the fear conduction actually pleaded with the experimenter to disconnect them from the shock generator and at least one subject prepared himself for his imminent demise, commenting later that, "[E]verybody has to go sometime. I thought this might be my time" (Ax, 1953, p. 435). Let me assure you that I don't think anyone could get away with doing something like this today. One must admit, however, that the procedures seemed to be effective in inducing real fear and real anger.

Ax found that fear and anger differed on seven of fourteen physiological measurements reflective of changes in the sympathetic nervous system, including cardiovascular activity, respiration, and muscle tension. Anger was characterized by increases in diastolic blood pressure and muscle tension, number of galvanic skin responses, and heart rate "falls," while fear was characterized by skin conductance increases, number of muscle tension peaks and respiration rate increases. Average heart rate increased during both anger and fear. These patterns, as Levenson, Ekman, and Friesen (1990) and others (e.g., Schwartz, Weinberger & Singer, 1981) were later to remark, represent the kinds of differences one would expect to see in the bodily responses of these emotions, given their role in the survival of the person. As fleeing from danger is the activity functionally associated with fear, one would expect to find bodily changes that ready one's body for vigorous exercise accompanying this emotion. A somewhat different pattern of bodily changes should be found for anger, which is associated with a very different kind of activity. This is indeed what Ax found. Similar results for anger were obtained by Funkenstein et al. (1954). Evidence that sadness and happiness ("mirth") could be differentiated at the level of the autonomic nervous system was found by Averill (1969).

Spinal-Cord Injuries and the Experience of Emotion I: Evidence in Support of James-Lange

Perhaps the most often cited study presenting evidence in favor of the James-Lange theory is one that James would have recognized immediately as fulfilling his requirements for an adequate test of his theory. In 1966, George Hohmann published a paper describing the results of research he had carried out on the emotional experience of a group of men who had sustained spinal-cord damage. Hohmann's subjects were twenty-five adult men whose spinal-cord lesions had left them with varying degrees of sensation from visceral feedback. Some of the subjects, those with cervical lesions, that is, lesions high on their spinal cords, were unable to experience any feedback from their autonomic nervous systems, whereas others, those with lumbar and sacral lesions, could experience some sensations from their viscera. Thus, Hohmann had the opportunity to examine whether the site of a spinal-cord lesion, and hence degree of feedback from the viscera, corresponded to the intensity of the experience of emotion. Through a series of structured interviews, Hohmann asked his subjects to make comparisons of their experience of fear, anger, grief, sentimentality, and sexual excitement before and after the injuries that had left them paralyzed.

Hohmann found that almost all of his subjects experienced marked decreases in their feelings of anger, fear, and sexual excitement. Moreover, the site of injury to the spinal cord showed a rough correspondence with the degree of decrease in feelings of fear and anger. Subjects with cervical and high thoracic lesions reported the greatest reduction in feelings of fear and anger, while subjects with lesions lower on the spinal cord reported the smallest reductions in fear and anger. Feelings of sexual excitement were reduced for all subjects (because, perhaps, of injury to other nerve tissue for subjects with lesions low on the spinal cord). Hohmann's subjects, especially those with lesions high on the spinal cord, described their emotions after they were injured as being qualitatively much different from their emotions before. Most often, they reported that their postinjury emotions were more "mental" and much less intense. In describing his feelings of sexual excitement, one subject commented, "It's a mental, thinking kind of thing rather than [a] physically driven feeling" (Hohmann, 1966, p. 149). Another subject, describing the changes in his experience of anger, reported,

> Now, I don't get a feeling of physical animation, it's sort of cold anger. Sometimes I act angry when I see some injustice. I yell and cuss and raise hell, because if you don't do it sometimes I've learned people will take advantage of you, but it just doesn't have the heat to it that it used to. It's a mental kind of anger. (Hohmann, 1966, p. 151)

Hohmann concluded from these findings that feedback from the viscera play an important role in the experience of emotion and, "that disruption of the autonomic nervous system and its afferent return causes notable disturbances in the mental correlates of emotion . . . the more extensive the Autonomic Nervous System disruption . . . , the greater the decrease in some emotional experiences" (Hohmann, 1966, p. 154). By implication, these findings thus offered strong support for the James-Lange theory; however, Hohmann's results were actually slightly more complicated. Interestingly, Hohmann found that the majority of his subjects, regardless of the site of their lesion, reported *increases* in what he called sentiment, the tendency to weep or get "choked-up" during the expression of tender feelings, while saying good-bye or in other "sentimental" situations. Hohmann speculated that the increased sentimentality in his subjects may have been related to depression, a condition that would not be uncommon among individuals with spinal-cord damage. Although Hohmann speculated further that depression may be accompanied by decreased autonomic arousal in intact individuals, he ultimately concluded that

> the factors responsible for this significant change are undefined. They may be physiological but, since they are found in all groups, they may be psychological. Even those with spinal cord injuries who appear to have made a good adjustment to their loss may still have a chronic, mild, pervasive feeling of depression. (Hohmann, 1966, p. 154)

One final interesting aspect of Hohmann's findings is the way they differed from those of an earlier study of emotional experience in paraplegic men by McKelligott (1959). McKelligott carried out essentially the same study a few years before Hohmann but obtained results opposite to those of Hohmann. McKelligott's subjects, some of whom would later participate in Hohmann's study, reported few differences between their pre- and post-injury experience of emotion. Upon questioning the subjects who had participated in the earlier study about the discrepancies in their reports, Hohmann discovered that many of the subjects had been reluctant to reveal any changes in their emotional experience to someone who was not also paralyzed, out of fear that he would regard them as "some sort of oddball" (Hohmann, 1966, p. 145). Hohmann reported that his subjects were much more forthcoming with him because he was also a paraplegic and would therefore "understand" their experience.

Ignoring the Evidence in Favor of James-Lange

By the mid-1960s, at least some researchers investigating emotions in the wake of Cannon's critique of James had obtained evidence that led them to believe that the James-Lange theory was essentially correct (Fehr & Stern, 1970). While the patterns of autonomic system differences among the emotions obtained by Ax, Funkenstein et al., and Averill tended to be small, they were differences nonetheless. Moreover, they were differences not only in degree or intensity but in direction as well, precisely the kind of patterning that the James-Lange theory would predict. Hohmann's study suggested that functionally separating the viscera from the brain resulted in a marked decrease in emotionality, just as James had predicted. In addition, a

re-evaluation of the James-Lange theory and review of research on peripheral involvement in the experience of emotion by Fehr and Stern (1970) that
included a thorough critique of Cannon, came out squarely on the side of
James-Lange. In spite of this evidence, the Zeitgeist of emotion theory
through the 1970s favored the view that all emotions, or at least all of the
emotions that usually concerned emotion researchers (i.e., fear, anger, happiness, sadness), were accompanied by feedback from the sympathetic nervous system that was more or less undifferentiated, that is, non-emotion-
specific. The prevailing view came to be that emotions were accompanied
by sympathetic arousal that was unidimensional, that is, either high or low
for particular emotions. George Mandler, a proponent of one cognitive approach to understanding how emotions are differentiated, summarized this
view in 1975 by arguing that

> the discriminated aspects of visceral arousal probably involve a general
> degree of arousal, and . . . [those] studies that have shown different pat-
> terns have failed to show that these patterns control emotional behavior.
> It is . . . also the case that widely different emotions show relatively little
> differences in physiological patterns . . . If, with different emotions, the
> patterns are similar, the argument can be made that it is highly unlikely
> the different emotions depend on different patterns. (Mandler, 1975,
> p. 133)

As we shall see, for Mandler and many other psychologists conducting research during this period, what differentiated emotions was not specific patterns of feedback from the viscera or other bodily sources but some
putatively cognitive process that allowed the undifferentiated feedback
from the body to be experienced as this or that emotion. This perspective,
Levenson et al. (1990) and others have argued, deflected attention away
from serious consideration of the role that autonomic feedback played in
determining the experience of different emotions.

Peter Lang, a contemporary psychophysiologist, has argued that the
view that the physiological responses associated with emotions are "a kind
of bubbling physiological soup, which is stirred up and given its distinctive
taste by the subject's cognitive appraisal" (Lang, 1979, p. 507), gained dominance over the James-Lange view partly for methodological reasons. According to Lang, the kinds of studies that could reveal the body's language
of emotion, studies such as Ax's, were simply too difficult to carry out for
both practical and ethical reasons. To these reasons, I think one must add
another, namely, that psychology during this period (the late 1950s through
the mid- to late 1970s) was dominated by behaviorism, which, with its emphasis on learning and the environmental determinants of behavior, may
have also inclined psychologists to ignore the physiological differences
among emotions.

For whatever reason, researchers in the 1960s and 1970s for the most part ignored or downplayed the evidence that supported the James-Lange theory and focused instead on cognitive and social factors involved in the genesis of emotion. One of the most important and seminal figures in this regard was Stanley Schachter, whose "two-factor" theory represents a kind of modified Jamesian approach to understanding emotions. Schachter, reacting to what he saw as the shortcomings of the James-Lange theory—primarily the absence of evidence of autonomic specificity—proposed a solution that reconciled the observation that emotions had to be about something and so required a cognitive component, with the understanding, more or less widespread at the time, that all emotions involved unidimensional sympathetic nervous system arousal.

The Body Has a Head: Stanley Schachter's Two-Factor Theory of Emotion

The first statement of Schachter's theory was published in 1962, in an article Schachter co-authored with Jerome Singer. Schachter and Singer's paper not only presented a new theory of emotion but described an elaborate and elegant experiment designed to provide support for the theory. In 1964, Schachter presented a more comprehensive statement of the theory and the evidence for it and the theory has been linked to his name alone ever since. I shall follow this convention and refer to the theory by Schachter's name only.

Schachter's theory rests on the notion that emotions consist of two components: *physiological arousal*, which is another term for what I've been calling autonomic feedback from the viscera or some other bodily source, and a *situationally-appropriate cognition*, which allows that arousal to be experienced as a particular emotion. "[A]n emotional state may be considered a function of a state of physiological arousal and of a cognition appropriate to this state of arousal" (Schachter & Singer, 1962, p. 380) or, as many an introductory psychology professor has written on the chalkboard: AROUSAL + COGNITION = EMOTION.

With this simple formulation, Schachter tied together a great deal of what was understood about emotions from the work of James and Cannon and provided psychology with an exceptionally rich theory that deeply influenced a generation or more of emotion researchers. That the theory is now regarded by many (see Reisenzein, 1983) as extremely flawed in no way detracts from the vital role that it had in stimulating a great deal of important research on emotions in the sixties, seventies, and eighties. Indeed, Schachter's theory was so filled with possibilities that it may be argued that it, and the research and theories it inspired, influenced the very course of social psychology during the two decades following its appearance.

Schachter explicitly considered his theory to be part of the Jamesian tradition (see Schachter, 1964, p. 70) and proposed the theory as a way to address the criticisms leveled at the James-Lange theory by Cannon. Schachter, like James, believed that some kind of bodily change was absolutely essential for the experience of emotion. Also, like James, he was somewhat unclear as to exactly what he meant by "bodily change." Preferring "physiological arousal" to the "more specific 'excitation of the sympathetic nervous system,'" Schachter argued that the "physiological" component of his model of emotion could refer to "a variety of bodily states" (Schachter & Singer, 1962, p. 380). In this he was much closer to the spirit of James than to that of Lange. Although he averred that Cannon's criticisms of the James-Lange theory had been weakened somewhat by new evidence, Schachter admitted that Cannon's arguments, "make it inescapably clear that a completely peripheral or visceral formulation of emotion, such as the James-Lange theory, is inadequate to cope with the facts" (Schachter, 1964, p. 50). The "facts," as Schachter saw them, were that the experience of particular emotions was underdetermined by feedback from the viscera or other bodily sources. In his view, there simply wasn't the kind of specificity in such bodily changes that would account for the great variety of emotions we can experience. Something else was needed: that something else was cognition.

Schachter argued, based on the findings of Marañon, (see above) and the replications of Marañon's study by Cantril and Hunt (1932) and Landis and Hunt (1932) that physiological arousal alone is not enough to initiate a real experience of emotion. So few of Marañon's subjects experienced genuine emotions because, although their bodies told them they were emotional, they had no appropriate cognition to explain to themselves why they felt this way. For Schachter, any time a person is in a state of physiological arousal—and remember, this can mean many different kinds of bodily states—that is not somehow already explained by the person's thoughts or surroundings, certain "evaluative needs" will be aroused in the person as well. The need to explain one's bodily state will then lead one to search for an appropriate explanation for one's arousal. Once that explanation is discovered, the person experiences the arousal as a particular emotion or other bodily state (such as hunger). To see how Schachter's model works, consider the following scenario:

You are sitting in a dimly lit campus-side bistro after a hard day of classes sipping your fourth or fifth cup of expresso when a very attractive classmate of yours from your social psychology class walks in. You've noticed him a couple of times in class when he's spoken and you've remarked to yourself once or twice how handsome he is. This evening, however, something about him really catches your eye and you decide to signal him over to your table and invite him to join you for a cup of coffee. This he does. (He's not only handsome and intelligent, but very agreeable to boot.)

You sit talking for a while and you manage to drink two more cups of expresso without really noticing it. (He's such a charming conversationalist!) After about half an hour you become aware of your heart pounding and your blood racing. You find that it's becoming difficult for you to think coherently. You have some vague sense that you are nauseous but the feeling isn't all that unpleasant. You notice that you are breathing so fast that you are almost panting. You glance over at your classmate, gaze deeply into his eyes for a moment and realize that you are falling in love.

The above scenario represents one of the ways in which an emotion can be generated according to Schachter's theory. First, some sort of bodily change takes place in a person. This change can be of a variety of types and can be due to a variety of factors. In this example, the powerful stimulant caffeine in the coffee initiates a number of physiological changes in the person. Second, the bodily changes are perceived by the person and the person is put into a state in which he or she is motivated to find an explanation for these changes. The search for the cause for the perceived bodily changes ends as soon as an appropriate probable cause is found. The search can end with the person either finding a cause for the changes of which he or she had previously been unaware, in this case, the realization that too much coffee makes one nervous, or reappraising the emotional significance of the situation and labeling the bodily changes as a particular emotion (cf. Reisenzein, 1983). The latter case will result in the experience of emotion, the former will not.

Although the situation described above is not the usual way in which emotions come into being, it has been the scenario that has most interested social psychologists and the one most typically studied in the laboratory (Reisenzein, 1983). In fact, designing experiments to reveal how people deal with the perception of unexplained arousal and to manipulate the attributions people make about such arousal—via what came to be called *misattribution*[5]—became something of a growth industry in social psychological research in the 1960s and 1970s, generating many interesting and clever studies, not only of emotions, but of many other phenomena assumed to involve undifferentiated arousal in need of cognitive labeling (e.g., eating, see Schachter, 1967; sexual arousal, see Cantor, Zillmann, & Bryant, 1975; and insomnia, see Storms & Nisbett, 1970, to name a few). The famous laboratory study that Schachter and Singer presented in their 1962 paper as support for the theory also involved just such an unusual situation (see later discussion).

Most emotions, however, are not generated in this manner. What comes first in everyday life is the appraisal of a situation in an emotional manner. This leads to the generation of physiological arousal and, simulta-

---

[5]*Misattribution* refers to occasions in which individuals misidentify the sources of their emotional arousal.

neously, a situationally appropriate label for the arousal. "In nature, . . . cognitive or situational factors trigger physiological processes, and the triggering stimulus usually imposes the label we attach to our feelings" (Nisbett & Schachter, 1966, p. 228). Note how remarkably similar this sounds to James' theory of emotion. The major difference, of course, is that, for James, "physiological processes" come with their own label, whereas for Schachter, that label has to be supplied by some form of cognition about the emotion-eliciting situation.

Offensive Questions and Wastebasket Hoops: Schachter and Singer's Evidence for the Two-Factor Theory

For Schachter, each component of emotion is necessary for the experience of emotion, one without the other—arousal without a label or a label without arousal—will not produce emotion. Schachter and Singer (1962) sought to demonstrate that both components were necessary by designing a study in which they could independently manipulate the physiological arousal their subjects experienced and whether or not their subjects possessed a situationally appropriate label for their arousal. Schachter and Singer's subjects were recruited to participate in a study of the effects of vitamin supplements on vision. Subjects were brought to a laboratory and were told that for the study they would be injected with an experimental vitamin supplement called Suproxin and, after the Suproxin had time to take effect, they would be given a test of their vision. This was all part of an elaborate cover story designed to disguise the true nature of the study.

After agreeing to participate in the study, subjects were randomly assigned to one of two groups. Subjects in one of the groups were given an injection of epinephrine, a drug that causes sympathetic nervous system arousal, while subjects in the other were given an injection of a saline solution. All subjects were then randomly assigned again, this time to one of three groups. The first group was given an accurate description of the effects of epinephrine; they were told that some people experience certain side effects after being given Suproxin, such as shaky hands, pounding heart, and flushed face. These were the *Epinephrine-Informed* subjects. Subjects in the second group were told that the injection was "mild and harmless and would have no side effects." These were the *Epinephrine-Ignorant* subjects. Subjects in the third group were given inaccurate information about the effects of epinephrine; they were told that their feet might get numb, they would feel itchy all over, and would get a headache. These were thus the *Epinephrine-Misinformed* subjects.

By means of the three kinds of information, Schachter and Singer were able to manipulate whether or not their subjects had an appropriate explanation or label for the arousal that would be induced by the epinephrine. Subjects given epinephrine along with an accurate description of its effects, according to Schachter's theory, would not be expected to report feeling emotional because their arousal already had a nonemotional explanation. They had the arousal without the appropriate emotional cognition. On the other hand, subjects given the saline injection were not expected to report feeling emotional either because they did not have the physiological arousal required for the generation of emotion. Subjects given epinephrine and either no information or inaccurate information about the effects of epinephrine should report feeling whatever emotion was appropriate to the situation in which they found themselves. Schachter and Singer manipulated their subjects' emotional context, and hence the availability of a situationally appropriate label for those subjects who did not already have one, in the following manner.

Once the subjects had been given the information about the effects of Suproxin, they were led to a room where they were told they were to wait for the Suproxin to take effect. Once this had happened, they were told, their vision would be tested. In the room, the subjects encountered another subject who was also waiting for his Suproxin to take effect. The second subject was actually a confederate of Schachter and Singer. He was placed in the room to provide the subjects with either one of two different emotional contexts for their arousal.

In the *euphoria* condition, the stooge, as Schachter and Singer called him, began an elaborately scripted routine that began with his doodling on scrap paper and ended with his shooting balled-up pieces of paper at the wastepaper basket and clowning around with a hula-hoop. In the *anger* condition, the subject and stooge were told they had to complete a questionnaire. The stooge, pacing his progress on the questionnaire with that of the subject, began his routine by remarking how long the questionnaire was and went on to become increasingly irritated and offended by the increasingly irritating and offensive questions it contained. When the stooge and subject got to the question "How many times each week do you have sexual intercourse?," the stooge exclaimed, "The hell with it! I don't have to tell them all this." A few moments later, he ripped up his questionnaire, threw the pieces to the floor and stomped out of the room, saying, "I'm not wasting any more time. I'm getting my books and leaving." The subject, if he continued filling out the questionnaire, was confronted with eight more offensive questions, the last of which was, "With how many men (other than your father) has your mother had extramarital relationships? 4 and under____ _____; 5–9_____; 10 and over_____."

Schachter and Singer took measures of their subjects' emotions in the anger and euphoria conditions by direct observation of their behavior (by means of a one-way window) and by a self-reported mood questionnaire that subjects completed after their session with the stooge. A crude measure of physiological arousal—pulse rate—was also obtained before and after the session with the stooge. Table 3.1 presents the results of the behavioral observations and self-report measures for the euphoria and anger conditions. Even though they presented them, Schachter and Singer argued that the self-report measures of their subjects' mood in the anger condition were not valid because they found that their subjects were unwilling to report that they were angry in any way that might potentially get back to the experimenter and jeopardize the extra exam credit they were promised in return for their participation. They note, however, that when subjects thought they were alone with another subjects they apparently felt more free to act in a manner congruent with their feelings.

Since the presence of physiological arousal was crucial to the usefulness of the study as a test of Schachter's theory, before examining their data, Schachter and Singer first checked to see if the epinephrine injection had indeed put their subjects into a state of arousal. Examination of their data revealed that subjects injected with epinephrine had significantly higher self-

TABLE 3.1   *Behavioral and self-report results of Schachter and Singer's (1962) test of Schachter's two-factor theory of emotion*

Euphoria		
Condition	*Self-Report Index**	*Behavioral Index***
Epinephrine-Informed	0.98	12.72
Epinephrine-Ignorant	1.78	18.28
Epinephrine-Misinformed [Euphoria only]	1.90	22.56
Saline-Injection	1.61	16.00
Anger		
Condition	*Self-Report index**	*Behavioral index***
Epinephrine-Informed	1.91	–0.18
Epinephrine-Ignorant	1.39	+2.28
Saline-Injection	1.63	+0.79

*The self-report index was derived by subtracting each subject's rating of how irritated, angry, or annoyed he felt (on a 5-point scale: 0—"I don't feel at all irritated or angry," 4—"I feel extremely irritated and angry") from how good or happy he felt (0—"I don't feel at all happy or good," 4—"I feel extremely happy and good").

**The behavioral index represents the extent to which subjects either joined in the stooge's activity in each condition or ignored or simply watched the stooge's activity. Higher numbers indicate high levels of emotion, lower numbers indicate the absence of emotion.

Source: After Schachter and Singer, 1962, Tables 2, 3 and 5.

ratings of physical symptoms characteristic of sympathetic nervous system arousal (i.e., palpitation and tremor) than did those subjects injected with saline. Epinephrine-injected subjects also had significantly higher pulse rates than did saline-injected subjects. Thus, Schachter and Singer concluded that the epinephrine increased subjects' physiological arousal. But, did the arousal, combined with the manipulation of the subjects' knowledge of the effects of the injection and their emotional context, have its intended effect?

As the top half of Table 3.1 indicates, the epinephrine-injected subjects who had a reasonable explanation for their arousal reported the least euphoria of any of the subjects. They also displayed the lowest level of euphoric behavior while in the presence of the euphoric stooge. Epinephrine-Ignorant and Epinephrine-Misinformed subjects reported the highest levels of euphoria in this condition and showed the highest levels of euphoric behavior. The finding that the Epinephrine-Ignorant and Epinephrine-Misinformed subjects were not that different from each other indicates that the difference between the Epinephrine-Ignorant and Epinephrine-Informed subjects was not due to simply giving subjects information about the side effects of the injection.

These results provide some support Schachter's theory (although it must be admitted that the obtained differences among the groups were not overwhelmingly large). If subjects experiencing sympathetic arousal have a plausible explanation for their arousal, as the Epinephrine-Informed subjects did, they will not experience the arousal as emotion. If they do not have a plausible explanation for their arousal, which was the case for the Epinephrine-Ignorant and Epinephrine-Misinformed subjects, they will experience the arousal as an emotion appropriate to their situational context. Examination of the lower half of Table 3.1 indicates that the difference between the Epinephrine-Informed and Epinephrine-Ignorant subjects was not limited to the euphoria condition. Epinephrine-Informed and Epinephrine-Ignorant subjects also differed significantly on the behavioral measures obtained in the anger condition.

The three groups differed in the predicted direction as well on the self-report measures of anger, although there is a curious anomaly in the patterns of self-report results for the euphoria and anger conditions. Setting aside Schachter and Singer's qualms about the anger self-report data, notice that subjects in the Epinephrine-Informed anger condition reported feeling the *most* euphoric of all the subjects in the study, while subjects in the Epinephrine-Informed euphoria condition reported feeling the *least* euphoric. In addition, Maslach (1979), in an important critique of Schachter and Singer's study, pointed out that, "the means of all conditions reflect a feeling of 'slight happiness,' regardless of the emotional cues provided by the euphoric and angry confederates" (p. 954). Apparently, Schachter and

Singer were not entirely successful in creating whatever emotion they wanted on top of the arousal they induced.[6]

Notice that there is another anomaly in the results presented in Table 3.1. Subjects who received a saline injection, an injection that should not have aroused them to any appreciable degree, reported higher levels of euphoria and displayed higher levels of euphoric behavior than did Epinephrine-Informed subjects. Saline-injected subjects in the anger condition showed a similar pattern. Since the saline-injected subjects did not have any unexplained arousal to account for, they should not have been affected by the emotional context in which Schachter and Singer placed them. Schachter and Singer accounted for this anomaly by examining the pulse rates of saline-injected subjects. They found that saline-injected subjects whose pulse rate increased during the experimental session and who thus were in a state of heightened arousal showed higher levels of both euphoria and anger relative to saline-injected subjects whose pulse rate decreased. The self-reported and observed emotion of the latter, in fact, were "quite comparable to the emotional level of subjects in the parallel [Epinephrine Informed] conditions" (Schachter & Singer, 1962, p. 395). Thus, Schachter and Singer were able to ultimately conclude that, "[w]hen either the level of sympathetic arousal is low or a completely appropriate cognition is available, the level of emotionality is low" (1962, p. 395) and that the anomalous data, when carefully examined, actually supported their hypotheses. Other researchers, commenting on their results have not been so sure (see Maslach, 1979, p. 954).[7] Their misgivings presaged major troubles for Schachter's theory, which I'll describe in a moment.

For a short time, however, Schachter and Singer's findings, and the results of several other studies carried out by Schachter and his collaborators (see Schachter, 1964) seemed to tidy up the mess left by Cannon's critique of the James-Lange theory. In particular, at least according to Schachter and Singer, the findings suggested that James was correct in arguing that bodily change is necessary for the experience of emotion but he was wrong to believe that bodily change alone will result in the experience of emotion. What transforms feedback from bodily changes into the experience of particular emotions is the "label" that gets attached to such bodily changes. Such labels are, in turn, a function of a person's perception of his or her surroundings.

---

[6]I thank one of the anonymous reviewers of the manuscript for this book for pointing these things out to me.

[7]Maslach (1979) found so many problems in Schachter and Singer's findings that she declared that, "[a]lthough their conclusion is provocative, a careful inspection of the findings suggests that it is not, in fact, supported by the evidence" (p. 954).

The Cruelty of History: Failures to Find Support for Schachter's Theory

While Schachter's reformulation of the James-Lange theory seemed initially quite promising and produced an extraordinary amount of research in its wake, much of that research, ironically, did not support the theory. The authors of two very extensive reviews of the research inspired by Schachter's theory and Schachter and Singer's classic study (Cotton, 1981; Reisenzein, 1983), concluded that the theory, at least in the form originally proposed by Schachter, is not entirely tenable. As Cotton (1981) has remarked, "time has not been charitable" (p. 372) to Schachter's theory. Curiously, studies attempting to replicate Schachter and Singer's original study or otherwise provide a direct test of Schachter's theory have generally not supported the theory, while other research, not explicitly intended to provide evidence for the theory—most notably research on misattribution—*has* supported the theory, at least in part. In this section I'll briefly summarize a few of the more important criticisms of and failures to replicate Schachter and Singer and conclude with a summary of research that can be seen as support for Schachter's theory. Since the literature on Schachter's theory is quite extensive, my review is necessarily selective. If you are interested in exploring the controversy over Schachter's theory in more depth, the excellent reviews by Cotton (1981) and Reisenzein (1983) will provide you with all of the detail you need (and then some!).

Plutchik and Ax (1967), in an early critique of Schachter and Singer's study, identified a number of problems with the latter's methodology. Among other things, they questioned the assumption that the epinephrine injections that Schachter and Singer gave their subjects actually produced a state of sympathetic nervous system arousal, arguing that the measure of arousal that Schachter and Singer used has been shown to be an unreliable indicator of such arousal. They also noted that the verbal index of emotion that Schachter and Singer used was inherently ambiguous. Schachter and Singer had constructed an index of their subjects' emotion by subtracting each subject's rating of how much irritation he felt from his rating of how happy he felt. A score of 0, Plutchik and Ax pointed out, could reflect either the complete lack of emotion or a mixture of the extremes of both emotions. Plutchik and Ax also called attention to the lack of any significant difference between the self-reported or observed emotions of subjects who had received a saline injection and those who had received a dose of epinephrine. Schachter and Singer's post hoc reanalyses aside, the failure to find such a difference posed a major threat to the theory as evaluated by Schachter and Singer's study. Finally, Plutchik and Ax questioned whether Schachter and Singer's findings had much relevance to the debate over autonomic differentiation of emotions. Although they did not explicitly invoke James, it is clear that they had his theory in mind when they argued that

> To show that one particular arousal agent such as adrenaline can be helpful in the development of two different emotions such as joy or fury in no way denies the possibility that both the cognitive and physiological systems are differentiated with regard to these two arousal states. (Plutchik & Ax, 1967, p. 81)

Attempts to replicate Schachter and Singer.   In two important attempts to replicate while improving the methodology of Schachter and Singer, Marshall and Zimbardo (1979) and Maslach (1979) found that, far from being affectively neutral, unexplained arousal was experienced by subjects as distinctly negative. Marshall and Zimbardo injected one group of subjects with either epinephrine or a placebo, gave them misleading information about the effects of the injection and placed them in the company of a euphoric confederate. To provide comparisons, Marshall and Zimbardo injected another group of subjects with epinephrine and exposed them to a neutral confederate. Another group was given accurate information about the effects of epinephrine but was injected with a placebo. Another was injected with a dose of epinephrine adjusted for body weight, and a final group was injected with epinephrine and then given a series of exercises to perform that were intended to increase the salience of any arousal they may have had from the injection.

Unlike Schachter and Singer, Marshall and Zimbardo found that the euphoric behavior of the confederate had little effect on subjects' self-reports of euphoria. The major influence on subjects' emotion was from the epinephrine injections and these were in a direction opposite to that predicted by Schachter's theory and Schachter and Singer's findings. Namely, subjects injected with epinephrine reported much more negative affect than did those injected with a placebo. This effect was especially pronounced for the two groups that received body-weight-adjusted doses of epinephrine. The presence of a euphoric confederate did influence the behavior of the subjects to some extent but this effect paled in comparison with that produced by the epinephrine injections. Marshall and Zimbardo, in summarizing their findings, concluded that

> [t]here is no evidence in the data generated by this study to warrant acceptance of the Schachter and Singer (1962) reported demonstration of the interaction of cognitive and physiological determinants of emotion. In particular, there was no instance in which subjects with inadequately explained epinephrine-produced arousal were significantly more susceptible than placebo controls to the induction of affect by exposure to a confederate who modeled euphoric behavior. (Marshall & Zimbardo, 1979, p. 980)

They concluded further that, "there are definite limitations to the power of cognitive control" (Marshall & Zimbardo, 1979, p. 982) and that

> [i]t is somewhat reassuring, especially considering their possible adaptive significance, that our true emotions may be more rationally determined and less susceptible to transient or whimsical situational determinants than has been suggested by Schachter and Singer. (Marshall & Zimbardo, 1979, p. 983)

Maslach, using hypnotically induced arousal, obtained results very similar to those of Marshall and Zimbardo. Subjects in her study, put into a state of unexplained arousal, also experienced that arousal as negative. They also displayed a clear difference between their behavior and their self-reported experience. These findings led Maslach to question seriously the validity of Schachter's theory and the research conducted by Schachter and his colleagues (i.e., Schachter & Wheeler, 1962) in support of the theory. She concluded that "people utilize far more sources of information in generating their emotional explanations than was initially suggested by Schachter and Singer's (1962) analysis," and that the emotional explanations of the subjects in her study, "appeared to be a complex function of their past experience, current life situation, and the immediate situational circumstances, rather than just the mood of the confederate" (Maslach, 1979, p. 965). With regard to the James-Lange theory, one particularly important source of information for subjects with regard to their current mood is the affective tone of any arousal they may be experiencing. The particular kind of sympathetic nervous system arousal induced by injections of epinephrine may very well be the same kind of arousal we experience when we are anxious.

A third replication of Schachter and Singer's study by Erdmann and Janke (1978) obtained results that were somewhat more promising from the point of view of Schachter's theory. Erdmann and Janke orally administered either ephedrine or a placebo to their subjects and then exposed them to one of four different emotional contexts, neutral, happy, angry or anxious. They found no difference in self-reported emotion for subjects in the placebo angry and placebo happy conditions, but subjects given ephedrine in the happy condition were significantly happier than subjects in the anger condition who had been given ephedrine. Thus, the presence of arousal was seen to significantly facilitate the experience of emotion, as Schachter's theory would predict. The implications of this finding for the theory were rendered somewhat ambiguous, however, by the additional finding that the various ephedrine conditions were not significantly different from their associated placebo conditions.

Misattribution studies. Schachter's theory has fared much better in some ways in studies using the so-called *misattribution paradigm* (cf. Cotton,

1981). One of the more interesting and useful implications of Schachter's theory was the notion that if a person could be persuaded that his or her arousal was not due to a particular emotion but was a consequence of some nonemotional factor, he or she would not experience the arousal as emotional. Therapists were quick to recognize in this a method of reducing the fears and anxiety of people placed in fear- or anxiety-arousing situations such as giving a speech. The logic behind studies using the misattribution paradigm is as follows.

Imagine for a moment that you have been asked on very short notice to give a speech in front of a large audience. The speech you have been asked to give is on a difficult topic you don't know much about and you've learned that the audience will be made up almost entirely of high-school English teachers who, you are told, will be mercilessly critical of your grammar. Shortly before you are scheduled to give your speech you suffer a minor allergy attack and take a nonprescription antihistamine/decongestant tablet. As your appointment with doom approaches, you notice that your hands are trembling and your heart is racing. You immediately attribute these symptoms to the drug you've just taken and not to the ordeal you are about to endure. As you begin your speech you notice that you are remarkably calm and you remain calm throughout your speech, which is greeted with thunderous applause.

The earliest misattribution study was carried out by Nisbett and Schachter (1966), who found that subjects given a pill that was described as having physiological effects similar to those accompanying anxiety (increased heart rate and respiration) tolerated higher levels of a painful electric shock than did subjects given a pill described as having anxiety-irrelevant effects (numbness and headache). Nisbett and Schachter argued that subjects did this because they attributed the arousal engendered by the shocks to the pill and not to the shocks themselves and so they experienced less pain. In research involving a variety of different types of stressful situations, from being in an overcrowded room (Worchel & Yohai, 1979) to watching an anxiety-provoking film (Girodo, 1973) to reading a speech in front of a camera (Olson, 1988), precisely the kinds of misattribution effects predicted by Schachter's theory have been found. There have been, however, many failures to find misattribution effects (e.g., Calvert-Boyanowsky & Leventhal, 1975), and some of the most theoretically interesting studies, most notably Storms and Nisbett's (1970) demonstration that misattribution could be used to alleviate insomnia, have never been replicated (see Kellog & Baron, 1975; Bootzin, Herman, & Nicassio, 1976). Moreover, as both Cotton and Reisenzein point out, while it is not uncommon for misattribution manipulations to work (e.g., reduce anxiety), actual measures of whether or not subjects are attributing their arousal to a neutral source have consistently failed to reveal the expected pattern of misattribution. This has led some researchers to propose alternative mechanisms for misattribution effects (see, for example, Allen, Kenrick, Linder, & McCall, 1989). Thus, it may be argued that misattribution studies offer only limited support for Schachter's theory.

Excitation transfer studies.   An extensive series of studies carried out by Dolf Zillmann and his colleagues (see Zillmann, 1978, for a review) on what is called *excitation transfer* provide some support for Schachter's theory, but, here again, while the behavior of the subjects in the studies conforms to predictions made by Schachter's theory, the mechanisms by which that behavior is produced remain largely unknown. In Zillmann's research, subjects are put into a state of high arousal by some nonemotional means, for example, by vigorously exercising on a stationary bicycle. They are then placed in an emotion-provoking situation and the effect of the prior arousal on their behavior is assessed. The idea is that the arousal induced by exercising will not have fully abated by the time subjects are placed in the emotion-provoking situation and thus the "transferred" arousal will facilitate whatever emotion is elicited in the second situation. Findings within the excitation transfer paradigm are quite robust and include a wide variety of both emotional and nonemotional behavior.

In one classic study within this paradigm, Zillmann and Bryant (1974) asked subjects to ride an exercise bicycle or engage in a non-arousing task. Subjects were then insulted by a confederate of the experimenters. When later given the chance to retaliate against the person who had insulted them, high-arousal subjects displayed considerably more aggressive behavior than did low-arousal subjects. Subjects in the high-arousal condition who were not provoked, however, did not display elevated levels of aggressive behavior, suggesting that, as Schachter's theory would predict, a situationally appropriate label was needed for the arousal to have its effect (cf. Cotton, 1981). Critical variables in the excitation paradigm include the timing of the task or event to which the exercise-induced arousal is to be transferred. If the events follow the exercise too closely, the transfer effect is not obtained, which also makes sense in light of Schachter's theory. Presumably, if subjects are put into an emotion-provoking situation immediately after engaging in strenuous exercise, they know exactly where their arousal has come from. The source of arousal for subjects put into an emotion-provoking situation after a delay, however, is much less salient and hence open to misattribution (see Zillmann, Johnson, & Day, 1974).

Negative-ion concentration and arousal.   Have you ever seen advertisements for those little "negative ion" air-cleaning devices that you plug into your car's cigarette lighter? Have you ever wondered what they might do in addition to ridding your car of unpleasant smells? A final bit of indirect evidence in favor of Schachter's theory comes from a recent series of very interesting and novel studies by Robert Baron and his colleagues on the effects of the high concentrations of negative ions produced by such devices on aggressive behavior (Baron, Russell, & Arms, 1985) and interpersonal attraction (Baron, 1987). Baron and his colleagues have found that the presence of high concentrations of negative ions facilitates aggressive behavior in subjects who have been angered and increases the perceived attractiveness of interaction partners. Baron (1987) reports that these effects are mediated through autonomic arousal, with high concentrations of negative ions heightening arousal. While there is no evidence in these studies that subjects are actually misattributing the source of their arousal, these findings can be conveniently explained by Schachter's theory.

Swaying Bridges and Swooning Tourists

What do the first-century, B.C., Roman poet Ovid and the writers for the television program *Miami Vice* have in common? Although they are separated by several centuries, each knows something about how to jump-start a romantic relationship. What they both know is reflected in one of the more inspired applications of Schachter's theory.

In one of the episodes of *Miami Vice,* Sonny, one of the program's heroes, is given an assignment to be the bodyguard for a famous singer who is being stalked by an assassin. Sonny is resentful at having been given such an assignment and his annoyance with the situation grows when he and the singer, Caitlin, do not hit it off. In fact, Sonny and Caitlin very quickly come to loathe each other and they spend most of their time together trading insults or sulking around. This goes on for quite a while until the inevitable scene in which Caitlin and Sonny are attacked by a large gang of machine gun–toting hitmen in fast, loud speedboats. Bullets whiz overhead in every direction and boats go out of control and explode as Sonny successfully fights off Caitlin's attackers. Caitlin has somehow managed to escape unhurt by crouching at Sonny's feet (*Miami Vice* did not go out of its way to question traditional sex roles) and as the last speedboat explodes and Sonny puts down his gun and kneels down to see if Caitlin is okay, he and Caitlin look meaningfully into each other's eyes and embrace passionately. Lots of kissing and that sort of thing follows and it is very apparent that the antipathy that Caitlin and Sonny felt for each other has been transformed into passion. A skeptical sort of person might ask, "Whoa, wait a minute! What just happened?"

Both Ovid and the social psychologist Elaine Hatfield would explain Caitlin and Sonny's situation in the same way, but they'd use somewhat different language. Hatfield, drawing on her use of Schachter's theory to explain passionate love, would say that Caitlin's and Sonny's initial dislike for one another put them into a state of physiological arousal. The fact that Caitlin and Sonny were continually at each other's throats probably kept them in a fairly high state of arousal most of the time. During the climactic attack scene, the whizzing bullets, exploding boats and general high level of chaos kicked up their arousal levels even higher. When the danger had passed, it is likely that their arousal levels were still very high (as Zillmann would predict). What happened next was a classic case of misattribution. Caitlin and Sonny, feeling themselves quite aroused, attributed this arousal to passion for each other. (You did the same in the campus coffee shop, remember?)

Hatfield's insight that, "perhaps it does not really matter how one produces an agitated state in an individual . . . As long as one attributes his [or her] agitated state to passion, he [or she] should experience true passionate love" (Walster [Hatfield], 1971, p. 90) was tested in a couple of inventive studies by Dutton and Aron (1974). Dutton and Aron arranged for an attractive young woman to meet single men at either the halfway point of a long, narrow footbridge high above a rocky gorge or on a much more solid bridge covering a less imposing expanse. The study took place at the Capillano suspension bridge just outside of Vancouver, Canada. The bridge is 450 feet long and about 250 feet high and I can testify from personal experience that it is quite thrilling, that is to say, arousing, to walk across (especially given the large numbers of small children who run back and forth across it trying to make it sway even more). Dutton and Aron reasoned that, if standing in the middle of the bridge were indeed arousing then it might be possible for someone to misattribute that arousal to some other source. And this is just what they found.

Dutton and Aron's confederate met men in the middle of the Capillano bridge or on the more solid bridge further upstream and asked them to tell her a story in response to an ambiguous picture. The purpose of this, she told them, was a study she was doing of the influence of scenery on creativity. When the stories were analyzed by a panel of judges unfamiliar with the study, the stories told by the men who were met in the middle of the Capillano bridge contained much higher levels of sexual imagery than did the stories of the men who were met at the safer bridge. Dutton and Aron's confederate had also given each of the men she met her telephone number in case they were interested in contacting her to get a copy of the results of the study. Only two of the men who were met on the safer bridge called her, but nine of the thirty-three of the men met in the middle of the Capillano bridge did. Dutton and Aron interpreted these results as strong support for Hatfield's theory of passionate love.

What does all of this have to do with Ovid? Ovid, in his *Art of Love*,* suggests that an excellent place to take someone you wish to have fall in love with you is to the gladiatorial games for, amid the excitement of the games, one's beloved is apt to mistake his or her excitement for passion:

On that sorrowful sand Cupid has often contested,
And the watcher of wounds often has had it himself.
While he is talking, or touching a hand, or studying entries,

*Ovid, *The Art of Love*, p. 110. Translated by Rolfe Humphries. Bloomington, Ind.: Indiana University Press, 1973. First published 1957.

Asking which is ahead after his bet has been laid,
Wounded himself, he groans to feel the shaft of the arrow;
He is victim himself, no more spectator, but show.

Schachter's Place in History

As the above suggests, the evidence regarding Schachter's theory indicates that the theory, as originally stated by Schachter, is almost certainly incorrect. Indeed, Schachter himself has moved considerably away from his theory and toward a more physiological reductionist account of emotions and emotional behavior (Schachter, 1980). Schachter was right in emphasizing the role that cognitive factors play in the generation of emotion, but his assumption that all emotions are accompanied and must be accompanied by undifferentiated arousal has not found much support. As Reisenzein concludes after his exhaustive review of research relevant to Schachter's theory,

> the available data seem to support only a rather attenuated version of Schachter's theory: that arousal feedback can have an intensifying effect on emotional states, and that this arousal-emotion relationship is mediated or modified in part by causal attributions regarding the source of the arousal. (Reisenzein, 1983, p. 258)

Reisenzein goes on to argue that, "the role of peripheral arousal has been overstated" (p. 258) and that the influence of feedback from the body on the experience of emotion may be more symbolic than real. However, as we will see in the next section, it is now clear that, at least for some emotions, feedback from the body, specifically, the face, can and does help determine the experience of particular emotions. Moreover, there is mounting evidence that autonomic differentiation of at least a small set of emotions does exist. Thus, while history has not been kind to Schachter's theory, it should be recognized that the theory generated an immense amount of research and, in many ways, was at least partly responsible for keeping the Jamesian tradition alive, as is illustrated by Winton's (1990) integration of James' and Schachter's theories.

Spinal-Cord Injuries and the Experience of Emotion II: Evidence Against the "Strong Form" of James-Lange

Given the importance of data about the influence of visceral feedback on the experience of emotion, and, hence, data about the emotional experience of people with spinal-cord injuries for testing the James-Lange theory, it is not surprising that Hohmann's conclusions that spinal-cord lesions lead to decreases in emotionality have not gone unchallenged. What is surprising, actually, is that there haven't been more studies of the effects of spinal-cord injuries on emotional experience. Attempting to remedy this situation and provide more definitive answers to the questions Hohmann raised, Chwalisz, Diener, and Gallagher (1988) replicated his study using more reliable measures of emotional experience than the open-ended and more impressionistic self-reports Hohmann obtained. They also included two control groups for comparison with subjects with spinal-cord damage, something that Hohmann had not done.

Chwalisz et al. interviewed a sample of eighteen young adults with damage to various sites along their spinal cords. All of the spinal-cord-injury subjects were wheelchair-bound. Chwalisz et al. also interviewed a group of fourteen young adults who were wheelchair-bound for reasons other than spinal-cord damage (e.g., due to cerebral palsy) as well as a group of twenty-four non-handicapped subjects. The second group of wheelchair-bound subjects was included to test the possibility that simply being handicapped could lead to the kinds of patterns of emotional experience Hohmann had observed. The three groups of subjects were roughly matched in terms of age and sex although there were more women in the non-spinal-cord-injury-handicapped group. All of the subjects were students, staff members, or alumni of a large university and constituted a somewhat more diverse group than Hohmann had interviewed.

Chwalisz et al. asked the subjects to complete a *standardized* test[8] of the intensity of their emotional experience, a life-satisfaction scale, a scale that separately measured the subjects' experience of positive and negative affect over a 1-week period, and a simple happiness scale. In addition, the subjects were asked to rate on a 7-point scale the intensity of their reactions to a number of emotion-provoking events, for example, "Your brother or sister goes in for very risky surgery and may not pull through," and to describe recent episodes of "any strong anger, joy, sadness, and love." Finally, as Hohmann did, Chwalisz et al. asked their wheelchair-bound subjects with spinal-cord damage to compare the intensity of their experiences of anger, sadness, fear, joy, love, and sentimentality before and after their injury. They also asked their wheelchair-bound subjects handicapped for other reasons to compare the intensity of their experience of these emotions with their experience of them during their early teens.

Complicating considerably the argument that feedback from the viscera is essential to the experience of emotion, Chwalisz et al. found *no differ-*

---

[8]*Standardized* tests are psychological measures for which normative information has been obtained. What this means for a particular measure is that the measure has been given to a group of people with known psychological characteristics. The scores on the measure for this group then serve as a standard against which the scores of other groups are compared. When psychologists refer to a measure as standardized, they also often mean that the *reliability* and *validity* of the measure have been established.

ences among the three groups of subjects on the overall intensity of their emotional experience or on the ratings of the intensity of their reactions to the individual emotion-provoking events. The spinal-cord-injury and other handicapped groups did differ significantly in the self-reported intensity of their experience of fear and love prior to their injury or early in their teens. However, the difference for fear was in the direction *opposite* to that predicted by the James-Lange theory. That is, subjects with spinal-cord injuries reported feeling fear *more* intensely after their injuries than before! Within the spinal-cord-injury group, Chwalisz et al. reported that over half of the subjects indicated that four of the six emotions they rated were, "stronger now than before the injury" (p. 823).

Chwalisz et al. did find, as Hohmann had, that the site of spinal-cord lesions had some effect on the experienced intensity of emotion. Specifically, when the emotional experiences of the spinal-cord-injury group were compared as a function of the site of their lesion, subjects with higher lesions (and hence, less feedback from the viscera) reported experiencing anger significantly less intensely than those subjects with lower lesions. Higher lesions were also found to be associated with lower overall emotional intensity scores, although the difference was not significant. In results that partly parallel but also partly contradict Hohmann's, Chwalisz et al. also found that the majority of subjects with high lesions reported *increases* in the intensity of their experience of joy, love, sentimentality, and sadness after their injury. Interestingly, Chwalisz et al. found no differences among the three comparison groups in terms of life satisfaction or happiness, although they did find that those spinal-cord-injury subjects with high lesions reported the least "acceptance" at the time of their injury than did spinal-cord-injury subjects with lower lesions. The latter finding is not surprising given the greater disability associated with higher lesions.

Chwalisz et al. concluded that the pattern of results they obtained was inconsistent with "strong" forms of the James-Lange theory, namely, the argument that feedback from the viscera is absolutely necessary for the experience of emotion. Instead of experiencing emotions less intensely, subjects with spinal-cord injuries experienced some emotions more intensely after their injury than before and more so than did subjects with no injuries. They approvingly quoted Ross Buck (1984) who had earlier argued that "visceral feedback does not appear to be either necessary or sufficient for all kinds of emotional experience" (p. 48).

Chwalisz et al. did, however, concede that their results could be taken as support for a weaker form of the visceral feedback argument, "the idea that autonomic arousal can amplify emotional feelings even though it is not essential to emotional experience" (p. 826). They noted that the site of spinal-cord injuries does seem to have some effects on the intensity of emotional experience, although the effects are not large. They offer the suggestion, however, that these results may be due to the restricted life-style of the spinal-cord subjects, as these did not differ greatly from the other group of handicapped subjects.

Chwalisz et al. also conceded that their study examined only a limited sample of the different kinds of bodily feedback potentially available to influence experience. As we have seen, James emphasized the importance of feedback from many bodily sources, not just the viscera, and so Chwalisz et al.'s findings do not rule out entirely the notion that emotional experience is dependent on bodily change. As we shall see, many modern-day Jamesians have focused their attention on the face and facial musculature as the most likely source of feedback from the body. Notice also that Chwalisz et al.'s results don't say anything about differentiation of emotions at the level of the viscera. As several studies I've already reviewed and some I've yet to discuss suggest, there does seem to be some *differentiation* of the visceral changes that accompany at least a small set of emotions. It could very well be the case that there is specificity to the visceral responses associated with emotions but that these responses do not directly affect emotional experience. As Winton (1990) has argued, "the important issue is not just whether emotion-specific bodily reactions can be documented, but whether bodily changes inform the individual of emotional quality" (p. 655). One simple way to approach the question of whether visceral changes influence the experience of emotion is to explore the extent to which people can indeed detect the kinds of visceral changes that accompany common emotions. Before I discuss what has been discovered about the role of feedback from the face in the experience of emotion, we need to examine research on the perception of visceral changes.

Visceral Perception

Can people accurately detect changes in their viscera of the sort James thought were the basis of emotions? This is an easy question to ask but a difficult question to answer. One early attempt to address the question involved devising a self-report measure of visceral perception. Mandler, Mandler, and Uviller's (1958) Autonomic Perception Questionnaire (APQ) was designed to assess the self-reported frequency and accuracy of peoples' perceptions of their autonomic activity. However, while Mandler et al. found that high scores on the APQ were associated with higher levels of anxiety and actual autonomic activity, subsequent research has revealed that the APQ is probably not a measure of the accuracy of visceral perception (see Katkin, 1985). Part of the problem in relying on self-reports of visceral changes is that such reports are influenced by a wide variety of factors and may reflect much more than the simple perception of bodily change (Pennebaker, 1982). Later attempts to answer the question have relied on more objective measures and some very sophisticated psychophysiological techniques unavailable to earlier researchers.

Edward Katkin, Jim Blascovich, and their colleagues (see Blascovich & Katkin, 1983; Katkin, 1985) have developed a method to determine objectively if people are able to detect autonomic activity, primarily their heartbeats, in both neutral and emotional conditions. What Katkin, Blascovich, and their colleagues do is monitor their subjects' heartbeats using a computerized recording device. As the computer is monitoring a subject's heartbeats, it generates two series of tones that sound something like the beating of a heart. One series of tones follows the subject's heartbeats by a fixed time interval, the other follows his or her heartbeats by a variable interval. That is, one of the series of tones accurately reflects the subject's heartbeats and the other does not. The task for the subject is to say which series of tones reflects his or her heartbeat.

You might be wondering why Katkin and colleagues went to all the trouble to devise such a complicated task. Why couldn't they simply monitor their subjects' heartbeats and ask them to describe them, for example, by saying "thumpa thumpa" or some such thing every time their heart beat? The trouble with such a procedure is that the researchers would have no idea what the subjects were actually discriminating. It could just as easily be their breathing or subtle muscle movements as heartbeats. Katkin et al.'s procedure has the advantage of allowing the researchers to know precisely what it is that their subjects are doing when they report a difference in the tone series, since the tones either are or aren't tied directly to their heartbeats and only their heartbeats.

Katkin, Blascovich, and their colleagues found in a series of studies using the above procedure that subjects can indeed learn to discriminate between the two series of tones. In one of their first studies (Katkin, Blascovich, & Goldband, 1981), subjects were to indicate which tone series reflected their heartbeats in each of 120 trials. After each trial, subjects were given feedback as to whether they had chosen the correct series. Subjects easily learned to discriminate the two-tone series, although some subjects learned the discrimination more easily than others (more about this in a minute). In a second session a week later, subjects were run through the same procedure but this time Katkin et al. played a trick on half of the subjects. These subjects listened to a recording of the tone series generated by their heartbeats from the *first* session. Thus, their attempts at discriminating the tones were not based on their heartbeats at the time of the discrimination task. Katkin et al. found that these subjects' ability to tell which tone series reflected their heartbeat dropped to chance levels. This finding indicates quite persuasively that in the first session the subjects were discriminating between the tones based on what their hearts were doing at the time. That is, they were in some way accurately detecting their heartbeats.

Katkin, Blascovich, and their colleagues have replicated this basic finding several times (see Katkin, 1985), as have others using slightly different procedures (see Davis, Langer, Sutterer, & Marlin, 1986), and each time they have found that some subjects are better at detecting their own heartbeats than are others. One of the largest and most persistent differences in this regard is that between women and men. Studies of the sensitivity of women and men to the emotional responses of other people, in which it is almost always found that women are more sensitive than are men (Hall, 1984), would suggest that women would be superior to men in visceral self-perception. Just the opposite is consistently found, however. In study after study, in the perception of not just heartbeats but other physiological changes as well (see Pennebaker & Roberts, 1992, for a review), men appear to be superior to women.

Interestingly, the gender difference in visceral perception is only apparent in studies conducted in the *laboratory*. That is, when subjects have other cues available to them about their emotional state, for example, cognitive or situational cues, women are as accurate as are men in detecting visceral changes. It is only when the only cues available are internal that men surpass women. James Pennebaker and Tomi-Ann Roberts (Pennebaker & Roberts, 1992; Roberts & Pennebaker, 1995) have attempted to account for the interaction of gender and setting in accuracy of visceral perception by pointing to differences in both the biology and socialization of women and men. They argue that, given already existing biological differences (men's physiological arousal, for example, takes longer to return to its resting state), differences in how women and men are taught to regard their bodies (having to do with, among other things, the fact that women menstruate and men do not) lead to women and men drawing on somewhat different sources of information when they experience emotion. Pennebaker and Roberts (1992) go so far as to say that women and men possess different "theories" of emotion, with mens' theories being more like what James had in mind and womens' theories being more "cognitive" in character (see next chapter).

This is a very provocative idea that will no doubt receive more attention in the years to come. For now, the take-home message is that the empirical research that led up to it clearly indicates that the emotional experiences of at least some people are influenced by the perception of visceral changes, as the James-Lange theory predicted (Blascovich, 1990, 1992). The relationship between the perception of visceral change and emotion, however, does not seem to be as strong as the theory would predict, and individual differences in visceral perception seem to be the rule rather than the exception (Blascovich, 1990). Thus, even though there do appear to be specific patterns of physiological change associated with certain emotions (more on this shortly), emotions may be differentiated by sources of bodily change other than the viscera. It is to one of the most likely sources of differentiation that we now turn.

The Facial Feedback Hypothesis

At the end of Lindsey Anderson's *O Lucky Man*, a film I must have seen a dozen times in my undergraduate days, the hero of the film, after having undergone a series of misadventures that include surviving a nuclear explosion, narrowly escaping being used as a guinea pig in a medical experiment by a mad doctor, being thrown in prison, and being chased and beaten by an angry mob, finds himself at an audition for a film and is asked by the director of the film to smile. The hero, understandably, replies that he can't. After asking the hero to smile a second time, the director hits him with the script for the film, whereupon the hero breaks into a bright grin. The scene then shifts and we see the hero dancing ecstatically with the other members of the cast as the film ends. I've always found the ending of the film to be particularly life-affirming, for it suggests that we can overcome our problems if only we struggle on and "just do it" when we feel most like giving up. The hero's smile at the end of the film is emblematic of the ever-present promise of transcendence in a world of adversity. What does any of this have to do with William James' theory of emotion? Quite a bit actually, for there is intriguing evidence that we may indeed transform our experience of the world in some situations if we are able to smile when we least feel like it. Putting a bit of a spin on James' idea that emotions are the bodily responses we have to emotion-eliciting events, the evidence suggests that emotional experience is determined from the outside in. In particular, many psychologists now argue that emotional experience is determined in part by the facial expressions that accompany our emotions.

The role of the face in the experience of emotion. As far back as 1924, the social psychologist Floyd Allport (1890–1978) argued that feedback from the face might play a crucial role in differentiating emotions. Allport, evincing a strong belief in the essential soundness of the James-Lange theory, proposed that the face was the ideal candidate for a source of bodily feedback as varied and complex as the range of human emotions required.[9]

> The facial expressions [of emotion] as well as bodily movements are strongly differential. Returning afferent impulses from these responses add to consciousness the distinguishing qualities which serve to differentiate the emotion of anger from that of fear. Without these impulses the two states would be simply unpleasant, and indistinguishable. (Allport, 1924, p. 92)

---

[9]"Theory it is, to be sure . . . ," he argued, "but it contains so much truth that it has been able to hold its ground against eminent critics" (Allport, 1924, p. 85)

Later, Sylvan Tomkins (1911–1991), in his very influential book on emotions published in 1962, proposed that feedback from the muscles of the face was a major factor in differentiating various emotions. Tomkins' proposal was in turn echoed in Carroll Izard's (1971, 1977) and Paul Ekman's (Ekman, Friesen, & Ellsworth, 1972) theories of emotion and in research carried out by John Lanzetta and his colleagues and by James Laird. In what came to be called the *facial feedback hypothesis* (Tourangeau & Ellsworth, 1979; Buck, 1980), the central notion is that, "awareness of one's facial expressions is the emotion" (Lanzetta, Cartwright-Smith, & Kleck, 1976, p. 367); that is, "different patterns of expressive activity of the body [specifically, the face] precede and cause in some way qualitatively different subjective experiences" (Laird, 1974, p. 476). As the face goes, one might say, so goes the experience of emotion.

One implication of the facial feedback hypothesis is that it should be possible to manipulate, that is, intensify or dampen, a person's experience of emotion by manipulating her or his face. The experience of anger, for example, should not be as intense if a person were to smile instead of grimace. Note how similar this is to James' proposal that emotions may be stimulated by simulating their characteristic expressions and postures. As both Robert Plutchik (1962) and Ross Buck (1980) have pointed out, this is an idea that may also be traced back to Darwin's *Expression of the Emotions in Man and Animals:* "The free expression by outward signs of an emotion intensifies it. On the other hand, the repression, as far as this is possible, of all outward signs softens our emotions" (Darwin, 1872/1965, p. 365).

Notice also how this proposal neatly sidesteps the criticisms Cannon made of the idea that emotions are differentiated by feedback from the viscera and of the more recent findings that visceral feedback may not be entirely necessary for the experience of emotion. Facial expressions, unlike visceral responses, are quick and are certainly as complex and as varied as the range of emotions we experience. Moreover, the muscles and skin of the face are extraordinarily sensitive and thus should provide an excellent source of feedback. The task facing those advocating facial feedback as an alternative to visceral feedback in Neo-Jamesian emotion theory is to demonstrate that the face really does provide us with differentiating information.

Evidence for and against facial feedback. In one of the earliest direct tests of the facial feedback hypothesis, Laird (1974) recruited a sample of male undergraduate students for a study of "the activity of facial muscles under various conditions" (p. 477). Subjects were told that during the study they would have the electrical activity of their facial muscles monitored via electrodes attached to their faces while they viewed some photographic slides. Subjects were told that "subtle emotional changes" while they were viewing the slides could affect the quality of the measurements that were being made of their muscles and so to check on this source of error, they would be asked to report their mood by means of an adjective checklist from time to time. Subjects were also told that measurements would be taken from some facial muscles that were relaxed and some that were contracted. To achieve this, an experimenter "arranged" each subject's face by telling him to contract certain muscles. The effect of this procedure was to produce an angry or happy expression on each subject's face. (At no time were subjects actually told to make an angry or happy expression.) Each subject was then shown a picture of children at play, once while his face was arranged into an angry expression and once while his face was arranged into a happy expression, and a picture of a group of Ku Klux Klan members, once for the angry expression and once for the happy expression. This rather elaborate set of procedures resulted in a situation in which Laird could assess subjects' moods while they viewed a pleasant and an unpleasant picture while their faces were composed into a happy or angry expression.

If facial expression is a significant determinant of emotional experience, as the facial feedback hypothesis would predict, then one would expect that making an angry or happy face should induce a corresponding angry or happy mood regardless of what slide a subject viewed. One would also expect that viewing an unpleasant slide while making an angry face would intensify any negative emotions one might experience in the presence of the slide and that viewing an unpleasant slide while making a happy face would diminish any negative emotions one might have. Correspondingly, a happy face in the presence of a pleasant slide should intensify the experience of positive emotions and an angry face should diminish them. These expectations were confirmed by Laird's results. Subjects were happier when their faces were manipulated into smiles and angrier (more aggressive) when their faces were manipulated into angry expressions. Having a happy expression intensified subjects' positive reactions to the pleasant slide and blunted their negative reactions to the unpleasant slide. Likewise, having an angry face intensified subjects' negative reactions to the unpleasant slide and diminished their positive reaction to the pleasant slide.

You might ask at this point whether Laird's results might be due to his subjects somehow guessing what emotion he wanted them to report. It is also reasonable to ask whether or not Laird might have somehow treated his subjects differently in the angry and happy face conditions, thus producing the effects he found. To control for the confounding effects of subject awareness, Laird gave all of his subjects a postexperiment interview in which he assessed the extent to which each of his subjects had guessed what the true nature of the study was. He then only analyzed the data from subjects who appeared to be unaware of the experimental hypothesis. To control for the second possibility, Laird ran subjects in pairs. During each experimental session, one subject had his face manipulated while a second did not. The second subject was treated exactly the same as the manipulated subject. In fact, they sat beside one another. When Laird analyzed the data from the nonmanipulated subjects, he found that their self-reported emotion did not differ as a function of which kind of expression the other subjects were making. Nonmanipulated subjects' emotions did differ as a function of what picture they viewed, however. Laird took this as evidence that when he was manipulating his subjects' faces into angry and happy expressions, he wasn't somehow communicating to them what emotion they were expected to report feeling.

Laird's findings seemed to provide strong support for the facial feedback version of the James-Lange theory, at least for the emotions of anger and happiness. Lanzetta, Cartwright-Smith, and Kleck (1976) obtained similar results for pain. They also found that one measure of the activity of the sympathetic nervous system, skin conductance, was also influenced by the manipulation of facial expressions. A study by Tourangeau and Ellsworth (1979), however, appeared to cast doubt on the reliability of Laird's and Lanzetta et al.'s findings.

Tourangeau and Ellsworth had subjects watch either a sad, fearful, or neutral film while making either sad, fearful, or nonemotional faces. Subjects were told that the purpose of the experiment was to study subliminal perception and that they had to hold their faces a particular way to prevent measurement errors. As in Laird's study, subjects were not told to make a particular emotional expression, but were given a set of detailed instructions on how to arrange their facial muscles. Tourangeau and Ellsworth also included a group of subjects who were given no instructions about how to arrange their faces. Unlike Laird's study, however, Tourangeau and Ellsworth used a between-subjects design in which each subject was given only one kind of expression to make and was shown only one of the films. Tourangeau and Ellsworth found that the films they showed their subjects had the predictable effect: the sad film made subjects sad, the anger-eliciting film made subjects angry, and the neutral film did not influence subjects' emotions. Tourangeau and Ellsworth, however, found that the kinds of expressions their subjects wore while watching the films had no effect on their self-reported emotions. They obtained some contradictory evidence that facial expression had some effects on measures of heart rate and skin conductance, but not enough to support the facial feedback hypothesis, especially in the absence of any effects on self-reported emotion. Tourangeau and Ellsworth concluded that

> the facial feedback hypothesis receives three major setbacks from the evidence of this study. First, adopting an emotional facial expression does not appear to be sufficient to produce the emotion . . . Second, adopting a nonemotional expression does not prevent emotional responding; thus, emotional expression does not seem necessary for emotional feelings . . . Finally, this lack of correlation [between expression and feel-

ings] constitutes especially damaging evidence against the theory. (Tourangeau & Ellsworth, 1979, p. 1528)

Defenders of the facial feedback hypothesis responded to Tourangeau and Ellsworth's findings with a variety of strongly worded objections to their claims (see Izard, 1981; Tomkins, 1981; Hagar & Ekman, 1981). Izard (1981), for example, criticized their study on both theoretical and methodological grounds, arguing that, among other things, their study was flawed because their subjects' facial expressions were voluntarily produced and were held for much too long a time. The fact that Tourangeau and Ellsworth's subjects' facial expressions were produced before the emotion-eliciting films began also meant that there was an incongruence between the feedback from the expressions and the emotional information coming from the films. Izard also concluded that Tourangeau and Ellsworth's study did not provide an adequate test of the facial feedback hypothesis because they tested the wrong hypothesis. What they should have tested, he argued, was whether or not spontaneous and "micromomentary" facial expressions influence emotional experience. Hagar and Ekman (1981), in their critique of Tourangeau and Ellsworth's study, focused on the possibility that the facial expressions Tourangeau and Ellsworth used were too difficult for their subjects to make and probably represented a mixture of expressions instead of just one. They also contended that Tourangeau and Ellsworth's procedures for getting their subjects to produce the facial expressions they used were not valid and that Tourangeau and Ellsworth did not demonstrate that their subjects in fact made the expressions they were supposed to make.

In a detailed reply to their critics, Tourangeau and Ellsworth (Ellsworth & Tourangeau, 1981) defended the validity of their study, reiterated the conclusions they originally made and took their critics to task for accusing them of testing an hypothesis unrelated to facial feedback. Tourangeau and Ellsworth took particular exception to the suggestion that their subjects' emotional experiences, while unrelated to the expressions they asked them to make, were instead related to exceedingly brief, micromomentary expressions that they could not detect. If this were the case, they argued, "it would mean that in ordinary social interaction we can see expressions that are useless in understanding our companions' emotions, whereas expressions we cannot see tell the true story" (Ellsworth & Tourangeau, 1981, p. 366).

Although Tourangeau and Ellsworth's study did not close the book on the facial feedback hypothesis, it certainly indicated that much more research was needed on the issue. Throughout the 1980s, that research was carried out by a number of researchers (see Adelmann & Zajonc, 1989, for a review), and it now appears that, indeed, facial expressions of emotion do seem to generate experiences appropriate to the expressions of at least a small number of relatively simple, "basic" emotions (but see Matsumoto,

1987, for a review and critique of this literature). A very cleverly designed study by Fritz Strack and his colleagues (Strack, Stepper, & Martin, 1988), for example, found that subjects induced to make a facial expression that inhibited the muscle movements involved in smiling by holding a pen in their lips, rated a series of cartoons as less funny than did subjects induced to make an expression that facilitated smiling by holding a pen in their teeth (see Figure 3.3 and try this yourself for 5 minutes to see if you feel any different while holding a pen in your mouth each way). Strack et al.'s procedures were specifically designed to rule out the possibility that subjects were somehow obtaining an awareness of the emotion that coincided with the expressions they were making. A recent study by Stepper and Strack (1993), in which subjects sat in a chair in an upright or slumped manner (by elevating or lowering a table on which they were writing), revealed that posture also has an influence on the experience of emotion, just as James predicted (see also Duclos et al., 1989, and Riskind & Gotay, 1982). Given the success of other researchers in producing facial feedback effects, it is unclear why Tourangeau and Ellsworth failed to find them. Laird (1984) has suggested that part of the answer may lie in his findings that not everyone is equally susceptible to the influence of facial feedback on their emotional experience.

Even though the basic phenomenon of facial and postural feedback seems to be well supported, there is considerable controversy about the mechanisms underlying these effects and their significance for understanding the experience of emotions in the real world. With regard to underlying mechanisms, the argument is over whether some sort of self-perception process is at work, a view favored by Laird (1984), or whether the effects of feedback are more direct and less cognitive, a view favored by Ekman and his colleagues (Ekman, Levenson, & Friesen, 1983). With regard to the significance of such feedback on the kinds of emotional experiences we have in everyday life, Buck (1980) and Winton (1990) remain unconvinced that facial or other bodily feedback does much more than influence the global direction and quality of our predominant mood at any one time. Winton (1990), indeed, cautions that

> only one published article has reported clear evidence for categorical effects of facial movement on mood (Duclos et al., 1989), and another such experiment yielded null results (Tourangeau & Ellsworth, 1979). Thus, although there is ample evidence that facial movements can directly produce global hedonic reactions, specific categorical effects have not been extensively documented at present. (Winton, 1990, p. 661)

By "categorical effects" Winton means the demonstration that different facial expressions can produce the experience of distinctly different emotions,

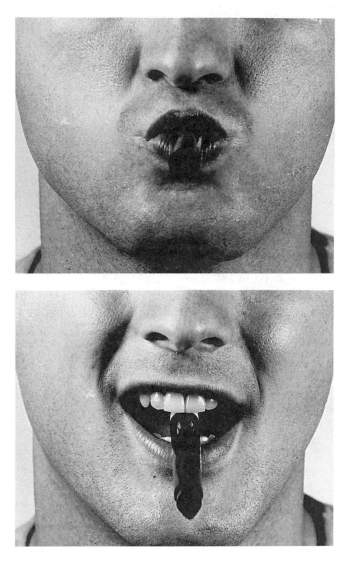

FIGURE 3.3. *Strack et al.'s technique to induce subjects to smile or not smile without their awareness. (From Strack et al., 1988, p. 771. Photographs courtesy of Fritz Strack.)*

say, fear, anger and sadness, rather than merely positive versus negative mood.

In light of the reservations of Winton and Buck, but recognizing the growing body of data that there are demonstrable effects for facial feedback, the most reasonable position would seem to be one that allows for emotions to be determined by feedback from the face and body as well as by other sources. Such a position is favored by Stepper and Strack (1993; see also Buck, 1980).

> On the one hand, we do not argue, as James (1890) did, that a particular bodily expression is the emotion or that an emotional experience is solely determined by a specific physical reaction. To feel proud, it is not sufficient to adopt an upright posture. Rather, specific noetic information (e.g., that of success in a difficult task) needs to be activated . . . On the other hand, unlike Schachter and Singer (1962), we do not assume that particular emotions are experienced as a consequence of identifying the causes of unspecific bodily feedback. Rather, we contend that a specific experiential representation is elicited if a certain configuration of specific bodily cues and noetic information matches a template . . . that the person has acquired both through learning and genetic endowment. (Stepper & Strack, 1993, p. 216)

Notice that for Stepper and Strack the emotional information provided by feedback from the body and face is always integrated, in a genuine emotion, with information from the person's environment that is received via the person's appraisal or evaluation of the environment. We'll explore what it means for a person to appraise his or her environment when we review the cognitive perspective in the next chapter. Before moving on, however, there's one more episode in the adventures of the James-Lange theory that we need to see.

The Vindication of William James: Representative Research on Emotion in the Jamesian Tradition

James and Lange made their predictions about the role of the body in the generation of emotion long before there were adequate techniques for studying what goes on inside the body during emotion. With the advent of modern psychophysiology, however, researchers have developed a set of extraordinarily powerful methods for listening to the body's language of emotion. What they have discovered has largely vindicated some of the features of James' theory of emotion.

Physiology follows facial expression.   The findings that emotions can be generated by the facial expressions and postures of emotion described in the previous section would not have surprised James, for he explicitly predicted that such things happen. In order to vindicate James and Lange fully, however, one would want to show that emotions can be differentiated in terms of more than just facial expressions and postures. One would want to be able to demonstrate differentiation at the level of the autonomic nervous system. Recent research has revealed that such differentiation indeed exists. What is interesting and remarkable about these latest findings is that autonomic differentiation was first demonstrated in studies of facial feedback in which it was found that physiology seemed to follow facial expression.

Paul Ekman, Robert Levenson, and Wallace Friesen published the results of a study in 1983 in which actors and facial expression researchers from Ekman's laboratory had a variety of their physiological indices of emotion monitored while they engaged in a "directed facial action task." The facial action task required them to voluntarily contract specific sets of muscles to produce the expressions for the six emotions regarded by Ekman and his colleagues as basic and universal, namely, anger, fear, sadness, disgust, happiness and surprise. What Ekman et al. found was that there were significant autonomic differences that paralleled the facial expressions for these emotions. In particular, while the facial expressions for fear, anger, and happiness all produced *increases* in heart rate, the expressions for fear and anger produced much larger increases than did that for happiness. The expression for disgust, on the other hand, produced *decreases* in heart rate. The expression for anger produced larger increases than did that for happiness in temperature at the tips of the fingers, an indicator of the amount of blood flow directed by the body to the extremities. The facial expression for fear produced a decrease in finger temperature. Similar (but not exactly the same) patterns of autonomic changes were found for a second task in which the same subjects were asked to attempt to imaginatively relive a past experience involving each of the six emotions.

I first heard of these results at an American Psychological Association convention when Ekman presented them to a packed room of emotion researchers. It's fair to say that many in the room were skeptical of his findings (I certainly was). What many of us wanted to know was, would the phenomenon extend to a nonspecialized group of subjects? After all, how like the rest of us are emotion researchers? These initial results have now been replicated a number of times by many different groups of researchers using samples of people from very different populations (see Levenson et al., 1990, or Levenson, 1992, for a review). It now appears that there are indeed reliable autonomic differences for at least a small number of simple emotions. In both directed facial action, "relived" emotion and related tasks, (1) heart rate increases are associated with anger, fear, and sadness, with the greatest increases being observed for anger, (2) heart rate decreases are associated with disgust, and (3) fear is associated with greater decreases in diastolic blood pressure and blood flow to the extremities than is anger. What, you might ask, do all of these differences mean? And, apart from that question, are the differences large enough to make any difference in the experience of emotion? (James once said that "a difference to be a difference must make a difference".)

Levenson admits that the "final tally of distinctions [among emotions] is likely to be small" (Levenson, 1992, p. 26) but he, Ekman, and Friesen nevertheless argue that the distinctions are important ones and that, moreover, they fit nicely into a developing picture of the evolution of emotions as response systems serving the survival interests of the organism (think here of Frijda's "action tendencies"). The increases in heart rate observed for anger, they argue, serve to prepare the organism for fending off antagonists, an activity that demands a great deal of energy, which an increase in heart rate and general sympathetic nervous system activity would supply. The increases in heart rate for fear, on the other hand, serve to prepare the organism for fleeing from predators or other dangers, also an energy-demanding activity. The observed differences between anger and fear on measures of blood pressure and blood supply to the extremities reflect the differences between the activities of fighting and fleeing. In fear, more blood is needed in the large muscles associated with rapid locomotion and, hence, fear is characterized by lower diastolic blood pressure and lower finger temperature (blood flow). The heart rate decreases seen in disgust may reflect the association of this emotion with the activity of expelling noxious substances, as it is characterized by increased salivation and gastrointestinal activity, which signal increased parasympathetic nervous system activation (Levenson, 1992; see also Rozin & Fallon, 1987).

William James would likely have no quarrel with the general outline of these explanations, for recall that central to his theory was the idea that our emotions represent our body's survival-related responses to the environment. The finding of reliable patterns of physiological differentiation of emotions and their explanation in terms of the functional significance of these patterns, if true, represent a kind of double vindication of James. Two puzzles remain, however.

First, it is reasonable to ask, why do physiological changes follow making faces? Levenson et al. (1990) propose a model in which voluntary muscle movements of the face that correspond to the expressions for one of the six basic emotions set in motion a parallel set of changes in the autonomic nervous system. It is not that the facial expressions cause the autonomic changes, rather

> when a voluntary facial [expression] is made, the signals that go out from the motor cortex [in the brain] to the facial nucleus to contract certain sets of facial muscles are accompanied by a set of parallel commands that go out to the organs of the autonomic nervous system. (Levenson et al., 1990, p. 381)

Levenson et al. argue further that these parallel connections are probably "hard-wired at birth" and that feedback from the face may not even be "necessary for emotion or for emotion-specific autonomic activity to occur"; all that is needed are the "central efferent commands for those movements"

(Levenson et al., 1990, p. 381). Thus, Levenson et al. would predict that even people afflicted with facial paralysis should show the autonomic response patterns as long as they are trying to contract the proper facial muscles. This notion would also account for the finding that spinal-cord lesions do not seem to result in the disappearance of emotion and that visceral feedback, even if highly emotion-specific, may not be as powerful a determinant of emotion as James thought. This will likely be a hot research topic in the next few years.

The second question to ask is, why does the autonomic differentiation seem so, well, limited? There are many more emotions than the Big Six that one could name and each of us probably experiences at least a few more than just these in daily life. Where is guilt? And, what about hope? Love? Resentment? The answer to the question of why the patterns of differentiation seem so slight is threefold. First, just as it was the case that the patterns discovered so far required advances in the technology of psychophysiology, so future discoveries will probably depend upon technological innovation. More differentiation will probably be discovered as we learn more about how to eavesdrop on the body.

Second, as Davidson (1993) argues, the methodologies used in the laboratory studies of autonomic differentiation have severely constrained the kinds of action tendencies available to subjects. As we'll see in Chapter 5, most emotions are associated with a number of often very different action tendencies. As Davidson points out, both approach and withdrawal, completely opposite behavioral tendencies, may be associated with the same emotion. Given the limited range of action tendencies associated with the emotions elicited by the directed facial action and relived emotion tasks, it is not surprising that the range of autonomic differentiation discovered thus far is so limited. Moreover, the evidence for differentiation that has been found, Davidson warns, is also likely to be misleading because of the artificial constraint on the action tendencies available to subjects.

> When . . . emotions occur spontaneously, they are often accompanied by widely varying patterns of action. On the basis of the likelihood that the same emotion is associated with different action tendencies in different contexts or individuals, corresponding differences in the autonomic changes that support these actions can be expected. (Davidson, 1993, p. 468)

Davidson's electrophysiological research suggests that emotions may indeed be differentiated by the action tendencies associated with approach and withdrawal (see Davidson, 1993).

The third reason why the autonomic differentiation observed so far is so limited is closely related to the idea that emotions are distinguished by the actions with which they are associated and that the latter depend on the context within which the emotion occurs and the person experiencing the emotion. Feedback from physiological responses *alone* will never account for all of the possible emotions we can experience because, to account for all of the variation and complexity in our emotional lives, we need to explore how we *think about* or appraise the situations in which we find ourselves. Research in the cognitive tradition has emphasized the importance of appraisal in understanding our emotional responses to the world, and it is to this tradition that we now turn.

Further Reading

JAMES, W. (1884). What is an emotion? *Mind, 9,* 188–205.

LEVENSON, R. W. (1992). Autonomic nervous system differences among emotions. *Psychological Science, 3,* 23–27.

SCHACHTER, S. and SINGER, J. E. (1962). Cognitive, social, and physiological determinants of emotional state. *Psychological Review, 69,* 379–399.

Feeling is Thinking

◆

The Cognitive Perspective

To arouse an emotion, [an] object must be appraised as affecting me in some way, affecting me personally as an individual with my particular experience and my particular aims. If I see an apple, I know that it is an apple of a particular kind and taste. This knowledge need not touch me personally in any way. But if the apple is of my favorite kind and I am in a part of the world where it does not grow and cannot be bought, I may want it with a real emotional craving.

—Magda Arnold (1960a, p. 171)

I spent the summer between my freshman and sophomore years of high school at my friend Mike's house in Key West, Florida. Mike and his family lived on a Navy base and their house was only a few feet from the ocean (actually, everything in Key West is only a few feet from the ocean). Mike and I spent the summer cruising around in his boat, waterskiing and snorkeling. One Friday afternoon we decided to mount an expedition to a well-known, abandoned house on stilts in the shallow water a couple of miles out in the Straits of Florida south of the city of Key West. There were many such houses in the shallows around Key West but this one held a particular fascination for us, as it was rumored to have once belonged to Ernest Hemingway. We decided that we would spend the night there on Saturday.

On Saturday morning we loaded all of our gear into Mike's parents' boat, including a 22-caliber rifle to protect us from sharks, and headed out to the house. We spent the rest of the day lounging around on what was left of the sun porch of the house, watching alligator gar and barracuda swim in the water 50 feet below us. Nightfall came and with the sound of gentle waves lapping against the sides of our boat, which we had tethered to the house's supports, we settled down into our sleeping bags for what we thought would be a peaceful, if humid, night's sleep. At about midnight, we were awakened by the sound of rain beating a furious tattoo on the tin roof of the house. A thunderstorm had blown our way as we slept and the house was under attack by heavy winds and pounding waves. Our first thought was to check to see if the boat was still securely moored to the stilts. To do this we had to go down to a kind of enclosed platform below the house and look through a hatchway where the ladder that ran down one of the stilts entered the house. Just as we got to the hatchway and turned our flashlight's beam in the direction of the boat, we heard a sickening double snap as both of the ropes tying the boat to the stilts broke.

The boat, in 5- to 6-foot seas, quickly drifted off into the darkness and disappeared. Without a moment's thought, Mike said, "I'm going after it! Stay here and shine the light on the water. If you see any sharks, shoot 'em." And with that, he put the keys to the boat in his mouth, climbed down the ladder, and dove into the water. In less than an instant he was out of sight. For what seemed like 20 minutes but must have only been 5, I clung to the rusty ladder, rain and salt spray slapping my face, one hand holding the rifle and the other the flashlight, whose feeble light illuminated about a 2-foot circle of swirling, dark water. At last, very far off in the distance, I heard the boat's engine turn over once, and then again, and then I heard the reassuring sound of its low rumble. A few minutes later, the boat appeared with Mike, wet but grinning, at the wheel. We decided that we would cut short our night at the house on stilts and return to Mike's house immediately. And so, leaving all of our gear in the house, I jumped down into the boat and we headed toward the lights of the city.

Our adventures at the house on stilts did not actually end there. We ended up spending the night in the boat, miserable and cold, on a sandbar about a mile from the city after we ran aground in the heavy waves of the storm, but that's another story. I want to use what happened to Mike and me on that summer night to illustrate one of the key concepts of the cognitive approach to emotion, namely, appraisal. As I was hanging from the ladder beneath the stilt house, the primary emotion I felt was fear. I knew how dangerous it was to swim in high seas at night, especially around rusty metal pilings. It was also not uncommon for us to encounter sharks and barracuda when we snorkeled in the area, and I could not help thinking about the possibility of Mike meeting a large, hungry shark out there in the darkness. Mike, however, appraised the situation very differently. Mike's overwhelming concern was to get the boat back. In talking with him after the incident, he said that he never even thought of the danger and felt no fear of the water at all. His only fear, he said, was what his parents would do if he lost the boat. Had Mike appraised the situation as I had, it is likely that we would have gotten a free ride to Key West courtesy of the U.S. Coast Guard.

To those psychologists working within the cognitive perspective, the reason why Mike and I experienced such different emotions lies in the fact that we thought about or appraised our predicament differently. *Appraisal* refers to the process by which we judge the personal relevance of our situation for good or ill. I appraised the situation as one of extreme danger (my oldest memory is of being on a sinking boat in a storm at sea, but that's another story also); Mike appraised the situation as challenging but not necessarily dangerous. Thus, the emotions we experienced were very different. In this chapter we will meet the major figures associated with the cognitive perspective and explore the meaning and mechanics of appraisal.

Emotions and Thought

If any one of the traditions or perspectives described in this book could be said to dominate the others, it would be the cognitive perspective. Although evolutionary and neo-Jamesian psychophysiological approaches to emotion are currently enjoying a great deal of popularity, much of the research on emotions in social psychology and related areas of psychology is either explicitly cognitive in nature or takes account of the process of appraisal in one way or another. There is even a scientific journal devoted specifically to exploring the relationship between cognition and emotion—titled, appropriately enough, *Cognition and Emotion*. This is not to say that everyone agrees that the cognitive approach is the best way to understand human emotions. Indeed, one of the most heated controversies in psychology in recent years, the debate between Richard Lazarus and Robert Zajonc that I describe later, involved a dispute over the role of cognition in generating emotions and how best to define cognition with reference to emotion. Nevertheless, cognition is widely recognized as an important if not critical aspect of emotions.

The modern cognitive perspective was born during the heyday of behaviorism in the mid-1960s and really only came into its own with the demise of radical behaviorism in the late 1970s and early 1980s (see Baars, 1986, and Sperry, 1993, for accounts of the "cognitive revolution" in psychology). By 1981, Campos and Stenberg observed that the "recent history of the study of emotion has been dominated by approaches stressing cognitive factors" (Campos & Stenberg, 1981, p. 273). By then, the triumph of the cognitive revolution was complete. The essence of the cognitive approach is the idea that in order to understand emotions, one must understand how people make judgments about events in their environment, for emotions are generated by judgments about the world. Emotions, in short, require thought. This is not a new idea, of course. The roots of the cognitive approach to emotion can be traced far back into the history of philosophy to such thinkers as Aristotle (384–322 B.C.) and Epictetus (ca. 50–138) (see Solomon, 1976, and Lazarus, 1991, for brief historical reviews, and Reisenzein & Schönpflug, 1992, for a description of a forgotten early modern cognitive emotion theorist), but the modern cognitive approach really got its start in the pioneering work of Magda Arnold.[1]

Magda Arnold and the Primacy of Appraisal

In 1960, Arnold published her two-volume *Emotion and Personality*, which consisted of an encyclopedic review of previous research into the psychological (Volume 1) and physiological (Volume 2) phenomena associated with emotion as well as a presentation of her own theory of emotion. Included in Arnold's review was a trenchant critique of both Darwin's and James' theories of emotion in which she faulted each for failing to explain adequately how emotions are elicited. The easiest way to begin to explore her theory is by examining her criticisms of James.

Where James went wrong. As we have seen, the problem for James was how best to conceive of the relationship between bodily changes and the experience of emotion. For Arnold, James' famous formulation of BODILY CHANGES = EMOTION begs the question of what process initiates the bodily changes in the first place. Although James had argued that "bodily changes follow directly the *perception* of the exciting fact" (James, 1884, p. 189), he never adequately defined what he meant by the term or explained how such a "perception" sets in motion the bodily processes that ultimately result in the experience of emotion. According to Arnold, it is not enough to say, as James did, that simple "association" provides an explanation for why certain stimuli come to have the power to elicit emotion, since (1) the new stimulus may have nothing to do with the original stimulus and (2), in any case, the emotion-eliciting power of the original stimulus is still left unexplained.

> James . . . explains the choice of attack or flight [say, from a bear] as a mechanical association of ideas based on past experience, and insists

---

[1] See Peters (1970), for a particularly clear and compelling philosophical account of the role of thought in emotion.

that this association of present situation with past danger produces the visceral changes felt as emotion. But mechanical association cannot account for the connection of this situation with a past dangerous one. We may have seen bears in zoos or pictures of bears innumerable times, may always have liked them and never thought of danger from them . . . Sheer association would bring back only the many earlier perceptions in which there was no hint of either fight or flight . . . In this explanation James really presupposes an appraisal that the bear is harmful. It is this realization that this bear means danger for us that makes this particular idea of "bear" overpowering by driving everything else from our mind. (Arnold, 1960a, p. 108)

In the example Arnold is critiquing, James had argued that we either flee from or fight a bear, "as he suggests an overpowering 'idea' of his killing us, or one of our killing him" (James, 1894, p. 518). However, as Arnold points out, "[t]he use of the term 'idea' . . . conceals the fact that this idea is not a simple perception as is the perception of the bear as a bear, apart from his intentions towards me or mine towards him" (Arnold, 1960a, p. 107). What distinguishes "mere" perception from emotional perception, Arnold argues, is the way in which the latter always involves a judgment of how the object of perception affects one "personally." By this she means that the perception of an object in an emotional sense involves an assessment of how an object may harm or benefit one.

To perceive or apprehend something means that I know what it is like as a thing, apart from any effect on me. To like or dislike it [that is, to perceive it emotionally] means that I know it not only objectively, as it is apart from me, but also that I estimate its relation to me, that I *appraise* it as desirable or undesirable, valuable or harmful for me, so that I am drawn toward it or repelled by it. (Arnold, 1960a, p. 171, emphasis added)

The nature of appraisals.   At the heart of every emotion, then, is this special kind of judgment that Arnold calls appraisal, "the direct, immediate sense judgment of weal or woe" (Arnold, 1960a, p. 175). Without appraisal there can be no emotion, for all emotions are initiated by an individual's appraisal of his or her circumstances. "To arouse an emotion, the object must be appraised as affecting me in some way, affecting me personally as an individual with my particular experience and my particular aims" (Arnold, 1960a, p. 171). For Arnold, the proper way to think about the sequence of events that culminate in the experience of emotion should be: PERCEPTION–APPRAISAL–EMOTION. Notice how, in her formulation, Arnold recognizes that a person's past experience and his or her goals are important aspects of the way that person appraises a situation, thus filling in the gap that James left. We will return to the question of goals and how they are involved in the genesis of emotion later.

FIGURE 4.1. *Magda Arnold in the 1960s. (Reproduced by permission of the Loyola University Chicago Archives and the author.)*

Arnold referred to appraisals as *sense judgments* to emphasize their "direct, immediate, nonreflective, nonintellectual, [and] automatic" nature (Arnold, 1960a, p. 174). Appraisals are judgments about the meaning of events, but they are not intellectual judgments. To use one of Arnold's examples, appraisals are much more like the kinds of judgments a baseball player makes in coordinating her movements with the speed and direction of a fly ball she is trying to catch. If the player stopped to think about the movement of the ball or her own movements, she "would never stay in the game" (Arnold, 1960a, p. 175). Appraisals, then, are judgments about our relationship to certain objects and events in our environment, they do not, and probably cannot because of the speed with which we make them, involve the kind of in-depth cognitive processing associated with knowing objects or events in a reflective sense. There is a world of difference between recognizing that an object is a rabid woodchuck and thinking about the various qualities and characteristics of rabid woodchucks or this particular woodchuck. For the emotion of fear to be elicited, it is enough simply to recognize the woodchuck as potentially dangerous. According to Arnold, this recognition is of the same order as perceiving the woodchuck as being near or far, moving or not moving, large or small, and so on.

I have gone into considerable detail on Arnold's distinction between appraisals and intellectual judgments because this is a point that is often overlooked by those who criticize the cognitive approach for over-intellectualizing emotions. As we will see below, much of the debate between Richard Lazarus and Robert Zajonc on the role of cognition in the experience of emotion is really about how to characterize the process of appraisal. The more or less immediate, automatic, nonreflective process that Zajonc sees as being the defining characteristic of emotional perception (see Zajonc, 1980) is not really all that different from the process of appraisal as described by Arnold.

Emotions as bodily responses and impulses to action. While Arnold emphasized the primacy of appraisal in her theory of emotion, she felt that bodily changes play an important role in emotions as well. Like James and the latter-day Jamesians, she believed that every emotion has its own distinct pattern of bodily activity. Like Darwin and James, she also believed that emotions serve survival-related purposes and that every emotion could be seen as an "impulse to action" (Arnold, 1960a, p. 178) or a readiness to respond to the environment in a particular way. Anger, for example, is accompanied by the "urge to strike and tear," whereas fear is accompanied by the urge to flee. Each of these actions follows directly from the kind of appraisals that we make about the events we encounter in our environment. To appraise a situation as dangerous, for example, implies that one should flee from the situation, and this is precisely the impulse to action that accompanies fear.

Arnold's treatment of the bodily responses associated with emotions is noteworthy for two reasons. The first is her argument that the bodily responses associated with each emotion serve as the motivation for the actions characteristic of the emotion. According to Arnold, appraising one's situation in a particular manner sets in motion physiological responses that are experienced as a kind of unpleasant tension. When the action implied by the appraisal, be it fleeing in fear or removing an obstacle in anger, has been completed, the physiological responses abate and we experience a relief from the tension. Thus, "[t]o flee as fear prompts us means not only escape from danger but relief from internal discomfort" (Arnold, 1960a, p. 179). This is an idea that was common to many so-called "drive reduction" models of behavior at the time Arnold was writing her book (e.g., Hull, 1943).

The second noteworthy aspect of Arnold's treatment of bodily responses is how she came to the conclusion that every emotion may be characterized by its own pattern of physiological activity. According to Arnold, "[s]ince different emotions urge us to different actions, and the physiological symptoms are relieved when we give in to this urge, we might expect that the physiological changes, taken by and large, will be as different as are the emotions" (Arnold, 1960a, p. 179). Thus, because different emotions seem to motivate our behavior in different ways, Arnold reasoned that underlying each emotion must be a distinct pattern of physiological activity. We know this intuitively, argued Arnold, because, "the physical sensations we feel are different in different emotions" (Arnold, 1960a, p. 179). We also know this in an indirect way, according to Arnold, because it forms the basis of how we recognize emotions in others.

Although it is certainly true that there may be individual differences in the expression of various emotions, "there will always be a core that is similar from person to person or even from man to animal" (Arnold, 1960a, p. 179). If such a core did not exist, she argued, we would have no reliable basis on which to make judgments about the emotions of others based on their expressions. It is interesting to note in this regard that Arnold assigned appraisal a crucial role in the process of making judgments of others' emotions. According to Arnold, "[t]here is no doubt that we recognize emotion by the same intuitive appraisal with which we respond to all situations that affect us in some way" (Arnold, 1960a, p. 205). Thus, while Arnold would not disagree with Darwin or James in seeing emotions as important, survival-related responses to the environment that are characterized by distinct patterns of physiological activity, she would maintain that essential to understanding how emotions work is an understanding of the process of appraisal.

Arnold's definition of emotion.   Given the emphasis she placed on appraisal, it is no surprise that Arnold ultimately defined emotion as

> the felt tendency toward anything intuitively appraised as good (beneficial), or away from anything intuitively appraised as bad (harmful). This attraction or aversion is accompanied by a pattern of physiological changes organized toward approach or withdrawal. The patterns differ for different emotions. (Arnold, 1960a, p. 182)

Notice how, like James, she considered feelings to be essential ingredients of emotion and, again like James, she saw the physiological changes that accompany emotions as being both the basis of the felt experience of emotion and as serving particular survival-related purposes. Arnold's lasting contribution to the science of emotion was her proposal that what initiated the physiological changes, feelings, and expressions characteristic of each emotion was the process of appraisal. In so doing, Arnold set the stage for the cognitive revolution in emotion research and provided an important set of concepts for other researchers to use in their attempts to understand the role of thought in emotion.

Arnold and Schachter

When I first sketched the outline of this book, I planned to place Stanley Schachter's two-factor theory of emotion within the cognitive tradition and discuss it in this chapter along with all of the other theories that emphasize the role of cognition in the generation of emotion. Schachter, after all, much in the same way Arnold did and other cognitive theorists would do, placed cognition first in the sequence of events leading up to the experience of emotion. The sequence Schachter envisioned, with physiological responses following directly from perception, sounds an awful lot like what Arnold had in mind. This is quite evident in one of the first examples Schachter used to illustrate how emotions are normally elicited:

> Imagine a man walking alone down a dark alley, a figure with a gun suddenly appears. The *perception-cognition* "figure with a gun" in some fashion initiates a state of physiological arousal; this state of arousal is interpreted in terms of knowledge about dark alleys and guns and the state of arousal is labeled "fear." (Schachter & Singer, 1962, emphasis added)

Unlike Arnold and the other cognitive emotion theories you'll soon meet, however, Schachter never closely examined the characteristics of the "perception-cognition" he identified. He simply took it for granted that such a process, in the normal course of things, sets in motion the physiological and experiential events we call emotion. Appraisal, as such, never plays a very prominent role in his theory. Thus, even though Schachter did spend considerable time examining the role of cognition in the labeling of physiological arousal, because arousal (and not appraisal per se) is so central to his theory, I decided that his theory would fit more comfortably with those that emphasize arousal rather than with those that emphasize cognition. Moreover, Schachter himself saw his theory as being a direct descendent of James' theory, albeit one that corrected James' faults. Indeed, at one point, Schachter even refers to his theory as "modified Jamesianism" (Schachter, 1964, p. 70).

"Short-Circuiting" Threat: Early Demonstrations of the Role of Appraisal in the Generation of Negative Affect

"Just keep telling yourself, 'It's only a movie!'" the advertisements for low-budget horror films tell us. Have you ever gone to one of those films and said this to yourself? Have you ever tried to get yourself through a particularly unpleasant visit to the dentist by telling yourself, "It'll all be over soon, and it really doesn't hurt that much anyway." If you have, then you've used a "cognitive coping strategy" that has been found by cognitive emotion researchers to be effective in reducing or "short-circuiting" stress (sometimes). This strategy involves changing the way we appraise a threatening or painful event, thus changing how we respond emotionally to it. The strategy's usefulness was demonstrated in a series of studies carried out by Richard Lazarus and his students and colleagues in the early 1960s.

Shortly after Arnold published her cognitive theory of emotion, Lazarus and his colleagues began a series of studies designed to show that a person's response to a stressful event could be minimized if the person could be induced to view the event in question in a nonstressful manner. In terms similar to those used by Arnold, Speisman, Lazarus, Mordkoff, and Davison (1964) argued that

> a stimulus must be regarded by the person as a threat to his welfare in order for stress responses to be produced. Thus, the same stimulus may be either a stressor or not, depending upon the nature of the cognitive appraisal the person makes regarding the significance [of the stimulus] for him. (Speisman et al., 1964, p. 367)

The stressful situation in which Speisman et al. chose to test this idea was watching an extremely gruesome anthropological film depicting a "rite of passage" ritual in which adolescent boys undergo a "subincision" operation. During the operation, the boys, who are about 13 or 14 years old, have the undersides of their penises cut with a sharpened piece of flint while they are restrained by a group of older men. While the boys appear to go into the operation quite willingly, they also appear to be very distressed during the actual subincision process; the operation is quite bloody and it is reasonable to assume that it is accompanied by a great deal of pain. I have seen the film and it is a bit of an understatement to say that it is *very* difficult to watch. To assess the hypothesis that changing the way a person appraises such a stressful event will change his or her emotional response to the event, Lazarus and his colleagues had male college students and airline executives individually view the film under one of four conditions while their affective responses to the film were monitored.

In a control condition, subjects simply watched the silent film. In a second, so-called *intellectualization* condition, subjects watched the same film with a sound track added to it that, "invited the viewer to observe in a detached manner, as anthropologists might, the interesting customs of the primitive natives" (Speisman et al., 1964, p. 368). The purpose of this sound track was to try to induce in the subjects a scientific attitude in which feelings were downplayed. In a third, *denial* condition, subjects were exposed to a sound track that denied that the subincision operation was painful or harmful in any way and that described the ritual as a "joyful" occasion that the young boys had anticipated with "enthusiasm." The idea here was to try to get subjects to experience the reverse of what they would ordinarily experience without the sound track. A fourth, *trauma* sound track emphasized the pain and danger involved in the operation and was intended to serve as a check on whether the content of the sound tracks was really the crucial variable in altering subjects' appraisal of the events depicted in the film. Notice that without such a condition, if the other two sound tracks proved to be equally effective in lowering the subjects' distress during the film, one could always argue that the subjects' distress was lessened merely by the presence of a sound track and not necessarily the content of the sound track.

Upon analyzing the data they had collected from their subjects' self-reports of distress immediately after the films and two physiological measures of stress recorded during the films, Speisman et al. found some support for the hypothesis that manipulating appraisals can "short-circuit" stress reactions. In particular, they found that their subjects' skin conductance responses to the films—skin conductance being a reliable indicator of sympathetic nervous system activity and hence, a person's response to a stressful event—differed according to what kind of sound track accompanied the film the subjects saw. Subjects in the *trauma* condition had the highest levels of skin conductance throughout the film, but particularly during an early scene in which the first subincisions are made. The skin conductance responses of subjects in the silent-film condition show a lower but still pronounced response to this scene, while the responses of subjects in the *intellectualization* and *denial* conditions to this scene are quite attenuated. While there were no differences among the four conditions for the self-report measures of distress, an outcome Lazarus and colleagues explain by arguing that by the end of the film the stressful events of the film are long past, Speisman et al. nevertheless concluded that, "the data presented have, in the main, supported the experimental hypothesis. Stress responses were greatest in the trauma track condition, next in the silent version, and significantly less in the [*denial* and *intellectualization*] sound tracks" (Speisman et al., 1964, p. 378).

The results of Speisman et al.'s study conformed nicely to what Arnold's theory would have predicted, namely, that the character of a person's emotional response to an event depends on how he or she appraises the event. Speisman et al.'s results were replicated and extended in a follow-up study by Lazarus and Alfert (1964) in which subjects' appraisals were manipulated by either accompanying the film with a sound track that denied the pain and suffering engendered by the subincision ritual or by providing subjects with the same information in written form *before* the film began. The results of Lazarus and Alfert's study provided even stronger support for Arnold's and Lazarus' ideas. As Figure 4.2 illustrates, the denial sound track led to an attenuated stress response to the film: compared with

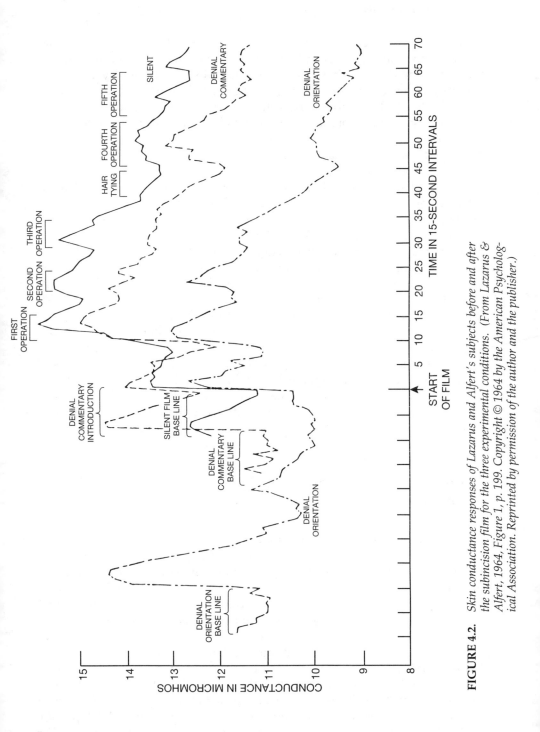

FIGURE 4.2. Skin conductance responses of Lazarus and Alfert's subjects before and after the subincision film for the three experimental conditions. (From Lazarus & Alfert, 1964, Figure 1, p. 199. Copyright © 1964 by the American Psychological Association. Reprinted by permission of the author and the publisher.)

a silent, control condition, subjects who heard the denial soundtrack showed much lower skin conductance levels throughout the film. Subjects who read the denial information before the film began, however, showed even lower levels of stress during the film. This finding is significant because it shows that emotional reactions to a stressful event can be influenced by changing subjects' expectations about the event *before* the event even takes place. The way an individual appraises an emotion-eliciting event, Arnold and Lazarus would argue, is a direct function of his or her expectations about the event.

The late 1960s to the late 1970s were boom times for researchers interested in the relationship between cognition and emotion. Scores of studies on the influence of cognition on stress and emotion were published during this period (see Lazarus, 1993, and 1991a), and in psychology departments all over the United States the excitement over this new perspective was nearly palpable. By the time I entered graduate school in 1975, cognition was *the* hot topic in the study of emotions. In fact, the first study I ever conducted as a graduate student (Cornelius & Averill, 1980) involved providing subjects with different kinds of information about a stressful event they were about to encounter, a cognitive manipulation. There is a definite advantage to being the first on the scene, however, as the results of these exciting new studies on cognition and emotion led Lazarus and his colleagues to offer one of the first self-consciously cognitive theories of emotion (Lazarus, Averill, & Opton 1970; see also Lazarus & Averill, 1972). Lazarus' work eventually culminated in his "cognitive-motivational-relational" theory of emotion.

Lazarus' Cognitive-Motivational-Relational Theory

Most, if not all, contemporary cognitive theories of emotion hold that specific emotions are preceded by specific patterns of appraisal (Smith & Lazarus, 1993; Lazarus, 1991), an idea Lazarus promoted in early versions of his theory (see, for example, Lazarus et al., 1970), and developed fully in his recent Cognitive-motivational-relational theory (Lazarus, 1991a). For Lazarus, emotions are responses to our perceived environments that "prepare and mobilise" us to cope in an adaptive manner with whatever harm or benefit we have appraised as being there (Smith & Lazarus, 1993, p. 234; see also Lazarus, 1991a, pp. 34–38). Central to Lazarus' model of the appraisal process is the notion that appraisals embody what he refers to as "relational meanings," the "specific implications for personal well-being" that a person sees in the situations confronting him or her (Smith & Lazarus, 1993, p. 236). Such relational meanings are a function of both what a situation has to offer a person for good or ill, and what a person brings to the situation in terms of his or her goals and intentions in the situation. For Lazarus, the former only take on meaning in the context of the latter. That is, in order to know how a person is going to react to a situation, we must know his or her expectations and goals with regard to the situation. Thus, Lazarus refers to his theory as "motivational-relational" because it describes how specific emotions arise out of the personal meanings that people bring to situations that have relevance to their knowledge and aspirations.

Lazarus and his colleagues describe the patterns of appraisal that express the relational meanings of the situations people encounter at two different levels of analysis. At the *molecular* level, *individual appraisal components* describe the, "specific judgments made by a person to evaluate particular . . . harms or benefits" in his or her environment (Smith & Lazarus, 1993, p. 236). At the *molar* level, the individual appraisal components are combined to yield *core relational themes*, which are a kind of summary of the emotional meaning of an event or situation.

Individual appraisal components.   According to Lazarus, at the most basic level, a person appraises a situation for the benefit or harm it might hold for him or her. This is accomplished through two kinds of appraisal, so-called *primary appraisal* and *secondary appraisal*.[2] Primary appraisals are about whether or not an event has any relevance for a person's well-being and, if so, how. Such appraisals involve a consideration of how much and what kind of impact an event will have on a person's goals. Receiving a failing exam grade, for example, can be expected to be appraised by a student as being highly relevant to and incongruent with his or her goal of passing a course. Secondary appraisals are about coping. These appraisals involve what a person might do to prevent further harm or acquire further benefit in the situation as well as who is to blame or receive credit for the situation. In the above example, the negative affect generated by receiving the failing exam grade may be mitigated somewhat by the student's knowledge that his or her professor is a pushover and can easily be convinced to change the grade to a higher one.

Core relational themes.   Lazarus argues that any one encounter between a person and a situation will result in several individual appraisals. In facing a particular event, a person will judge whether the event is relevant to his or her goals, whether it will hinder or facilitate the attainment or his or her goals, whether he or she can do anything about the event, and so on. According to Lazarus, these individual appraisals combine to reveal the larger "relational meaning" of the encounter. These larger meanings are what he refers to as *core relational themes*. A core relational theme, he says, is

---

[2] Arnold (1960a) made a similar distinction (see pp. 180–181).

the, "central (hence core) relational harm or benefit in adaptational encounters that underlies each specific kind of emotion" (Lazarus, 1991a, p. 121). Each emotion is associated with a specific pattern of individual appraisal components and a particular core relational theme.

The core relational theme for anger, for example, is "a demeaning offense against me and mine" (Lazarus, 1991a, p. 122), which involves appraising an event as one that is relevant and incongruent with one's goals and in which another is blameworthy (Smith & Lazarus, 1993). Suppose, for instance, I overhear a friend of mine make a sarcastic comment about me. This event is relevant to my goal of maintaining a friendly relationship with this person and is incongruent with that goal. It is also an event for which the other is to blame. In this situation, according to Lazarus, the individual appraisal components involve "motivational relevance," "motivational incongruence" and "other-accountability" (Smith & Lazarus, 1993), which come together to form the core relational theme of "a demeaning offense against me" for which another is to blame, thus generating the emotion of anger. Notice that the appraisal that the other person is to blame for the event involves a quite complex set of attributions. These include interpreting the other person's behavior toward oneself as being both voluntary and unjustified (see Averill, 1982). Notice also that if this last appraisal component were different, say, if it were *me* who made the sarcastic remark, the core relational theme for the event would be different and so would the resulting emotion. In this case, guilt, and not anger, would result. Table 4.1 presents the core relational themes for several emotions.

Perfidious friends and nasty teaching assistants: Testing Lazarus' theory. Smith and Lazarus (1993) provided a test of Lazarus' model of the relationship between appraisals, core relational themes, and emotion by having a group of undergraduate students from the University of California

TABLE 4.1. *Lazarus' core relational themes for several emotions*

Emotion	Core Relational Theme
Anger	A demeaning offense against oneself
Anxiety	Facing uncertain threat
Fright (fear)	Facing an immediate, concrete, overwhelming physical danger
Guilt	Transgressing a moral imperative
Sadness	Experiencing an irrevocable loss
Happiness	Making progress toward the realization of a goal
Love	Desiring or participating in affection, usually but not necessarily reciprocated
Compassion	Being moved by another's suffering and wanting to help

Source: Adapted from Lazarus, 1991a, Table 3.4, p. 122.

at Berkeley read written scenarios designed to elicit different appraisals and relational themes and, hence, different emotions.[3] Subjects were instructed to imagine themselves as being in the scenarios and to report, by means of structured questionnaires, how they appraised the situations described in the scenarios and how they would feel in each situation.

Each subject first read one of four basic scenarios. Two of the scenarios, one in which the subject is betrayed by a friend (*Friend scenario*) and one in which he or she is persecuted by a teaching assistant (*TA scenario*), were designed to elicit the relational theme of "other-blame." The other two, one in which the subject learns that a beloved relative has cancer (*Cancer scenario*) and one in which the subject receives a low grade in an important course (*Course scenario*), involved the theme of "loss/helplessness." After completing the questionnaire about their reactions to the scenarios, subjects were given a second scenario to read that represented a second episode in the basic scenario they had just imagined themselves in. Each subject read one of four different versions of this second scenario. Each version of the second scenario emphasized a different relational theme. One version emphasized "other-blame" and was designed to elicit anger; one emphasized "self-blame" and was designed to elicit guilt; a third emphasized "threat" and was designed to elicit fear or anxiety; and a fourth emphasized "loss/helplessness" and was designed to elicit sadness. All of the events described in the scenarios were assumed by Smith and Lazarus to be high in motivational relevance and incongruence.

Smith and Lazarus predicted that the subjects' reactions to the first scenarios would differ in terms of both their appraisals and their emotions, and this is indeed what happened. Subjects' appraisals of other-accountability and other-blame were higher in the *Friend* and *TA* scenarios than they were in the *Cancer* and *Course* scenarios, and subjects reported higher levels of anger in the former two scenarios than in the latter. In addition, subjects' appraisals of loss/helplessness and pessimism about coping were higher in the *Cancer* and *Course* scenarios, as were their self-reported levels of sadness. It is interesting to note, however, that the *Friend* scenario also produced relatively high levels of sadness. Smith and Lazarus expressed surprise at this last finding, although I think it is perfectly reasonable to expect someone to feel sadness over the loss of a friendship, no matter how the friendship ended.

In analyzing subjects' appraisals and emotional responses to the second scenarios, Smith and Lazarus found that the sadness scenario was not particularly effective in inducing sadness. However, the anger scenario did

---

[3]Actually, the test was of Smith *and* Lazarus' model, which, for all practical purposes, is essentially the same as Lazarus', particularly with the regard to the general proposition that emotions are dependent on appraisals.

indeed elicit anger, the threat scenario fear/anxiety, and the guilt scenario feelings of guilt. Moreover, the individual appraisal components and core relational themes associated with each of these emotions were found to be not associated with any of the other emotions. Thus, for all of the emotions they examined except sadness, Smith and Lazarus found strong support for their predictions and, thus, for their model of the appraisal process.

"Preferences Need No Inferences": Zajonc's Challenge to Lazarus

In 1980, Robert Zajonc, whose theory of facial efference we encountered in the previous chapter, issued a no-holds-barred challenge to the cognitive perspective (Zajonc, 1980). Although Zajonc's critique was not aimed specifically at Lazarus' work, indeed, Lazarus is not even mentioned in Zajonc's original paper, the objections that Zajonc raised about the cognitive approach to emotions went to the heart of Lazarus' theory. It is not surprising, then, that Lazarus answered Zajonc's challenge with a forceful reply (Lazarus, 1982). Zajonc followed with a response to Lazarus' reply (Zajonc, 1984), which made for quite a lively little scientific debate.

The essence of Zajonc's position is the assertion that cognition and emotion are independent systems and that it is possible to generate emotions without the participation of any cognitive processes, thus countering Lazarus' claim that cognition is both a necessary and sufficient condition for emotion (see Lazarus, 1991a, pp. 177–190, for a detailed discussion of this issue). According to Zajonc, those who argue that emotion is "postcognitive," believe that

> [a]n affective reaction, such as liking, disliking, preference, evaluation, or the experience of pleasure or displeasure, is based on a prior cognitive process in which a variety of content discriminations are made and features are identified, examined for their value, and weighted for their contributions. (Zajonc, 1980, p. 151)

Zajonc takes issue with the notion that, "[o]bjects must be cognized before they can be evaluated" (Zajonc, 1980, p. 151), arguing instead that many affective reactions can be shown to have occurred when no cognitive activity has taken place or, equivalently, before any cognitive activity has had time to take place. Table 4.2 presents eight features of affective reactions Zajonc identifies that suggest that affect and cognition are separate and at least partially independent systems. For our purposes, the most important items on this list are the first, "Affective reactions are primary," and the seventh, "Affective reactions need not depend on cognition."

Zajonc bases his conclusion that affect need not depend on cognition

TABLE 4.2. *Eight reasons why affect and cognition should be seen as separate systems*

1. Affective reactions are primary. ("Feelings come first," cognition follows.)
2. Affect is basic. (Phylogenetically, emotional responding comes before cognition.)
3. Affective reactions are inescapable.
4. Affective judgments tend to be irrevocable.
5. Affective judgments implicate the self.
6. Affective reactions are difficult to verbalize.
7. Affective reactions need not depend on cognition.
8. Affective reactions may become separated from content.

Source: Adapted from Zajonc, 1980.

on studies of the "mere exposure effect" (Moreland & Zajonc, 1977, 1979). In such studies, subjects are exposed to a series of stimuli, such as tones of different wavelengths, Japanese ideographs, or complex polygons. Some of the stimuli, unbeknownst to the subjects, are presented repeatedly. After the initial presentation of the stimuli, subjects are presented with another set of stimuli that contains some of the stimuli they have already heard or seen and are asked to identify which stimuli they have heard or seen before. Because of the unfamiliarity or complexity of the stimuli (or both), or the presence of a distracter task, subjects are not very good at doing this. However, subjects are also asked which stimuli they like or "prefer." Their preferences, it turns out, are strongly related to how many times they have been exposed to the stimuli. Thus, subjects are shown to have a positive affective reaction to stimuli they don't even recognize! In arguing that affect precedes cognition, Zajonc points to studies by cognitive psychologists (see, for example, Posner & Snyder, 1975) in which reaction times to make affective judgments about a stimulus were shown to be faster than were reaction times for recognition of the stimulus.

The results of these and other studies led Zajonc to conclude that "to arouse affect, objects need to be cognized very little—in fact, minimally" (Zajonc, 1980, p. 154). How could it be otherwise, Zajonc asks, given the role of emotion in quickly preparing the body to deal with potentially life-threatening, survival-related events in the world. Thus, by implication, Zajonc argues that the view taken by Lazarus and others that events or objects must always be appraised before emotional reactions can take place is false.

In his reply, Lazarus, while acknowledging the validity of the empirical studies Zajonc cites, argues that Zajonc's conclusions about the meaning of those studies are based on a faulty definition of appraisal. According to Lazarus, Zajonc equates cognition, and hence, appraisal, with conscious, deliberate, rational thought that involves a more or less complete processing of the information contained in a stimulus. Following Arnold, Lazarus instead sees appraisal as a much more automatic, nonreflective, and not necessarily conscious process and asserts that, however minimal the processing of information from the stimulus and however "irrational" the outcome, some type of appraisal is *always* necessary before emotions can be elicited (Lazarus, 1982). In fact, appraisal is such an integral part of the process of generating emotions, Lazarus argues, that the two cannot meaningfully be separated. Herein, I think, is the key to resolving the differences between Lazarus and Zajonc.

The difference between the positions of Lazarus and Zajonc boils down to how one ultimately defines cognition and appraisal. For Zajonc, the amount of processing of the information from a stimulus necessary for affect to occur is, as he says, "minimal." Because he seems to equate cognition with at least as much information processing as is needed to identify a stimulus, he must argue that cognition cannot be involved in the kind of quick and automatic judgments that are involved in the generation of affect. Notice that Zajonc doesn't argue that *no* information is being processed, only that the processing is minimal and may involve the detection of special features of the stimulus in question (something he calls *preferenda*). When Lazarus talks about the characteristics of appraisal, he is talking about a very similar kind of processing—very fast, automatic, and only of the features of the stimulus essential for making judgments about the personal significance of the stimulus. Lazarus prefers to call this appraisal and consider it a kind of cognition, Zajonc does not. Thus, the difference between their positions is largely, I think, definitional. This is not to say that matters of definition are trivial, far from it. Definitions are at the heart of scientific theory making. Zajonc, in his response to Lazarus' reply to his original article, accuses Lazarus of trying to address the problem of how much cognition is involved in emotion by definitional sleight of hand while he addresses the problem by reference to "the facts" (Zajonc, 1984). It has long been recognized by philosophers of science that what one wishes to call "the facts," however, depends very much on how one's theory defines them (Kuhn, 1962). The failure to recognize this tendency sometimes leads scientists to believe that facts precede theories, when just the reverse is the case.

Apples and oranges.   There is another important definitional difference between Lazarus' and Zajonc's views of the nature of appraisal that, I think, is more interesting and potentially more important than how each defines cognition. This difference has to do with what each chooses to call emotion. Notice that Zajonc equates emotion with "affective reaction." Affective reactions are defined by Zajonc as, "liking, disliking, preference, evaluation, or the experience of pleasure or displeasure" (Zajonc, 1980, p. 151). Indeed, his paper is subtitled "*preferences* need no inferences" (emphasis added). Notice also that the studies Zajonc presents to provide support for his position all involve very simple kinds of affective judgments, usually liking. These affective judgments are very different from the kind of emotional phenomena considered by Lazarus. Nowhere does Zajonc discuss the kinds of cognitive processes involved in anger, sadness, fear, love, or guilt, and yet *these* kinds of emotions are Lazarus' central focus. Thus, one can make the argument that Zajonc and Lazarus are really talking about apples and oranges: Zajonc's concern is with very simple positive or negative affective judgments and Lazarus' concern is with more complex emotions. An appraisal that a "demeaning offense" has been committed against me is a far cry from (and much more complex than) my getting a vague sense that I don't like a person. Given their differences in focus, it may be the case that *both* Lazarus and Zajonc are right. Lazarus' model applies to complex emotions and Zajonc's applies to very simple affective reactions.[4]

Before We Were So Rudely Interrupted: Mandler's Theory of Emotion

In 1975, George Mandler published a book entitled *Mind and Emotion* in which he presented his theory of the cognition-emotion relationship in the wider context of an information-processing view of mental events. Mandler was one of the first emotion theorists to make full use of the information-processing approach to cognitive phenomena stimulated by Ulrich Neisser's influential book *Cognitive Psychology* (1967). Mandler's theory of emotion is in some ways similar to that of Schachter (as described in the previous chapter) in that he posits an important and essential role for autonomic nervous system arousal in the generation and experience of emotion. His theory also emphasizes the role of the "cognitive interpretation" of that arousal and of the events in the environment that elicit such arousal. His theory is different from Schachter's and more "cognitive" in that it contains a much fuller consideration of the role of cognition in the genesis and experience of emotion.

For Mandler, the starting point for the generation of emotion is arousal, defined as "the activities of the autonomic nervous system, particularly its sympathetic division" (Mandler, 1975, p. 66), and the perception of arousal. Like Schachter, Mandler believes that arousal is relatively undifferentiated and that it varies simply in terms of its intensity. Sympathetic nervous system arousal is occasioned by a number of environmental events having survival value to us. One of the most important of these events is the "interruption of ongoing plans and actions" (Mandler, 1975, p. 66). Mandler assigns special status to interruptions as a class of events having special

---

[4]The recent neurophysiological work by LeDoux (1987) on the two emotion pathways in the brain supports this conclusion (see Appendix).

adaptive significance because an interruption in a person's plans and actions often, "signals important changes in the environment, which often lead to altered circumstances of living, adapting, and surviving" (Mandler, 1975, p. 153). So important is interruption as a cause of sympathetic nervous system arousal that Mandler argues that interruption is a "sufficient and possibly necessary condition for the occurrence" of such arousal (Mandler, 1975, p. 153).

The arousal of sympathetic nervous system activity has two functions, according to Mandler. One function is simply to prepare the organism physiologically to respond to whatever events in the environment elicited the activity. This is the familiar preparatory response recognized by many emotion theorists from Darwin on. The second function of sympathetic nervous system activity is to "signal" consciousness "for attention, alertness, and scanning of the environment," an activity that "demands interpretation and analysis" (Mandler, 1975, p. 67). Once such a signal has been registered, a person's "sensory and cognitive systems" engage in a search for information as to the source of the autonomic arousal and/or the person's environment. Thus, anything that sets in motion sympathetic nervous system activity also sets in motion a search for the causes of the activity. This search involves a reorienting of our consciousness. Herein lies one of the most important functions of emotions according to Mandler, namely, to call attention to events in our environment that have possible adaptive significance for us.

For Mandler, the experience of emotion and the behaviors that sometimes accompany such experiences are the "interactional result" of sympathetic nervous system arousal and the "cognitive interpretation" of such arousal. Such cognitive interpretation includes a search of one's surroundings for the possible causes of the arousal (compare this with Schachter's similar notion) as well as an assessment of one's ability to deal with the situation, what Lazarus would call coping. The end result of this cognitive activity in the presence of the arousal is the experience of emotion.

Notice here how Mandler's theory, even though it acknowledges the importance of autonomic activity, emphasizes the conscious experience of emotion. Indeed, emotions, for Mandler, are intimately bound up with consciousness and what he calls the "troubleshooting" function of consciousness (Mandler, 1975, p. 171). Emotions, being at least partly signals to consciousness that a reorienting of one's attention, plans, and, perhaps, activities is necessary, of course, require consciousness. Thus, Mandler's theory can be seen as a theory of mental life and consciousness in general as well as a theory of emotion. It is for this reason that Mandler insists that his task is not to develop a theory of emotion per se, but to describe "a system that has as its product some of the observations that have been called 'emotion'" (Mandler, 1975, p. 2–3).

Video games psychologists play: Testing Mandler's theory.   Mac-
Dowell and Mandler (1989) devised a fiendishly clever test of Mandler's notion that interruptions are important causes of autonomic arousal and emotion. MacDowell and Mandler first gave a group of undergraduate students
the opportunity to become proficient at a video game called *Rogue* (written
by one of the author's assistants). In the game, players move a character, the
Rogue, through the mazes and passageways of a series of dungeons. The
object of the game is to find one's way out of the dungeon while avoiding
being killed by the various monsters that one encounters along the way. The
monsters in the dungeon have different strengths and abilities and whether
or not one survives an encounter with a monster depends on the skill one
has acquired in fighting other monsters and where one is in the dungeon,
monsters encountered later in the game being more powerful than monsters
encountered earlier. In addition to battling monsters successfully, winning
the game also depends on the amount of treasure one has when one finds
the exit. After playing the game for a relatively brief period of time, players
come to expect particular monsters and objects such as pieces of gold at particular points in the game.

Once their subjects had become accomplished players and had built
up a set of expectations as to what would happen when in the game, Mac-
Dowell and Mandler reprogrammed it so that the subjects would experience a set of both positive and negative unexpected events, for example, en-
countering 1,000 pieces of gold when only 70 were expected, or being killed
by the "Jackal," a monster normally incapable of killing the Rogue. Mac-
Dowell and Mandler predicted that such unexpected events, being interruptions in the subjects' plans and ongoing activities, would elicit higher levels
of autonomic arousal than would comparable expected events. Degree of
arousal, in turn, was predicted to be related to the subjects' "subjective intensity of experience," with greater arousal being associated with greater affective intensity.

The subjects in the study had their heart rate and skin conductance
continuously monitored while they played the game, though MacDowell
and Mandler never describe what their subjects thought of this. In addition,
subjects were asked, via the computer, to describe the intensity of their feelings on a 7-point scale after both expected and unexpected events. Thus,
MacDowell and Mandler collected information on their subjects' autonomic
arousal and self-reported affect in response to the events in the game. Upon
analyzing these data, MacDowell and Mandler found that their subjects'
arousal was indeed higher in response to unexpected than expected events,
but only when measured by heart rate. This was true regardless of whether
the event was positive or negative. Subjects' heart rates did change more
rapidly in response to negative than positive events, however.

In line with their second prediction, MacDowell and Mandler found evidence that the intensity of their subjects' affective experiences while playing the game was related to the degree of their autonomic arousal. Specifically, there was a high correlation between the intensity of the subjects' self-reported affect and the rate of change of both heart rate and skin conductance in response to the unexpected events, even though there was no difference between the intensity of subjects' self-reported affect in response to the expected and unexpected events.

MacDowell and Mandler interpret these results as supporting two of the important claims of Mandler's theory, namely, that the interruption of a person's ongoing activities brings about changes in autonomic arousal and that this arousal contributes to the intensity of the person's emotional response to the interruption. The results MacDowell and Mandler present are quite complex, however, and do not provide unambiguous support for the theory. For though it is true that their subjects did respond to unexpected events with increases in arousal, the intensity of subjects' self-reported affect did not always parallel the degree of arousal, and Mandler is quite insistent that, "arousal produces the intensity" of emotional experience (MacDowell & Mandler, 1989, p. 106). Leaving aside the problem of specifying the mechanisms by which arousal "produces" intensity of felt experience, given the ambiguity of the results, it is far from clear just how much support the results provide for this aspect of Mandler's theory. The extent to which the arousal elicited by the unexpected events in the video game was due to the way they interrupted the subjects' ongoing activities or simply to their novelty is also not clear.[5] Nevertheless, at least to some extent, the results of MacDowell and Mandler's study are consistent with the broad outlines of Mandler's theory. Interruptions in ongoing activity do appear to generate autonomic arousal and the specific quality of the emotions that are occasioned by that arousal are related to the nature of the expectations that are violated by the interruptions.

The Best Laid Schemes o' Mice and Men: Oatley and Johnson-Laird's "Communicative" Theory of Emotion

A theory similar to Mandler's in many ways is Keith Oatley and Phil Johnson-Laird's "communicative" theory of emotion (Oatley, 1992; Oatley & Johnson-Laird, 1987). Oatley and Johnson-Laird's theory is also concerned with the consequences of interruptions, although its focus is specifically on the interruption of goals (Oatley, 1992, p. 50). Oatley and Johnson-Laird's theory is unique among current cognitive theories of emotion,

[5]I thank one of my anonymous reviewers for pointing this out.

however, in that it was developed within the larger context of *computational* models of language and cognition from the discipline of cognitive science.[6] By developing such a theory of emotion, Oatley and Johnson-Laird hoped to address the almost complete absence of emotions from computational models of cognition and to offer a theory that some day might be amenable to "formal" testing, that is, testing by means of computer simulations. With regard to the former, it is interesting to note that Oatley and Johnson-Laird have argued that emotions, rather than being phenomena that are best left out of models of human thought, "are central to the organization of cognitive processing" (Oatley & Johnson-Laird, 1987, p. 30).

Emotions and modules. At the heart (or should I say brain?) of Oatley and Johnson-Laird's theory is the idea that human cognitive processes are "modular" and have the need to communicate with one another. What this means is that human cognition is accomplished by means of a system of more or less autonomous processing modules. Each module is designed to carry out a particular task or process, say, searching memory for a name to attach to a face, and, once it has been activated, it will complete its specialized task unless it is interrupted (Oatley & Johnson-Laird, 1987). To account for the order that collections of such modules must have so that they don't routinely interfere with one another, Oatley and Johnson-Laird envision them as being organized hierarchically. Higher-order modules control lower-level modules and can call upon them to carry out their particular tasks. At the top of the hierarchy of modules is a kind of executive module or operating system analogous to the operating systems of computers. Such systems coordinate the activity of the modules they control, fulfilling plans and achieving particular goals by calling upon them to carry out their tasks at specific times in specific sequences. Included within the operating system, according to Oatley and Johnson-Laird, is a model or representation of the system itself as a whole. This is a crucial component of the operating system as it is involved in the generation of emotions, for one of the "goals" of the operating system, and hence of the system as a whole, is self-preservation.

Emotions and communication among modules. In order for such a system of autonomous modules to carry out any kind of complex task, of course, the individual modules must communicate with one another. Lower-level modules must pass information to higher-level modules and high-level modules must integrate information received from many lower-

---

[6]*Computational* models of language and cognition liken the human brain to a computer and regard cognition as being akin to the kinds of transformations of symbols that computers carry out. Cognition is computational in the sense that it involves nothing more than what any self-respecting, reasonably intelligent computer could do. For more information on the computational approach to cognition, see Churchland (1988) or Gardner (1985).

level modules and respond appropriately to each. According to Oatley and Johnson-Laird, coordination among the modules in the human cognitive system involves two very different kinds of communication, and this is where emotion comes in.

The first kind of communication is "propositional" or symbolic in nature, and involves what might be thought of as factual information about the world, for example, "I met her during my second year of college" or, "To get to Triangle Street, turn left on Pleasant Street." The second kind of communication is nonpropositional or emotional in nature and serves not to pass information among modules but to set them into particular states or "modes." Oatley and Johnson-Laird propose that the function of this class of communications is to interrupt the ongoing activity of the system as a whole and to place and maintain the various modules in the system into a state of readiness or "emotion modes" (Oatley & Johnson-Laird, 1987, p. 32). This kind of communication has the capacity to override whatever else is going on in the system and ready the modules in the system to respond in some manner. These signals, which are evoked by the perception of certain survival- or goal-related information in the (internal or external) environment function in a manner analogous to the "global interrupt" command found in some computer programs. When these are issued, new priorities are quickly established for the various individual modules in the system and for the system as a whole.

> Emotion signals provide a specific communication system which can invoke the actions of some processors [modules] and switch others off. It sets the whole system into an organized emotion mode without propositional data having to be evaluated by a high-level conscious operating system . . . The emotion signal simply propagates globally through the system to set it into one of a small number of emotion modes. (Oatley & Johnson-Laird, 1987, p. 33)

To understand how this works, imagine that you've just bumped into someone with your shopping cart at the local market. As you mumble an apology and make eye contact with the person, you get a vague feeling that you know her. Before you can recall her name, however, you are overcome with a sense of fear and dread as you realize that she teaches the English class you've skipped for the past 2 months and that she recognizes you. What has happened here, according to Oatley and Johnson-Laird, is that the activity of all of the many modules involved in your ongoing cognitive activity at the time—from comparing the unit price of two brands of tofu to wondering when you'll have time to wash your car—have been suddenly reset and placed in the service of fulfilling a higher-level goal, in this case, coming up with a quick and plausible explanation for why you haven't been in class.

Notice how, except for the computer analogies, Oatley and Johnson-

Laird's theory is similar to Mandler's in giving priority to the way emotions signal important events in the environment and prepare one both cognitively and physiologically for activities that may involve changing one's plans or goals and altering one's current behavior. Emotion signals are seen to do this very quickly and without the aid of consciousness.

Like Ekman (see Chapter 2), Oatley and Johnson-Laird assume that there are a small number of basic emotions, although they refer to them as "emotion modes" (Oatley & Johnson-Laird, 1987). They think of happiness, sadness, anxiety/fear, anger, and disgust as states of readiness to respond to the environment in particular ways in the presence of particular stimuli. All of these emotion modes are elicited by stimuli in the environment that are relevant to a person's goals. Anxiety/fear is elicited, for example, when one's goal of self-preservation is threatened. Anger is elicited when a plan one is carrying out in order to reach some goal is frustrated. Happiness is elicited when a goal is achieved (Oatley & Johnson-Laird, 1987, Table 1, p. 36). Unlike Ekman or Izard, Oatley and Johnson-Laird do not think of complex emotions such as regret or embarrassment as *combinations* of simpler, basic emotions. Rather, they see complex emotions as consisting of basic emotion modes with an added "propositional evaluation which is social and includes reference to the model of the self" (Oatley & Johnson-Laird, 1987, p. 46).

Emotions and social communication.   Oatley and Johnson-Laird call their theory "communicative" because one of the central functions of emotions within the human cognitive system as they see it is to carry out a particular kind of communication among the modules of the system. Oatley and Johnson-Laird also regard emotions as communicative in a social sense in that many of the more complex emotions serve to communicate information about the mutual plans and goals of interdependent social actors.[7] Anger, for example, is a complex, social emotion as well as a basic emotion in that it arises when one person's plans or progress toward a goal are interrupted by another person's behavior. Displays of anger communicate in no uncertain terms that a person feels his or her expectations (and rights) have been violated. Drawing on some of the work of James Averill (1982), which we'll examine in the next chapter, Oatley and Johnson-Laird argue that, in a broader sense, anger may be seen as one of the ways in which social actors "renegotiate" their roles in complex systems of social interaction (Oatley, 1992, see pp. 211–214).

---

[7]It is interesting to note in this context that Oatley and Johnson-Laird draw extensively on the computer scientist Marvin Minsky's (1986) "society" theory of mind in building their model of the human cognitive system. The "agents" in the society of mind that Minsky describes look much like the interdependent social actors described by Oatley and Johnson-Laird (and most social psychologists).

Best-laid and other schemes.   Oatley entitled his recent book about his and Johnson-Laird's theory *Best Laid Schemes*, taking the title from the well-known poem "To a mouse on turning her up in her nest with the plough" by Robert Burns in which, "The best laid schemes o' Mice an' Men" are seen as leading to, "nought but grief an' pain." According to Oatley and Johnson-Laird, our schemes, whether best laid or not, bring us not only grief and pain but all of our emotions. Emotions arise at what they refer to as the "junctures" of our plans, when our plans have been interrupted but also when they have been fulfilled. Emotions communicate important information within our cognitive system but also within our social systems. Oatley and Johnson-Laird's theory is a bold attempt to outline what a computational model of human emotions might look like and to indicate the ways in which emotions function at both the intra- and interpersonal levels. Being so new, it is too soon to be able to say much about the validity of the theory, although it appears to fit the available data as well as any other current theory (but see Averill, 1994, and Frijda et al., 1989, for critiques), and Oatley has done a marvelous job of "testing" the theory by drawing upon novels such as George Eliot's *Middlemarch,* Leo Tolstoy's *Anna Karenina,* and the poems of Sappho, among other literary works, to illustrate how the theory works.[8] Time will tell, of course, whether the theory will come to "grief an' pain," but, given its scope and potential power, it may be one of the most important cognitive theories to come out of the 1990s.

BOX 4.1

Can Your Computer Tell When You're Feeling Sad?

The question of whether or not computers can experience emotions has long been a staple of both science and science fiction. Sophisticated computers have now become such a part of many people's daily lives that the question is no longer simply an academic one (Turkle, 1984). Emotion researchers, appropriately enough, have found the question a difficult one to ignore as well (see Frijda & Swagerman, 1987). The question of whether or not computers can feel emotions is certainly an interesting one, as is the question of whether computers can tell what *you* are feeling. As an alternative method of exploring the nature of the appraisal process, Klaus Scherer (1993) developed a computer "expert system" that attempts to ascertain what emotion a person is experiencing by asking the person a series of questions about his or her appraisals.

    Scherer's GENESE (Geneva Expert System on Emotions) contains a detailed, theoretically derived "knowledge base" that consists

---

[8]Oatley's book is quite a literary, as well as philosophical and psychological, achievement in its own right. It deserves to be read by any serious student of emotion.

of information on what kinds of appraisals are associated with what kinds of emotions based on Scherer's own appraisal research (Scherer, 1988). Various appraisal dimensions are associated with fourteen different emotions in the program by a series of "weights." These weights are essentially the theoretically derived probability that a particular kind of appraisal is associated with a particular emotion. The user of the program is asked a set of fifteen questions about a particular emotional episode such as, "Did the situation that elicited your emotion happen very suddenly or abruptly?," "Did the event help or hinder you in satisfying your needs, in pursuing your plans or in attaining your goals?," and "Did you feel that you had enough power to cope with the event— i.e., being able to influence what was happening or to modify the consequences?" The user responds to each question on a quantitative scale, for example, "(0) not pertinent, (1) not at all, (2) a little, (3) moderately, (4) strongly, (5) extremely."

Once the user has answered all of the questions, the program compares the pattern of the user's answer with the pattern of answers that, theoretically, should be associated with a particular emotion. The program then presents the user with a list of the fourteen emotions ordered from most likely to least likely. If the computer correctly predicts the user's emotion, the user tells the computer so. If the computer's prediction does not match what the subject feels his or her emotion was, the user enters "incorrect" and the program then issues a second prediction. An extremely interesting feature of Scherer's system is what happens if the computer misses the ball twice. If the second prediction is also incorrect, the program asks the user to tell it the correct emotion. The program then takes this information and constructs an appraisal-emotion data base for that particular user. Thus, the system is able to "learn" new appraisal-emotion relationships via the feedback it receives from individual users.

Scherer assessed the accuracy of the system by examining how often it correctly predicted the 282 emotional episodes entered by a sample of 236 people (some users entered more than one episode). After culling the incorrectly entered episodes and user-entered emotions that made no sense (such as "le spleen total"), Scherer found that the system correctly predicted users' emotions on the average 77.9% of the time. The accuracy of the system varied considerably, from a high of 100% for joy/elation, contempt/scorn, and desperation/grief to a low of 14.3% for anxiety/worry. Scherer accounts for the low accuracy for anxiety by pointing out that anxiety and fear situations are emotional episodes that often change very quickly and that the users of the system may have been entering information from a variety of points in the episodes, thus conflating the "danger anticipation *and* the resolution part of the emotion process" (Scherer, 1993, p. 347).

Whatever its present shortcomings, it is clear that Scherer's system may provide a valuable tool for exploring the relationship between appraisal and emotion (see Chwelos & Oatley, 1994, for a friendly critique). The system seems to hold particular promise as a way of studying individual differences in patterns of appraisal.

Other Cognitive Structural Theories of Emotion

By now you should be fairly convinced that thought is indeed intimately involved in emotion or at least convinced that a number of scientists are convinced that thought is intimately involved in emotion. The question of how specific thoughts or appraisals are related to specific emotions, however, has not been fully answered. The question, as you might imagine, is a very important one. Either implicitly or explicitly, all of the cognitive emotion researchers whose theories we have examined assume that particular patterns of appraisals or cognitions are associated with particular emotions and that emotions can, in fact, be *predicted* from their associated cognitions.

The task of precisely specifying the relationships between particular cognitions and particular emotions has been undertaken by a number of researchers whose research is carried out within a variety of different but related theoretical frameworks (Frijda, 1986; Frijda et al., 1989; Lazarus, 1991; Oatley, 1992; Ortony, Clore, & Collins, 1988; Roseman, 1984; Roseman, Spindel, & Jose, 1990; Smith & Ellsworth, 1985; Scherer, 1988). Following Frijda et al. (1989), I consider the theories employed by these researchers and by Smith and Lazarus to be "structural" theories in the sense that they are all concerned, like Smith and Lazarus, with specifying the unique cognitive structures associated with each emotion.[9] Cognitive structural theorists assume that all of the cognitions associated with a particular emotion can be seen as reflecting a relatively small number of underlying meanings or "dimensions." In a hypothetical and very simple dimensional theory, fear, for example, might be seen as reflecting the withdrawal end of an "approach-withdrawal" dimension, while love might be seen as reflecting the approach end of the dimension. The cognitive structure of emotions refers to the supposedly invariant patterns of these underlying meanings, with each emotion having a particular pattern of values along several underlying dimensions (see Frijda et al., 1989, p. 212) . The claim is that the particular patterns of meaning underlying the appraisals or cognitions associated with each emotion, *cause* the emotion. The variability that is seen in our responses to the same situation is a result of differences in how we appraise the situation, or more precisely, in the cognitive structure of our appraisal of the situation (Roseman et al., 1990): The same cognitive structures always give rise to the same emotions, but people differ in what cognitive structures are elicited by a particular situation because their goals and motivations differ (Lazarus, 1991). Since this is all rather abstract, let's explore a particular structural theory to see a little more concretely what this all means.

---

[9]This is somewhat different from the way that de Rivera (1977), in *his* structural theory of emotions, uses the term. De Rivera, drawing on the work of Jean Piaget, uses the term to refer to the way in which emotions form a coherent system: "while individual emotions each have an identity, they are not separate entities but are parts of a whole—a system of object relations or a 'structure'" (p. 36).

Why You Feel Guilty When You Forget to Call Your Mother: Roseman's Structural Theory

There are currently several more or less fully elaborated, cognitive structural theories of emotion competing for the attention of students of emotion (see earlier discussion). Each of them seems to make the same assumptions about the nature of emotion, and the cognitive dimensions they see as underlying most emotions are quite similar (see Roseman et al., 1990, and Scherer, 1988, for detailed discussions of the similarities among them). For the sake of brevity, I will confine my discussion of them to Ira Roseman's theory. However, given the similarities among the various structural theories, except for specific details, what is said about one theory may be said about them all. You may want to track down Ortony et al.'s (1988) excellent book *The Cognitive Structure of Emotions*, and compare their theory to Roseman's. The basic assumptions of the two theories are quite similar but they differ in their details and in what they emphasize.

Five dimensions = fourteen emotions. Roseman (1984; Roseman et al., 1990) proposes that underlying the cognitions associated with each of fourteen emotions is a set of five dimensions or "sets of alternative appraisals of events . . . [that] determine whether an emotion will occur and which discrete emotion that will be" (Roseman, 1984, p. 17).

1. *Situational state* refers to whether the events one encounters in a particular situation are *consistent or inconsistent with one's motives* in the situation. If one's goal in a situation is to, say, complete some task such as eating lunch, then anything that interferes with that goal, say, an untimely phone call or finding aphids in one's salad, will be appraised as inconsistent with one's motive. Events that are consistent with one's motives lead to positive emotions, whereas events that are inconsistent with one's motives lead to negative emotions. This dimension is similar to the much simpler "harmful/beneficial" dimension proposed by Arnold (1960a).

2. *Probability* refers to how *certain* or *uncertain* one is that a particular event or outcome in a situation will occur. According to Roseman (1990), uncertain events lead to emotions such as fear or hope and certain events lead to relief, joy, sadness, or disgust.

3. *Agency* refers to who is responsible for the events in a particular situation. Events caused by *oneself* may lead to guilt, whereas events caused by *another person* may lead to anger. Events occasioned by *circumstances beyond one's control* may lead to sadness.

4. *Motivational state* refers to whether the events one encounters involve *obtaining a reward or avoiding punishment.* Roseman (Roseman et al., 1990) terms these *appetitive motivation* and *aversive motivation,* respectively. In a particular situation, obtaining a reward might lead to joy, whereas avoiding punishment might lead to relief.

5. *Power* refers to whether one perceives oneself as *weak* or *strong* in a particular situation. Appraising oneself as weak in a situation might lead to fear, whereas appraising oneself as strong might lead to frustration or anger.

Roseman argues that particular patterns of where one's appraisals are located on these five dimensions lead to particular emotions. As illustrated in Figure 4.3, hope, for example, follows from the appraisal that an event is consistent with one's motives, that it is caused by circumstances outside of one's control, and that the outcome of the event is uncertain. An appraisal that a motive-inconsistent event caused by another person in a situation in which one perceived oneself as strong would lead, on the other hand, to anger. Perceiving oneself as weak under the same circumstances, according to Roseman, would lead instead to a feeling of dislike.

Fear and loathing at Yale: Testing Roseman's theory.   Roseman (1984; see Roseman, 1991, for a more complete description), tested the adequacy of an earlier and somewhat different version of his proposed five dimensions by having Yale University undergraduates read brief vignettes about people in emotion-eliciting situations in which information about each of the appraisal dimensions was systematically varied. Roseman constructed forty-eight different versions of eight stories describing a person involved in situations such as taking an exam or having a romantic relationship threatened by infidelity. The versions differed along the dimensions of *certainty/uncertainty* (probability), *presence/absence* (situational state) of a *rewarding/punishing* (motivational state) event, whether the event was *deserved/undeserved* (legitimacy) and whether the event was *caused by the protagonist/another person/circumstances* (agency). His subjects read one version of each of the eight stories and rated on an 11-point scale how intensely the protagonist in each story would experience, "joy, relief, hope, warmth-friendliness (liking), pride, distress, sorrow, fear, frustration, coolness-unfriendliness (disliking), anger, regret, and guilt" (Roseman, 1984, p. 24).

Analysis of the subjects' intensity ratings strongly supported the hypothesis that the various emotions would be associated with the specific patterns of appraisal proposed by Roseman. The results of the self/other responsibility (agency), probability, and motivational state manipulations, however, were much closer to what Roseman had predicted than were the results for the situational state and deserved/undeserved (legitimacy) manipulations (Roseman et al., 1990; Roseman, 1984). This led Roseman to revise his situational state dimension to become *motive-consistent/motive-inconsistent* rather than simply *presence/absence,* and his legitimacy dimension to become *power* (appraising oneself as weak or strong) (Roseman, 1984, pp. 25–29).

You can't always get what you want. To assess the validity of his re-

divulgence

FIGURE 4.3. *Appraisal dimensions associated with fourteen emotions, as proposed by Roseman, Ira, "Cognitive Determinants of Emotion" in P. Shaver (Ed.), Review of Personality and Social Psychology, vol. 5, p. 18. Copyright © 1984 by Sage Publications, Inc. Reprinted by permission of Sage Publications, Inc., and the author.*

	Positive		Negative		
	Motive-Consistent		Motive-Inconsistent		
	Appetitive	Aversive	Appetitive	Aversive	
Circumstance-Caused					
Unknown	Surprise				
Uncertain	Hope		Fear		Weak
Certain	Joy	Relief	Sorrow	Discomfort, Disgust	
Uncertain	Hope		Frustration		Strong
Certain	Joy	Relief			
Other-Caused					
Uncertain			Disliking		Weak
Certain	Liking				
Uncertain			Anger		Strong
Certain					
Self-Caused					
Uncertain			Shame, Guilt		Weak
Certain	Pride				
Uncertain			Regret		Strong
Certain					

vised appraisal dimensions, Roseman et al. (1990) conducted a study in which students from several universities were asked to recall either two negative or two positive emotions, for example, sadness and fear, regret and guilt, joy and relief, from a set of sixteen, and to write brief descriptions of two situations in which they experienced these emotions. The subjects were then asked to answer a set of forty-four questions about the appraisal dimensions related to each of the emotions. To assess the situational state dimension, for example, subjects were asked, "At the time, did you think of [the event that elicited the emotion] as consistent with what you wanted or as inconsistent with what you wanted?" The appraisal questions were all rated on 9-point scales, for example, *"Very much consistent with what I wanted* (1) to *very much inconsistent with what I wanted* (9)" (Roseman et al., 1990, p. 914).

Upon analyzing their subjects' ratings of the appraisal dimensions associated with each of the two emotions they experienced, Roseman et al. (1990) found strong support for the hypothesis that

> the particular emotion(s) experienced in response to an event depend(s) on whether the event is perceived as inconsistent or consistent with a person's motives; whether motives relevant to the event involve decreasing one's punishments or increasing one's rewards; whether one sees oneself as weak or strong in the situation; whether the event is seen as caused by circumstances, other persons, or the self; and whether the event's occurrence is judged to be uncertain or certain. (p. 909)

Events giving rise to anger, for example, were rated by the subjects as highly motive-inconsistent (low situational state), as very undeserved, morally wrong and unjust (low legitimacy), and as caused by another person (other person agency). Events involving guilt were also rated as highly motive-inconsistent, but were seen as caused by the self (self-agency) (see Roseman et al., 1990, Table 1, p. 907) . In general, according to Roseman et al., the patterns of their subjects' appraisal ratings conformed very closely to what Roseman's theory predicted. Thus, at least for the sixteen emotions Roseman et al. studied, there appears to be substantial evidence that specific emotions are indeed associated with specific patterns of appraisal or cognitive structure. It is important to note in this regard that Roseman et al. included in the list of emotions they studied not only "the usual suspects"— happiness (joy), anger, fear, sadness, surprise, and so forth—but also some emotions not usually examined by emotions researchers, for example, hope, pride, guilt, shame, regret. Because of this, the strength and clarity of their findings, and the ways in which they attempted to synthesize their research with that of other cognitive structural theorists, Roseman et al.'s study can be regarded as a contribution of central importance to the cognitive tradition.

Representative Research on Emotion from the Cognitive Perspective

Most of the research discussed in conjunction with the theories presented in this chapter (e.g., Smith & Lazarus, 1993; MacDowell & Mandler, 1989; Roseman et al., 1990) is relatively recent and fairly representative of the kind of research that is currently being conducted within the cognitive tradition. This being the case, in what follows I describe a somewhat unusual but still representative study of the appraisal-emotion relationship. This study is unusual because it was carried out in the "real world," and involved assessing people's reactions to a real emotion-provoking event (as opposed to people's memories of such events), namely, taking a midterm examination in psychology. I realize that some people might think that a college psychology class is not the real world and that taking an exam is not a very meaningful emotional event. Before you make this criticism, however, try telling an anxious sophomore who hasn't studied for the exam that his or her emotions are not real or meaningful and see how far you get.

Hoping for the best, fearing the worst: Patterns of appraisal before and after a midterm exam.   Smith and Ellsworth (1987) asked a class of introductory psychology students at Stanford University to complete a questionnaire on their thoughts and feelings 20 minutes before they were to take their midterm examination and, about 2 weeks later, immediately after they had received their grades on the exam. On the questionnaire, the students were asked to rate on a series of 9-point scales how much they were experiencing each of twenty-five emotions "right now." The students also rated, by means of a series of 11-point scales, how much each of eighteen different appraisal items described how they were thinking about the exam, their preparations for it, their reactions to the grade they received, and so forth. These items were designed to tap eight appraisal dimensions—pleasantness, anticipated effort, attentional activity, certainty, responsibility, control, legitimacy, and perceived obstacles—that had been proposed in an earlier study (Smith & Ellsworth, 1985).

Consistent with the results of other studies of the appraisal process (see especially Folkman & Lazarus, 1985) and with what they had expected, Smith and Ellsworth found that, with the exception of guilt, the emotions their subjects experienced before and after the exam were associated with distinctive patterns of appraisal along the eight proposed dimensions. Hope, for example, which was experienced more before the exam than after it, was characterized by appraisals of self-agency, high effort, and high certainty. Hope was also associated with appraising the exam as very important, an appraisal dimension that emerged out of Smith and

Ellsworth's analysis of their subjects' appraisal ratings. Fear, which was experienced more before the exam than after it, was characterized by appraisals of unpleasantness, high effort, and difficulty, and by the appraisal of the exam as an obstacle. Anger, on the other hand, which, along with happiness and guilt, was experienced more after the exam than before it, was characterized by appraisals of high other-agency and low legitimacy (that is, by the exam being considered unjust) and by the exam being perceived as an obstacle.

By subjecting these data to a *multiple regression analysis*,[10] Smith and Ellsworth found that, again with the exception of guilt, the emotions their subjects reported experiencing before and after the exam could be *predicted* from their appraisals along at least one of the dimensions. Anger before and after the exam, for example, was predicted by the subjects' legitimacy appraisals. Happiness, on the other hand, was predicted by subjects' appraisals of the pleasantness of the situation both before and after the exam, while hope was predicted by subjects' appraisals of the amount of effort involved in dealing with the exam. These findings are extremely important, for they show that the predicted relationships between appraisals and emotions can be found not only within the somewhat artificial confines of emotion-recall studies but also in situations involving matters of real consequence for subjects (for another study of emotional appraisal in the real world, see Smith & Pope, 1992).

Emphasizing the importance of conducting research on appraisals in real-world settings, Smith and Ellsworth found that a number of the appraisal-emotion relationships they had observed in their earlier study (Smith & Ellsworth, 1985) did *not* show up in their results. In commenting on this finding (or, rather, lack of findings), Smith and Ellsworth suggest that, while theoretically or prototypically, certain patterns of appraisal *should* be associated with particular emotions, in the real world, not all of these are essential for the experience of a particular emotion.

> [A]lthough *typical* instances of anger involve appraisals of certainty and high anticipated effort, and although *typical* instances of happiness involve appraisals of certainty and a desire to attend to the situation, these appraisals do not appear to be essential to the experience of these emotions . . . It may well be that certain dimensions are especially important for some emotions, and not so important for others. Appraisals along *different* dimensions may be central to the experience of different emotions. (Smith & Ellsworth, 1987, p. 486)

---

[10]*Multiple regression analysis* is a statistical technique that allows one to ascertain how well a set of variables, in this case subjects' ratings of the various appraisal dimensions, individually and in combination, predict another variable, in this case, the subjects' emotion ratings.

Problems Facing the Cognitive Perspective

As Smith and Ellsworth suggest, one of the key questions facing researchers studying the appraisal process involves specifying what dimensions are important for which emotions. Although there are remarkable resemblances in the dimensional structures of the appraisals identified by different researchers using different methodologies and theoretical frameworks (Roseman et al., 1990), the dimensions proposed by the various cognitive emotion theorists are clearly different (see Scherer, 1993, Table 1, p. 327). As Scherer (1993) argues, "the question of how many and which appraisal criteria are minimally needed to explain emotion differentiation is one of the central issues in research on emotion-antecedent appraisal" (p. 331). Future research on the nature of the cognition-emotion relationship will undoubtedly involve specifying more precisely the patterns of appraisal associated with different emotions. In order to truly demonstrate its usefulness in constructing a comprehensive account of emotional differentiation, such research must investigate not only the patterns of appraisals underlying the simple, "basic" emotions such as fear, anger, and happiness but the more complex emotions and emotion "blends." The fact that appraisal researchers routinely include complex emotions such as hope and guilt in their studies suggests that the cognitive tradition has already taken a major step toward proving its mettle in this regard.

Researchers investigating the appraisal-emotion relationship also face the problem of considering appraisal as a *process*, that is, as an ongoing series of evaluations of and reactions to environmental events that include a person's more or less continuous *re*-evaluation of his or her environment based on his or her responses to it (what Arnold and Lazarus thought of as "secondary appraisal"). As Scherer has recently argued, "there can be little doubt that we need to talk about *emotion episodes* that are characterized by continuously occurring changes in the underlying appraisal and reaction processes" (Scherer, 1993, p. 329) and further, it may be assumed that "the appraisal process is *constantly operative* with evaluations being continuously performed to update the organism's information on an event or situation (including the current needs or goals or the organism and the possibility to act on these)" (Scherer, 1993, p. 330). Most of the research on appraisals has, at least methodologically, implicitly assumed that appraisal is a one-step, one-shot process, with appraisal being a single, discrete event. Given that emotions happen in "real time" and constitute the mechanism by which organisms continually respond to changes in their environment (cf. Mandler's conception of emotion), it would seem that, in order to have any ecological validity whatsoever, the next generation of cognitive emotion theories must seriously consider appraisal as a process.

Another problem facing appraisal researchers concerns the failure of many of the existing appraisal theories to appreciate the *social* nature of the appraisal process. In their study of the factors involved in appraisal, Manstead and Tetlock (1989) found evidence that appraisals for guilt, shame, embarrassment, and even joy involved a consideration of other people in an important way. Guilt, for example, was characterized by appraisals having to do with, "inconsistency of behaviour with private and public standards, harm done to another or others," as well as "personal responsibility" (Manstead & Tetlock, 1989, p. 229). By including appraisal scales having both a "self" and "other" component, for example, "inconsistency with own standards," and "inconsistency with others' standards," Manstead and Tetlock were able to uncover a hitherto hidden dimension of the appraisal process, namely, the extent to which we routinely take others' standards and reactions into account when appraising a situation.[11]

This is a convenient point to begin exploring the social constructivist perspective on emotions, for, as their name implies, social constructivists argue that, in order to understand human emotions, it is absolutely essential to consider emotions in their social context. For social constructivists, in fact, it makes no sense to think of emotions outside of the social contexts within which they occur.

Further Reading

ARNOLD, M. B. (1969). Human emotion and action. In T. Mischel (Ed.), *Human action: Conceptual and empirical issues* (pp. 167–197). New York: Academic Press.

LAZARUS, R. S. (1991b). Progress on a cognitive-motivational-relational theory of emotion. *American Psychologist, 46,* 819–834.

OATLEY, K. (1992). *Best laid schemes: The psychology of emotions.* Cambridge: Cambridge University Press.

ROSEMAN, I. J., SPINDEL, M. S., & JOSE, P. E. (1990). Appraisals of emotion-eliciting events: Testing a theory of discrete emotions. *Journal of Personality and Social Psychology, 59,* 899–915.

---

[11]This is something sociologists, at least since George Herbert Mead (1863–1931), have always assumed (see McHugh, 1968).

5

Emotions and the Politics of Everyday Life

◆

The Social Constructivist Perspective

[E]motional syndromes are among the roles societies create, and individuals enact . . . Often, an emotional role is built upon, or incorporates elements from, one or more biological systems of behavior. But the meaning of the emotion—its functional significance is to be found primarily within the sociocultural system. The emotions are not remnants of previously serviceable habits, as Darwin maintained. Rather, they are presently serviceable, and one of the tasks of theory is to shed light on the functions that emotional syndromes now serve.

— James Averill (1980a, p. 337)

During the doldrums of my graduate student career when I was casting about for a dissertation topic, I happened to attend a screening of the Vietnam War documentary *Hearts and Minds*. My last-minute decision to go see the film on a night when I had many other things to do proved to be a good one, for the film was not only deeply moving but it also provided me with a topic for my dissertation.

Hearts and Minds is an unflinching look at how the United States conducted the war and the effects and aftereffects of the war on those who, in one way or another, were involved in it. In the film there are two interviews that I found particularly intriguing. One was with a former bomber pilot who described how he came to oppose the war and his role in it after visiting one of the sites he had bombed. Seeing the devastation he had brought to a small village and the people who lived in it, and realizing he was responsible for the devastation, transformed his understanding of his "job" as a bomber pilot. He realized that he could no longer look at what he did as simply a series of technical tasks to be carried out with efficiency and precision. Piloting his plane to a particular set of coordinates and pushing a switch to release his load of bombs was now inexorably linked with the knowledge that the bombs he dropped killed and maimed not only the enemy soldiers they were meant to kill and maim, but innocent civilians as well. During the course of relating his story of personal transformation, the pilot wept, and I think it's fair to say that many in the audience were also moved to tears by the story he told. The second interview was with Daniel Ellsberg, the Pentagon analyst who leaked the so-called Pentagon Papers to the press and subsequently became a highly visible opponent of the war. At one point in the interview, as Ellsberg related the profound effects of the war and the release of the Pentagon Papers on his life, he wept as well.

The emotional displays of these two men had a powerful effect on me at the time, as I realized that, outside of a few fictional portrayals in films and on television, I had only seen one other man weep (that's another story). As I started thinking about why so few men weep in public in American culture, I also realized that I had found a dissertation topic. Almost from the moment the film was over I began gathering all the information I could on why humans weep. Even though, surprisingly, there was relatively little solid empirical research on weeping at the time, it was very apparent that there was a large gender difference in the propensity to weep in the presence of others and there was considerable cultural variation in the form and propensity to weep as well. My project was thus framed quite early on by the assumption that the gender differences and cultural variations in weeping that I and others had observed were not due to "natural," biological factors but were the result of cultural influence. In starting from this assumption, I had placed my research squarely within the social constructivist perspective on emotions.

Social constructivists believe that emotions are not merely influenced by culture, in the way, say, Paul Ekman speaks of "display rules" overlaying and regulating natural emotional displays (see Chapter 2), they are, rather, *products* of culture.[1] Thus, in the case of weeping, while it would be difficult to deny that human weeping is a physiological response that is part of our evolutionary heritage, social constructivists argue that

---

[1]Depending on whom one reads, this perspective is called social construct*ivist* or social construct*ionist*. Since I've never really understood the difference between the two terms, if there is a difference, and since I first became acquainted with the perspective as *social constructivism*, I refer to it by this term throughout my discussion.

emotions are not just remnants of our phylogenetic past, nor can they be explained in strictly physiological terms. Rather, they are social constructions, and they can be *fully* understood only on a social level of analysis. (Averill, 1980a, p. 309)

This is a radical assumption with far-reaching implications for how we understand what emotions are all about. It is also an assumption that is hotly contested by emotion researchers working within other perspectives, especially the Darwinian and Jamesian (see, for example, what Shaver, Wu, & Schwartz, 1992; and Izard & Phillips, 1989, have to say about the perspective).

Research on emotions from a social constructivist perspective is part of a larger social constructivist program in psychology (Gergen, 1985; Gergen & Davis, 1985), anthropology (Rosaldo, 1989), sociology (Coulter, 1989), and related disciplines (e.g., feminist studies; see Garry & Pearsall, 1989), that seeks to understand the socially constructed nature of not only emotions, but mind, self, sexuality, gender, and even rationality and science (see McMullin, 1988). Social constructivists examine the ways in which phenomena such as emotion, self, sexuality, and gender are embodied in a culture's social practices, including its language, participate in and partially constitute the moral order of the culture, and serve to maintain that moral order.

Although some of the ideas of social constructivism have been around a very long time (e.g., in the work of Marx and Durkheim[2] and their followers in sociology), as an identifiable tradition of emotion research and theory in psychology, it is relatively young. Indeed, it could be said that the perspective really only came into its own in the 1980s with the publication of two important texts, Rom Harré's *The Social Construction of Emotions* (1986a) and Kenneth Gergen and Keith Davis' *The Social Construction of the Person* (1985). There now exists a sizable body of work in psychology that can be called social constructivist (see Gergen, 1985, for a more general introduction to the methods and subjects of social constructivist inquiry). Much of the social constructivist work on emotions, however, has been carried out by scholars who are not psychologists. Harré, for example, is a philosopher, and Catherine Lutz, the author of an extensive investigation of emotion in one non-Western culture, the wonderfully titled *Unnatural Emotions* (Lutz, 1988), as well as the editor of an important volume on the social construction of emotions (Lutz & Abu-Lughod, 1990), is an anthropologist. Nevertheless, since this is a book about psychology, let's begin exploring the social constructivist perspective on emotions by examining the work of one of its most widely published representatives, the psychologist James Averill.

I should mention here that Jim Averill was my graduate school mentor and that I consider myself a social constructivist, albeit one who gives con-

[2]Emile Durkheim (1858–1917), French sociologist, author of *Suicide* (1897). Karl Marx (1818–1883), German political philosopher, author of *Das Kapital* (1867).

siderable credence to Darwinian approaches to the study of emotion. (How these two seemingly mutually exclusive perspectives might coexist is a topic I take up in the next chapter.)

The Incredible Hulk and Other Social Roles: Averill's Social Constructivist Theory of Emotion

A very different definition of emotion.   Making a break with traditional definitions of emotion every bit as dramatic as that made by William James 125 or so years ago, Averill (1980a) considers emotions to be a special kind of *social role*. More specifically, he defines an emotion as, *"a transitory social role (a socially constituted syndrome) that includes an individual's appraisal of the situation and that is interpreted as a passion rather than as an action"* (Averill, 1980a, p. 312). Since this is a complex and, to many, unfamiliar definition of emotion, let's examine each of its aspects carefully.

FIGURE 5.1.   *James Averill in the 1970s. (Photograph by Rod Kessler.)*

Emotions as syndromes. Averill asks us to first consider how emotions may be thought of as "syndromes." A syndrome is a set of events that occur together in a systematic manner. Physicians often speak of a collection of symptoms that are often found together as syndromes, as in the fever, coughs, sore throat, and aching joints that are typical symptoms of influenza. Like diseases, Averill argues, emotions have a variety of more or less easily identifiable components that tend to occur together. These include *subjective experiences, expressive reactions, patterns of physiological response,* and *coping reactions* (Averill, 1980b). *Subjective experiences* are the particular feeling qualities associated with emotions, *expressive reactions* are the facial expressions and bodily postures that may accompany particular emotions, *physiological responses* are the autonomic nervous system and other bodily changes that accompany some emotions, and *coping reactions* are the behaviors we engage in while we are emotional. A moment's reflection about even a small set of your own emotional experiences will tell you that this list includes most of the phenomena associated with emotion. It should also tell you, however, that *not every emotion is associated with all of the components.* A typical instance of fear, for example, may be characterized by all four components, but what of a typical instance of an emotion such as hope? So far as anyone now knows, there is no particular facial expression that is always associated with hope, nor is hope associated with a particular pattern of physiological responses (Averill, Catlin, & Chon, 1990).

Some emotions, then, are associated with all of the components, whereas others are associated with only one or two or, perhaps, none. Further, a moment's reflection should tell you that *not every instance of any particular emotion need include all of the components.* It should be relatively easy for you to think of an instance of, say, anger in which you *did not* scowl in a manner "typical" of anger or do the things one "usually" does while one is angry, such as hurling insults at the person who made you angry.

These observations are important, for they reveal that it is still possible to "be" emotional in the absence of the phenomena that we typically think of as defining emotions. For Averill, this is a crucial point, for, in his way of thinking, although some of the components of emotion may be associated more closely with some emotions than others, "there is no single response, or subset of responses, which is *essential* to an emotional syndrome" (Averill, 1980b, p. 146). That is, while particular subjective experiences, physiological responses, expressive reactions and coping behaviors may sometimes be *sufficient* to define a specific instance of emotion, none are absolutely *necessary.* It is possible for one to be described legitimately as being afraid when one is not physiologically aroused or making the facial expression typical of fear. This view contrasts sharply with that of someone like Ekman, who defines emotions in terms of specific characteristics, such as facial expressions, that *must* be present in order for something to qualify as an emotion (see, for example, Ekman, 1984, pp. 329–340).

There's no "there" there.   Averill explicitly rejects the notion that the essence of emotions is to be found in how we feel, how our bodies react, or what we do while we are emotional. For him, there are far too many exceptions to definitions of specific emotions that consist of finite sets of characteristics. Emotional syndromes, he says, are "polythetic," that is, "not definable in terms of a limited number of characteristics" (Averill, 1980a, p. 308): "[A]n emotional syndrome may include many diverse elements, some of biological and some of social origin, but none of which is essential to the identification of the syndrome as a whole" (Averill, 1980a, p. 308). What, then, makes emotional syndromes "hang together?" The answer is to be found in Averill's description of emotions as "transitory social roles."

Emotions as social roles.   A role, according to Averill, is, "a socially prescribed set of responses to be followed by a person in a given situation" (Averill, 1980a, p. 308). The diverse components of emotions are given coherence by the socially determined rules associated with particular emotional roles. Emotions, as social roles, represent the temporary enactment of a "prescribed set of responses" in which a person may be seen as following a set of rules that tell him or her the "proper" way to appraise a situation, how to behave in response to the appraisal, how to interpret his or her bodily reactions to the appraisal, and so on (Averill, 1984). Central to the notion of rules here is the idea that the rules of emotion are *learned*. According to Averill and other social constructivists, part of what we learn by virtue of our being socialized into a particular culture are sets of rules that implicitly govern our emotional performances (Armon-Jones, 1986a, 1986b; Averill, 1984; Cornelius, 1984).

To get an idea of how emotions can be thought of as social roles, imagine for a moment what you might do if a good friend of yours deliberately made humiliating remarks about you in the presence of several other people. If you grew up in the United States or another Western country, you will probably recognize this as a situation in which it would be "appropriate" to become angry (you might also feel hurt by your supposed friend's insensitivity). In fact, in most Western cultures and particularly in the United States, if you did *not* become angry in a situation such as this, people might think you were a fool for letting someone take advantage of you (Spellman, 1989).

Recognizing this as an appropriate occasion for the expression of anger, think of what you might do to "express" your anger. Again, if you grew up in a Western culture, you might take your friend aside and, in no uncertain terms, tell him how his remarks made you feel. You might also begin crying, slap your friend's face, or shake your fist at him. You could, however, outwardly do nothing, but inwardly coolly plot your revenge. All of these would be recognized as appropriate responses to such an event. In another culture, however, they might not be. If you grew up in Japan, for example, as the Japanese psychoanalyst Takeo Doi once told me, you might simply smile at the person who angered you, and you would try at all costs to avoid confronting your friend. If you grew up among the Utku Eskimos of the Canadian Northwest Territories, it is also likely that you would try to avoid a confrontation (Briggs, 1970). The fact that we recognize some situations as appropriate provocations to anger and others as not appropriate and some behaviors as appropriate for the angry person and others as not appropriate reveals the rule-governed nature of the appraisals and behaviors associated with anger, as does the considerable cultural variation in what "counts" as anger (see Averill, 1982, and Mesquita & Frijda, 1992, for extensive discussions of these issues).

Emotional appraisals.   Averill was a student of Richard Lazarus (see Chapter 4) and collaborated with him on some of his work on the nature of appraisals, and so it is not surprising that Averill places considerable importance on how a person interprets or appraises situations giving rise to emotions. There is, more generally, a close affinity between the cognitive perspective and the social constructivist perspective, and in many ways it could be said that social constructivism is an outgrowth of the cognitive revolution of the 1970s (Harré, 1994). Central to the cognitive perspective is the assumption that emotions are dependent on particular kinds of evaluative cognitions, or appraisals, that provide a link from the person to the environment and serve to differentiate a person's emotional responses to his or her environment. Social constructivists like Averill agree with this assumption but go one step further, arguing that how a person appraises his or her environment is *culturally determined.* As the philosopher Claire Armon-Jones put it in a recent outline of the constructivist position, according to constructivists,

> emotions are characterized by attitudes such as beliefs, judgments and desires, the contents of which are not natural, but are determined by the systems of cultural belief, value and moral value of particular communities. (Armon-Jones, 1986b, p. 33)

Thus, Averill would disagree with the argument made by Oatley (see Chapter 4) and several other emotion theorists (see, for example, Plutchik, 1980) that appraisals represent innate responses to evolutionarily significant events.

Note should be taken of Armon-Jones' use of the terms *value* and *moral* in the passage quoted above. Averill and other social constructivists see cultural values, what is considered right and wrong and good and bad by a culture, as important determinants of emotional appraisals. Emotions, some constructivists argue, are to a large extent *moral judgments* about events in the world (see Solomon, 1976, for a discussion of emotions as judgments; and Sabini & Silver, 1982; and Schoeman, 1987, for several illustrations of the ways in which emotions are intimately bound up with moral judgments) and, as moral values show considerable individual and cultural variation, so too do the emotions based on them. Thus, one of the crucial ways in which emotions may be said to be social constructions is through their relationship to culturally determined systems of values that are learned by individuals socialized into particular cultures (and subcultures).

Although Averill maintains that there is no necessary "core" to emotions, likening emotions more to onions than artichokes (Averill, 1980b), appraisals play a central role in defining emotions in his theory. As we shall see below, the most important characteristic of anger is the way in which the person defines or appraises the situation. Indeed, with regard to anger, if a person does *not* appraise a situation as one involving an unjustified transgression against him or herself, he or she will not enact the transitory social role that is anger (Averill, 1982). Making such an attribution requires a great deal of cultural knowledge, to be sure, making the relationship between the appraisal and the emotion a contingent one, but it is an attribution that is nonetheless essential for anger to take place. A similar assertion could be made about most emotions. For Averill, as for other cognitively oriented emotion researchers, then, the way a person appraises a situation determines the emotion he or she will have. Thus, in spite of Averill's appeals to the polythetic nature of emotional syndromes, within his theory, appraisals appear to be a necessary (but not sufficient) condition for the generation of emotion. Indeed, appraisals provide the crucial link between the individual and culture that undergirds the entire social constructivist program, in that what one acquires when one learns to appraise a situation in a particular manner is a system of cultural meanings that constitute the emotion (see Averill, 1980b, especially pp. 148–149). These meanings define the social role that is the emotion.

Emotions as passions.   What we call emotions were at one time routinely referred to as "passions," a word that emphasizes the experience of passivity associated with many emotions (Averill, 1980a). Descartes' 1637 treatise on emotions, for example, was entitled *Passions of the Soul* (Descartes, 1637/1911). Even though we no longer call emotions passions, Averill argues that we still very much think of them in this manner. To see how this is so, consider the words we use to describe our emotions, especially those that often involve conflict. We are said to be "gripped" by fear, "seized" by anger, "paralyzed" by anxiety, and "haunted" by remorse. This kind of language is not restricted to unpleasant or negative emotions, for we "fall" in love and are "overcome" by happiness. In these expressions and others, emotions are represented as things that happen to us, things that are outside of our personal control. As Averill says, by speaking of emotions in this way, "[i]t is as though emotions were alien forces which 'overcome' and 'possess' an individual" (Averill, 1980b, p. 151). Averill argues that this way of speaking about emotions is primarily metaphorical and reveals part of a widely shared cultural theory of emotions (Averill, 1990b).

For Averill, the fact that emotions are experienced as passions does not reveal their deep-seated biological nature or the fact that they are "located" in the more primitive parts of our brains, as some have maintained (see Averill, 1974, for a detailed discussion of the psychophysiological symbolism found in most traditional theories of emotion). Rather, it reveals the complex way in which we interpret our own experience when we are emotional (see also Mills & Kleinman, 1988). Emotions, Averill argues, are *actions* rather than passions. They are meaningful behaviors we engage in to accomplish particular social and individual goals. They do not just happen to us, they are things that we do, willfully. We nevertheless *experience* them as passions. The experience of passivity associated with emotions is an *interpretation* or attribution we make about our own behavior. We do this, says Averill, for both individual and social reasons, but primarily to disclaim responsibility for what we do while we are emotional.

I have found that this is one of the most difficult aspects of Averill's theory for people to understand, probably because it goes against so much of our received wisdom about emotions, not to mention our immediate experience of them. To get a sense of what Averill is talking about, think for a moment about what it means to say, "I was beside myself with anger," as in, "I'm sorry I threw your plaster statue of Elvis at the television. I was beside myself with anger." This apology contains within it a very powerful excuse, namely, "I am not to blame for my actions, because I wasn't myself when I did them." In essence, I am asking you to excuse my actions because they were not *my* actions, I was temporarily not myself when I engaged in the actions; the I who I usually am was "displaced" by my anger. Appealing to our emotions, particularly those Averill calls the "conflictive" emotions, the best examples of which are anger and romantic love, allows us to do things we would very much like to do while not being held accountable for doing them (Averill, 1980b; see also Solomon, 1976). Romantic love is similar to anger in that we are "allowed" to do things while under the influence of love that we would not otherwise be able to get away with or at least not get away with without considerable public censure (Solomon, 1981). Claiming that I am in love, for example, partly excuses the boorish way in which I treat my friends when I devote all of my attention to my newfound beloved and none to them. Were I to turn my back on my friends for some other reason, they might indeed think of me as a boor, and I might feel ashamed of my behavior. Since I am in love, however, we all have a ready explanation for my actions that effectively insulates me from criticism.

The experience of anger or romantic love as a passion is, to repeat, an interpretation that we place on our actions, or, more precisely, an interpretation that our culture places on our actions. In a very real sense, our culture has already made the interpretation for us, for if we are sufficiently well socialized, we will automatically come to experience emotions as passions, because the experience of passivity is part of what it means to be emotional in our culture (see Frijda & Mesquita, 1994, for a parallel discussion of cultural influences on how emotions are experienced).[3]

The Incredible Hulk.   I have always thought that the comic book and television character the Incredible Hulk serves as a fine example of how emotions work in Averill's theory. In the comic book and later in the television series, nuclear scientist Dr. David Banner is exposed to a massive dose of gamma rays while saving the life of a young person who has unwittingly wandered onto a secret atomic bomb test site (Horn, 1976). The gamma rays turn Banner into the Incredible Hulk (originally, in the comic, simply the Hulk). Banner, however, is not *always* the Hulk; he only becomes the Hulk when he is provoked to anger, and so he spends a great deal of time desperately trying to not become angry. When Banner is angered, he literally becomes another "person": He turns green, grows to enormous size, and develops superhuman strength. He also acquires a very nasty disposition that generally predisposes him to a great deal of snarling and smashing things up. Banner is essentially completely out of control while he is the Hulk. However, no matter how out of control the Hulk seems to be, his rage follows a predictable course. After smashing up enough things and rampaging around for a while, Banner returns to "normal," usually with a healthy dose of guilt over what he has done while he was the Hulk. Significantly, the Hulk usually manages to exact retribution from whoever made Banner angry in the first place. Not surprisingly, this person or persons always turn out to be the bad guys.

Following Averill's theory, I would argue that each of us is a bit like the Incredible Hulk when we become angry. We may not turn green and shred our clothes when we are provoked, but we do act in ways that we would not ordinarily, and, more often than not, while we are angry, we are able to get back at the person or persons who incurred our wrath. If our behavior is called into question, we can always apologize by claiming that we

---

[3]The idea that there are times when we may not be responsible for our actions is explicitly codified in jurisprudence in the concepts of "crimes of passion" and "not guilty by reason of insanity." Under both of these notions, a person may be excused from certain crimes because he or she was suffering from a "defect of reason" when they were committed. Emotions in everyday life, Averill argues, are much like little crimes of passion (see Averill, 1982, for a discussion of these issues with reference to anger).

could not help ourselves. We were, after all, angry. Since Averill has devoted considerable attention to the social construction of anger (Averill, 1979a; 1982, 1983), let's take a look at anger from his perspective in a bit more detail.

Aspects of the Social Construction of Anger

Averill begins with the premise that anger is not a primitive response to frustration and it is certainly not simply another name for aggression (see Averill, 1982, pp. 30–31). Anger is a highly sophisticated, socially constituted, emotional syndrome that serves to regulate *human* interpersonal behavior. Describing instances of what nonhuman animals or human babies do as anger is to use the term metaphorically, for anger is an emotion that requires considerable cognitive and social sophistication and, by Averill's definition, is an emotion that only humans display (see Averill, 1980b, p. 146).

A little touch of Ari' in the night.　Like Aristotle, who defined anger as "an impulse, accompanied by pain, to a conspicuous revenge for a conspicuous slight directed without justification towards what concerns oneself or towards what concerns one's friends" (*Rhetoric*, 1378a32), Averill argues that the instigation to anger is the perception that one has been wronged in some manner, or that, more generally, some acceptable standards of behavior have been violated by the instigator.[4] Moreover, the behavior in question, as Averill found in two extensive studies of the everyday experience of anger (reported in Averill, 1982), must be seen as voluntary and unjustifiable. That is, you would not get angry at me if I *accidentally* stepped on your toe. However, if I went out of my way to step on your toe, and did it "for no good reason," you would be quite justified in becoming angry at me. Notice how natural it is to speak of anger being "justified." Following Averill, this points to the ways in which anger is part of a behavior system that enforces normative standards. Anger is not simply a response to frustration, although it is often that, it is also a response to what we believe is morally wrong (Sabini & Silver, 1982). Table 5.1 presents the factors Averill found to be involved in the instigation of anger in a sample of university students and residents of a medium-sized town in Massachusetts.

Two points are important to make here. First, Averill never precisely specifies what counts as a voluntary, unjustified transgression. The list of possible behaviors that may be interpreted in this manner is probably end-

---

[4]The quotation from Aristotle is from *The Rhetoric and the Poetics of Aristotle*, W. R. Roberts (Trans.) (1954).

TABLE 5.1.   *Factors involved in the instigation of anger as described by Averill's subjects*

Instigations to Anger	Mean Rating (0 = Not at All, 1 = Somewhat, 2 = Very Much)	Percentage of Subjects Marking "Somewhat" or "Very Much"
1. Frustration or interruption of some ongoing or planned activity	1.38	82
2. An event, action, or attitude that resulted in a loss of personal pride, self-esteem, or a sense of personal worth	1.02	64
3. Violation of expectations and wishes that are important to you but that may not be shared by others	.99	68
4. Violation of socially accepted ways of behaving or widely shared rules of conduct	.90	63
5. Possible or actual property damage	.29	19
6. Possible or actual physical injury or pain	.23	14

Source: Averill, *Anger and Aggression: An Essay on Emotion,* Table 8-4, p. 174 (New York: Springer, 1982). Reprinted by permission of the author and Springer-Verlag.

less. Being assaulted because one is wearing a Boston Red Sox cap is almost certainly an unjustified transgression, but thoughtfully remembering someone's birthday, in certain circumstances, may be interpreted as an unprovoked attack and so may also elicit anger. How a particular behavior is interpreted depends on the person, his or her motives, personality, and history, and his or her interpersonal and cultural context. Through socialization, a person learns what his or her culture considers to be appropriate circumstances for anger. A person also acquires idiosyncratic ways of interpreting his or her own and others' behavior. This is why Averill says at one point that emotions are constructions of both the individual and his or her culture (Averill, 1980a). The second point to note here is how complex the attributions involved in the instigation to anger are. These are not the kind of attributions that nonhuman animals or infants are believed to be able to make. Anger, for Averill, is really only something that more or less fully-developed humans (over the age of about 5) can experience.

"That makes me so mad I could . . . "   One of the things psychologists routinely do that makes Averill really angry is to confuse anger and aggression. Being aggressive is only *one* of the many things a person may do while angry, and though anger may indeed facilitate aggression, anger need not be followed by aggression, nor does aggression require anger (Averill, 1983). In asking people to describe what they typically did and felt like

doing when they were angry, Averill found that, while many of his subjects reported they indeed felt like engaging in some form of physical aggression, only a very small percentage (10%) actually did so. As the data in Table 5.2 illustrate, Averill's subjects reported they were much more likely to engage in "calming activities" or talk about the incident that instigated their anger with either the person who made them angry or an uninvolved person than they were to engage in direct or indirect aggression.

Take a look at Table 5.2 and think for a moment about how any number of different behaviors might count as "verbal or symbolic aggression" or "denial or removal of some benefit." Averill's data seem to accord very well with his notion of anger as a polythetic syndrome. To be sure, Averill found that *some* of his subjects reported experiencing the expressive and physiological reactions that other researchers have identified as components of anger, for example, an increase in muscle tension, frowning, a rise in temperature (see Averill, 1982, Table 9-6, p. 200), but their anger was not *defined* by these reactions. Nor was it defined, as we have seen, by aggressive behavior. Given the appropriate circumstances, almost any expressive reaction, including no expressive reaction, and any behavior, may be seen as constituting anger. If aggressive behavior only rarely accompanies anger,

TABLE 5.2.   *Instrumental behavior during anger reported by Averill's subjects*

Type of Response	Percentage of Subjects Marking "Somewhat" or "Very Much"	
	Impulses Felt	*Actual Behavior*
Direct aggression		
Verbal or symbolic aggression	82	49
Denial or removal of some benefit	59	41
Physical aggression	40	10
Indirect aggression		
Telling a third party in order to		
get back at the instigator	42	34
Harming something important to		
the instigator	25	9
Displaced aggression		
Against a nonhuman object	32	28
Against some person	24	25
Nonaggressive responses		
Engaging in calming activities	60	60
Talking the incident over with a		
neutral party	59	59
Talking the incident over with the		
offender without hostility	52	39
Engaging in activities opposite to		
the instigation of anger	14	19

Source: Averill, *Anger and Aggression: An Essay on Emotion,* Table 9-5, p. 193 (New York: Springer, 1982). Reprinted by permission of the author and Springer-Verlag.

why is aggression so often identified with anger? Part of the answer has to do with what Averill sees as the social functions of anger.

Let's make up and be friendly.   Significantly, when Averill asked his subjects whether their anger at another person was harmful or beneficial, most (62.5%) said it was beneficial, even though the affective reactions that lingered after their anger were rarely pleasant (see Averill, 1982, Table 9-8, p. 204). Most of the anger incidents described by Averill's subjects involved a person with whom they shared some kind of personal relationship and it was very clear from Averill's data that the anger incident often improved the relationship between the person who was angered and the target of the anger. This was true whether the subject was describing being angry at another person or being the target of another's anger (see Averill, 1982, Table 10-8, p. 223, for the reactions of subjects who were the target of another person's anger). The anger incidents also helped the targets of another's anger to realize their own faults, presumably those relevant to their relationship to the person they had angered.

The picture that emerges here is of an emotion that plays an important role in regulating interpersonal relationships via the communication that one feels one's standard's or expectations have been violated. Aggression is involved in anger only insofar as the threat of revenge for having been transgressed against is part of the social meaning of anger (compare this with Aristotle's definition of anger). Indeed, if we have been wronged, we are *expected*, in one way or another, to seek just retribution (Spellman, 1989). Herein lies the key to understanding anger as a social construction.

Anger, Averill argues, serves to mediate between two contradictory social norms. What might be called the *norm of retribution* says that if we have been wronged, we are justified in forcefully seeking retribution (see Moore, 1987). This includes using the threat of aggression. However, what might be called the *norm of conciliation* says that we should avoid deliberately hurting or threatening to hurt others to get our way. How can we both seek our just retribution by threatening and *not* threatening others? By becoming angry, of course! Anger, according to Averill, because it is experienced as a passion, allows us to seek retribution but not be held (entirely) responsible for doing so in a forceful manner. If we go too far in seeking retribution, of course, we are in trouble, but more often than not, the communication that one believes one has been wronged, coupled with the threat of retribution that is part of the social meaning of anger, is enough to transform, if only briefly, our relationship to the target of our anger into one more to our liking. These individual and social functions of anger are neatly summarized in Averill's definition of anger. According to Averill, anger is

> a socially constituted response which helps regulate interpersonal relations through the threat of retaliation for perceived wrongs, and which

is interpreted as a passion rather than as an action so as not to violate the general cultural proscription against deliberately harming another. (Averill, 1979a, p. 71)

Emotions and the politics of everyday life. As should be evident from his analysis of anger, Averill sees emotions as having important social functions. Emotions for Averill, as for other social constructivists, are part and parcel of how our interpersonal lives are governed. Emotions may indeed have important functions within the person, alerting us to potentially life-threatening discrepancies between our goals and what the environment holds for us, or preparing us for vigorous action, but they also do a certain amount of *social work* for us and for our culture. If politics can be defined as the tactics and stratagems used to obtain or maintain power or control, to the extent to which our emotions are involved in helping us to regulate and acquire influence in our interpersonal relationships, emotions are political. Emotions, it could be argued, are the stuff of the politics of everyday life (Abu-Lughod & Lutz, 1990).[5]

The Function of Emotions in Social Life

It is easy to recognize the social functions that an emotion like anger might have—one need only look at the effects that one's anger has on other people to see the ways in which anger serves to regulate social interaction—but what of a much less social, seemingly more primitive emotion such as fear? As Armon-Jones (1986a) has noted, "[s]ince fear is understood . . . as the archetypal primary emotion, it would appear to be the most resistant to the constructionists' explanatory principles and so deserves particular consideration" (p. 62). Can fear indeed be covered by the social constructivist account of emotions?

The answer to this question depends, first, on whether or not common objects of fear can be seen to have significant "sociocultural content" (the term is Armon-Jones') and, second, on whether it can be shown that fear has social, as opposed to individual/species survival-related functions. The ethnographic research of Catherine Lutz (1983, 1985), which I review in the next chapter, convincingly demonstrates that the objects of fear may be culturally determined and that fear may have important social functions. In anticipation of that discussion, here are some general comments on these two issues.

Fear of people with AIDS (see Pryor, Reeder, & McManus, 1991;

---

[5]This is a notion that comes through very clearly in Aristotle's treatment of anger. Indeed, Aristotle's analysis of anger is part of his discourse on rhetoric, which is the art of influencing others.

Young, Gallaher, Belasco, Barr, & Webber, 1991), of urban spaces (see Middleton, 1986), and of pesticides and contraceptives (see Cutter, Tiefenbacher, & Solecki, 1992) are just a few examples of fears whose objects have significant cultural content, and that, moreoever, are of recent origin. Even though these are related to more "natural" fears in that they involve the perception of danger and, perhaps, the desire to flee, these similarities, though certainly real, are trivial. What is significant is the fact that these are fears of the modern world, not of the Pleistocene savanna. It would be odd indeed if evolution had not equipped us with the capacity to learn new kinds of fears. As the anthropologist David Scruton has remarked, the list of human fears is, "not limited to things that long ago went bump in the night or hissed in the grass. How useless fear would be, if it only protected us against threats mainly experienced by humans who have been dead for untold millenia!" (Scruton, 1986, p. 40).

It is clear that the objects of fear may be culturally determined, but what might be the social functions of fear? In an argument that I examine more closely in the next chapter, Armon-Jones (1986a) asserts that some of the kinds of social objects that children are taught to fear are "instrumental in sustaining social values" (p. 63). What she means by this is that such fears, more often than not, are about behaviors and objects of more than passing moral significance to a society. Children quickly acquire fears of naturally occurring dangers, such as unfamiliar animals or fire, but most of them also acquire fears of forgetting to do their homework or interacting with morally suspect individuals, such as strangers who offer them candy. Such fears certainly have the effect of keeping us out of harm's way, but many of them also, to put it bluntly, have the effect of keeping us in our place (Valentine's, 1989, feminist analysis of women's fears is especially instructive in this regard). Reflecting on this social function of fear, Scruton (1986) asserts that

> [n]o human society can tolerate unrestrained departure from normative behavior expectations. We must live and act within more or less clearly defined limits on what we are free to do. To venture outside those limits is to invite some kind of collective retribution. The character and severity of the retributive response will depend on a cultural definition of the event and its significance as well, perhaps, as on the social features of the one who strays. But in general terms, members of a society are encouraged to be afraid of departing from what is expected of them and what is tolerated. (p. 41–42)

Fear, according to the social constructivist perspective, then, can be seen as one of the means by which social norms are maintained. Fear, in this sense, is a regulator of social behavior no less than is anger. What is said of anger and fear may also be said of other emotions, such as shame, grief, and guilt (see Frijda & Mesquita, 1994). Once attention is shifted away from the experience of emotion and the physiological changes that may accompany emotion, one can see the important social functions that even the simplest emotions have and the ways in which experience and even physiology contribute to those functions (Kitayama & Markus, 1994a, 1994b).

Cross-Cultural Studies of Emotion Viewed from a Social Constructivist Perspective

Recognizing that cultures differ in how they are organized, what they value and devalue, what aspects of the self they promote, and so forth, one would expect that the emotional lives or everyday politics of people in different cultures would differ as well. Indeed, this is a claim that is central to the social constructivist account of emotions (see also the various contributions to Kitayama & Markus, 1994a). It is to the question of cross-cultural differences in emotional experience that we now turn.

In Chapter 2 we examined the evidence produced by Paul Ekman and his colleagues on the universality of facial expressions of emotion. Recall that Ekman and others have found that people in many different cultures, even those with little or no contact with other cultures, reliably recognize the facial expressions associated with a small number of emotions. Ekman contends that these results indicate that people everywhere share at least a small set of basic emotions. Some have argued, however, that Ekman's studies really only demonstrate that people in different cultures are capable of matching simple emotion labels to a small number of facial expressions and that, moreover, they do not do this with 100% accuracy over even the small number of emotion labels that have been studied (see Fridlund, 1992, 1994; Russell, 1994). Further, there is suspicion among anthropologists who study emotions that the single-word or brief sentence descriptions of emotions used by Ekman and his followers in their matching tasks might not be good representations of the emotion knowledge or experience of a people and that such terms may not even function as labels for facial expressions or feelings in many languages (Lutz & White, 1986). The fact that Ekman and others always start with English emotion terms and then translate them into the language of whatever group they are studying is also troubling to those who take a social constructivist view of emotion (see Wierzbicka, 1986). Notice that the standard for accuracy is almost always what North American college students can do. Thus, in the opinion of many of those who take a social constructivist position, studies demonstrating the universality of facial expressions associated with a small set of emotions cannot be used as evidence that the emotions themselves are universal (see Ortony & Turner, 1990, pp. 320–321, for a cogent statement of this argument).

The finding that subjects can match simple labels to faces does not necessarily imply that they do indeed categorize and experience emotions in terms of such labels. According to the social constructivist position, such studies are likely to miss the real meanings of emotion terms and descriptions because no attention is paid to the larger, everyday context within which such terms and descriptions are used. Before one can gauge how accurately the people of a particular culture can match facial expressions with their putative labels, one must first explore what emotion terms exist in that culture and how those terms are used in everyday discourse within the culture. By comparing the emotional lexicons of different cultures, we can get a sense of what emotions are important to a people and what emotions are not important to them (Heelas, 1986; Mesquita & Frijda, 1992). If the emotional lexicons of two cultures differ, one can expect the kinds of emotions experienced in the two cultures to differ as well. As Rom Harré, the pre-eminent philosopher of social constructivism, says, "Historians and anthropologists have established conclusively that there are historically and culturally diverse emotion vocabularies . . . it follows that there are culturally diverse emotions" (Harré, 1986b, p. 10).

Language matters.   Implicit in this argument is the notion that the language of emotion is a vital part of the experience of emotion. The claim is that *how we talk about our emotions has a major influence of how we experience emotions.* As the developmental psychologists Michael Lewis and Carolyn Saarni assert in their account of the socialization of emotion, "it is clear that emotional experience . . . requires that organisms possess a language of emotion" (Lewis & Saarni, 1985, p. 8). For social constructivists, "emotion talk," which includes the words for emotion in our language, how we use those words, and the way we talk about emotion in our language, is a critical component of emotion because such talk embodies the meanings of the emotions recognized by our culture (Ochs & Schieffelin, 1989). This is why Lewis and Saarni see the acquisition of a culturally appropriate emotional lexicon by children as a vitally important aspect of the socialization of emotions and as *the* major determinant of changes in children's *experience* of emotion: "[o]f particular import for the socialization of emotion in general and experience in particular is the acquisition of an emotional lexicon" (Lewis & Saarni, 1985, p. 8; see also Lutz, 1985).

In this regard, think for a moment about Averill's observation that many of the ways in which we refer to emotions portray them as things that happen to us. I'll bet you've never heard anyone say, "I climbed into love," but you've heard many people say, "I fell in love." In Averill's view of emotions, these expressions partially constitute and help to determine our experience of love as a passion. Zoltán Kövesces, in his richly detailed analysis of the metaphors and metonyms of emotion in English (see Box 5.1), starts with a similar assumption: "[T]he conventionalized language we

BOX 5.1

Hot Under the Collar: Metaphors of Anger in English

In a novel attempt to explore the emotion concepts used by English-speaking people, Zoltán Kövecses (1990) produced an extensive catalog of the metaphors and metonyms for various emotions in the English language. In assembling his lists of emotion metaphors, Kövecses began with the assumption that "the conventionalized language we use to talk about the emotions can be an important tool in discovering the structure and contents of our emotion concepts and that . . . the emotion concepts we have can reveal a great deal about our experiences of emotion" (Kövecses, 1990, p. 3). Kövecses further assumed that people carry around in their heads "certain prototypical cognitive models associated with particular emotions" (1990, p. 4), and that these cognitive models, which represent emotions in terms of their prototypical or "best" features, are the means by which we organize our experience of emotions. After having assembled as many of the everyday English expressions for anger and its kin that he could find, Kövecses determined that the model of anger contained in the metaphors and metonyms we use to talk about anger in English has the following features.

The physiological effects associated with anger *stand for* the emotion. Anger is thus revealed by the presence of

- *Body heat,* as in the expression, "Don't get *hot under the collar.*"
- *Internal pressure,* as in the expression, "I was so angry I was *ready to explode.*"
- *Redness in the face and neck,* as in the expression, "She was *red* with anger."
- *Agitation,* as in the expression, "I was *shaking* with anger."
- *Interference with accurate perception,* as in the expression, "I was *blind* with rage." (Kövecses, 1990, p. 52)

This system of metonyms combine to produce the concepts of anger contained in the following metaphors.

- *The body is a container for anger:* "He was *filled with* anger."
- *Anger is the heat of a fluid in a container:* "I had reached the *boiling point.*"
- *When the intensity of anger increases, the fluid rises:* "My anger kept *building up* inside me."
- *Intense anger produces steam:* "She got all *steamed up.*"
- *Intense anger produces pressure on the container:* "I could barely *contain* my rage."

- *When anger becomes too intense, the person explodes:* "She *blew up* at me."
- *When a person explodes, parts of him [or her] go up in the air:* "She *flipped her lid.*"
- *When a person explodes, what was inside him [or her] comes out:* "His anger finally *came out.*"
- *Anger can be let out under control:* "I *gave vent* to my anger." (Kövecses, 1990, pp. 53–58)

Anger is also seen and experienced by English speakers as *insanity,* as *a dangerous animal,* as *an opponent,* as well as *a burden* (Kövecses, 1990).

Kövecses, in an argument that should sound familiar to you, asserts that these metaphors are central to and, indeed, shape our experience of anger. To the extent that we, for example, think of anger as a "fluid under pressure," when we are angry, we will act in ways that are consistent with that metaphor, finding ways to safely "vent" our anger. To the extent to which we think of anger as an "opponent" against which we must "struggle," we will attempt to avoid becoming angry, and so on.

use to talk about the emotions can be an important tool in discovering the structure and contents of our emotion concepts and . . . the emotion concepts we have can reveal a great deal about our experiences of emotion" (1990, p. 3). Talk may be cheap, but it has major effects on how we experience emotions.

When considering the role that language plays in the experience of emotion, it is important to keep in mind that the language of emotion is woven out of the fabric of a culture's more general discourse about social life (Harré, 1994). The judgments of right or wrong that are part of the appraisals associated with anger, for example, are intimately connected with what a person understands to be the moral order of his or her culture and his or her immediate relations within the culture. Implicated in such appraisals are also concepts of the self and self-worth, of the importance of keeping promises or meeting societal expectations, the meaning of friendship, the desirability of speaking up for oneself, and so on (Harré, 1986b; see also Harré, 1979). As the anthropologist Paul Heelas observes in his survey of the emotion words used in different cultures, "emotion talk does not exist in isolation from other domains of knowledge" (1986, p. 236). Thus, emotion talk is never simply about emotions; it is about all of the issues associated with interpersonal relations within a culture. This is why it is appropriate to think of emotions as the lingua franca of the politics of everyday life. This is why it is also difficult to come up with a definition of emotion that can be applied to all cultures at all times.

Apples and oranges (again).   Comparing the emotional vocabularies of different cultures might seem like an easy task: all one has to do is to make lists of the words for emotion in each culture and then compare them, right? Immediately upon embarking on such a task, however, one encounters a very knotty problem, namely, how to define emotion in such a way as to allow the comparison of cultures that define emotion differently. To quote Heelas again,

> A number of cultures . . . do not make distinctions of the 'mental-physical', 'body-mind' and 'emotion-cognition' variety. Ethnographers studying societies which do not employ the category 'emotion' clearly have not found it easy to identify what counts as emotion talk. It is difficult to elicit satisfactory replies to the question, 'Does "x" term refer to an emotion?' if the respondents' replies could be referring, for example, to what we consider to be bodily states of affairs . . . There are in fact many interpretative and linguistic problems to do with establishing what counts as emotion talk—and, for that matter, to do with establishing the nature of forms of emotion talk. (Heelas, 1986, p. 237)

Thus, one must be careful not to define emotions entirely by the way they are defined by people in North America and then look for the way analogous concepts are used in other cultures (Wierzbicka, 1986). One must first establish the "domain" of emotion talk for a particular culture, exploring whether, for example, emotions are treated as internal events, as expressive movements or gestures, or as relations among people, and so forth. As is clear from even the briefest cross-cultural survey of definitions of emotion, there are wide variations in how people of different cultures define what counts as emotion. Indeed, some languages do not even have a term for emotion. Thus, not only do different cultures identify emotions not found in Western cultures, the very way the concept of emotion is defined varies as well.

Lutz, for example, found that emotions are defined by the *situations* in which they occur for the inhabitants of Ifaluk, a tiny atoll in the South Pacific. "While Americans define emotions primarily as feeling states . . . the Ifaluk see emotions as evoked in, and inseparable from, social activity" (Lutz, 1986, p. 283). Likewise, Lutz reports, emotions are considered by Samoans, Pintupi Aborigines, and some of the inhabitants of the Solomon Islands to be "statements about the relationship between a person and an event (particularly those involving another person) rather than as statements about introspection on one's internal states" (Lutz, 1986, p. 267). Lutz and others have also found that the underlying dimensions of meaning of groups of specific emotion terms vary as a function of culture.

In a classic cross-cultural study of the meaning of affective terms, Charles Osgood (1916-1991) and his colleagues (Osgood, May, & Miron, 1975) used a statistical technique called *multidimensional scaling* to examine how the affective terms in the languages of several cultures form clusters based on similarities in their meanings.[6] The first dimension of meaning to "emerge" from the similarity ratings of emotions by people from several cultures, Osgood et al. found was *evaluation* and the second was *potency*. Evaluation refers to the way in which the words for emotion in a language can be ordered in terms of whether they refer to events that are good or bad, pleasant or unpleasant. Potency refers to how emotions vary in terms of their intensity. Applying multidimensional scaling to the emotion terms in the language spoken on Ifaluk, Lutz also found that the first and second dimensions to emerge were quite similar to the evaluation and potency dimensions identified by Osgood et al., but the ways in which evaluation and potency were expressed were unique to Ifalukan culture.

Specifically, certain emotions and the situations in which they occur are considered "bad" in Ifalukan culture because they result from the unequal distribution of resources (Ifalukan culture emphasizes sharing). "Good" emotions are associated with obedience and cooperation, even when they may be experienced as unpleasant, as is the case with an emotion called *metagu*, which is sort of a combination of social fear and anxiety. Among the Ifaluk, "strong" emotions, that is, those high in potency, are those associated with a person being in a position of higher rank than others, or having more resources or self-control than others. Thus, potency, in Ifalukan culture, does not necessarily describe how strong or weak the emotion experienced is. Rather, it refers to a person's social position. These observations led Lutz to observe that, "[w]hile it appears to be universally the case that people sort the environment into the categories of 'good' and 'bad,' these latter words are themselves multidimensional and must be placed and interpreted in cultural context" (Lutz, 1986, p. 278). Lutz's finding that the dimensions of meaning underlying Ifalukan emotion words refer to social matters is not surprizing given that, as she sees them, the Ifaluk view most of the emotions they experience as being engendered by their interactions with others.

Fago, liget, amae, *and other challenges to universalist claims.*   Consistent with the social constructivist assumption that cultures whose social life is organized differently from that of Western cultures should identify different emotions, Lutz found that the Ifaluk described several emotions that have no exact analogs in Western cultures. *Fago* is a combination of compassion, love, and sadness that is seen by the Ifaluk as being similar to

---

[6]*Multidimensional scaling* is a complex statistical technique that essentially transforms a set of similarity judgments of a group of words into a picture. Words that are seen as similar to one another form "clusters," words that are seen as dissimilar appear in different clusters. The physical distance among words and clusters in the picture is a measure of how similar the words or clusters are. One examines how the clusters are arranged in the picture for clues as to the dimensions of meaning that "produced" the clusters.

four other emotions that are associated with being away from one's family and friends, *lalomweiu* (loneliness/sadness), *liyeman* (longing), *pak* (homesickness), and *laloileng* (insecurity). *Fago*, however, is not simply a kind of sadness, for it refers to "one's relationship with a more unfortunate other" (Lutz, 1986, p. 273). Interestingly, it is the most frequently used word in the cluster of emotion words associated with what Lutz describes as "connection and loss."

As described by the late anthropologist Michelle Rosaldo (1944–1981), *liget* is a word used by the Ilongot of the island of Luzon in the Philippines to refer to "[p]eople, spirits, and certain objects, like wind and rain, liquor, illness, chili peppers, and fire . . . as a noun or adjective [it suggests] potency, energy, intensity, the irritating heat of chili peppers, the rush of rapids, or the forces of wind" (Rosaldo, 1980, p. 45). It is a word that has some of the meanings of *anger* but also much more.

> For people to *si liget*, or "have anger," means that they are neither shy nor fearful, not unduly quiet or reserved. *Liget* points in human life to a readiness to be "different" or take offense . . . , to stubbornness and conviction, but also to the fact that one is quick moving, youthful, active . . . , and "tied up tight" or "strong." (Rosaldo, 1980, p. 45)

Like anger, *liget* results from "insults, slights and other intimations of inequality" (Rosaldo, 1980, p. 47) and can lead to revenge and retribution. Also like anger, but much more so, *liget* is seen as having both negative and positive qualities. *Liget* is associated with "wild violence," "chaos, separation, and confusion," but also with the emotions necessary to be a successful hunter or warrior: "'I am full of *liget* when I hunt' a man says, 'because I do not fear the forest'" (Rosaldo, 1980, p. 49). "'Without *liget* to move our hearts,'" the Ilongot say, "'there would be no human life'" (Rosaldo, 1980, p. 47).

Amae is a widely reported emotion in Japan for which there is no exact translation in English (Doi, 1973). *Amae* can be seen, very loosely, as a kind of positive dependence on another person, as the desire to put oneself in a dependent, almost childlike relationship and to "merge" with another, or the behavior involved in eliciting such a relationship. The latter is often translated as "coaxing" (Morshbach & Tyler, 1986). The various meanings of *amae* center on "passive dependency needs in hierarchical relationships" (Morshbach & Tyler, 1986, p. 300), most of which would be seen as alien or even pathological to North Americans.[7] Indeed, Americans would regard the kind of "coaxing" described by Morshbach and Tyler (1986) in their study of *amae* in Japanese literature and popular culture as being typical of *amaeru* (the

---

[7]Tellingly perhaps, the Chinese ideograph for *amae* is thought to have originally depicted a mother's breast (Morshbach & Tyler, 1986).

verb form of *amae*), as embarrassingly childish. For the Japanese, although it is possible to express the emotion inappropriately, in general, engaging in the behavior associated with *amae* does not have this connotation.

Takeo Doi, in his detailed examination of *amae* and the role that it plays in Japanese culture, argues that *amae* is an emotion that is ubiquitous in and central to Japanese family and social life in that it provides the bond that holds the various personal and social relationships that a person may have together. Indeed, the Japanese regard it as a basic emotion that is even found in animals (Doi, 1973, p. 15). Although *amae* is an emotion that children express toward their parents, it is considered to be a learned emotion, not observable in children under 1 year of age (Morshbach & Tyler, 1986, p. 302). It is also an emotion, in spite of its ubiquity, that is not usually spoken of. The reason for this may be seen as an aspect of the meaning of *amae* in Japanese social life. As Doi observes, the

> Japanese feel that the use of words can chill the atmosphere, whereas Americans, in contrast, feel encouraged and reassured by such communication. I think this is clearly related to the psychology of *amae*, because the Japanese idea is that those who are close to each other—that is to say, who are privileged to merge with each other—do not need words to express their feelings. One surely would not feel merged with another . . . , if one had to verbalize a need to do so! (Doi, 1973, p. 387; see also Morshbach & Tyler, 1986)

Emotions: Universal, or Culturally Specific?

Cross-cultural surveys by those who adopt a social constructivist perspective emphasize the differences among cultures in the emotions they identify. When a culture appears to share an emotion with North American culture, the unique relationship between the emotion and its wider cultural context is highlighted. As the above brief review indicates, there *are* differences among cultures in how emotions are defined and in what they mean, but what are we to make of these differences? Do the differences indicate that "anything goes" and that cultures are free to invent whatever emotions they wish? Or are there ways in which, underneath the surface variations, emotions in all cultures everywhere are similar or the same? That is, are there physical, biological, or other constraints on how cultures organize the emotional lives of their members? Philip Shaver and his colleagues, whom we met in Chapter 2, dispute the social constructivist notion that emotions differ appreciably across cultures. Recall that, for them, in spite of their apparent dissimilarities, all of the cultures so far studied show an impressive degree of similarity in the meaning of the terms they use to describe emotions.

Shaver, Wu, and Schwartz (1992) specifically take Lutz to task for downplaying the ways in which emotions in North American culture may be seen as being about social activity as well as being "feeling states" (Russell, 1991b, offers a similar critique). Shaver et al. did this after reanalyzing some 600 descriptions of emotion episodes collected earlier by Shaver, Schwartz, Kirson, and O'Connor (1987). In their reanalysis, they categorized each episode in terms of whether or not it involved the "subject's relationship to another person or group of people" (Shaver et al., 1992, p. 201). Shaver et al. found that 100% of the episodes describing love, 91% of the episodes describing anger, and 90% of the episodes describing sadness involved another person or persons. From these results, Shaver et al. concluded that

> U.S. accounts are concerned with the same general issue that Oceanic people's emotion accounts are: the relationship between a person (with desires, goals, and values) and an event, usually an event involving at least one other person. (Shaver et al., 1992, p. 201)

Shaver et al.'s conclusions may be misleading, however, for while emotions such as love and anger for North Americans do indeed involve other people, centrally, they are nevertheless experienced as internal feeling states and this may be quite different from the way the Pacific islanders studied by Lutz and others experience emotions. The fact that North Americans experience emotions as embodied feeling states is illustrated quite nicely by Shaver et al.'s own discussion of the metaphors of anger (see pp. 204–205) as well as Averill's (1982) examination of the everyday experience of anger (see especially pp. 199–201). Given that so much of the language of emotion in English is "body talk," it would indeed be surprizing if we did not experience emotions as internal feeling states (see also Wierzbicka, 1994). Notice, however, that there need be no necessary contradiction in viewing emotions as both internal feeling states and as about other people. The "aboutness" of an emotion is its object, that which incited it or that to which it is directed. This does not necessarily say anything about how the emotion is experienced (see Averill, 1980b, pp. 148–150, on the objects of emotions).

Back to Basics: Social Constructivism and the Problem of Basic Emotions

As we saw in Chapter 2, many of the theorists who identify with the Darwinian approach to the study of emotions posit the existence of a relatively small number of so-called basic emotions, the Big Six (or Seven). Even though they disagree on how many basic emotions there are, Ekman, Izard, Tomkins, and Plutchik, for example, all argue that humans everywhere come into the world with a set of basic emotions or the capacity to develop a set of basic emotions with which to deal with their environment. As described in Chapter 4, Oatley and Johnson-Laird, working from within the cognitive tradition but influenced by evolutionary thought as well, also contend that human beings possess a small set of basic emotions. For most of these theorists, because all human beings share the same biology and ancestral environment, they have evolved a relatively small set of responses to the particular survival-related environmental contingencies they have faced over the course of their evolutionary history (see also Tooby & Cosmides, 1990, for a detailed and cogent statement of this position). Basic emotions are associated with our species' primitive biological responses to problems in the environment that are considered in some way to be "basic" or of fundamental importance to the survival of the organism (Ortony & Turner, 1990). Thus, fear may be considered a basic emotion because its function is to help us deal with the basic problem of dangers in our environment. Anger is basic because it is associated with the basic problem of defense, and so on. As you might imagine, social constructivists take a somewhat different view.

According to Averill,

[f]rom a constructivist point of view, there are an indefinite number of emotions. That is, societies can shape, mold, or construct as many different emotions as are functional with the social system. (Averill, 1980a, p. 326)

For a theorist like Averill, there is no necessary reason why some emotions should be seen as more basic than others. While it is true that some emotions may display more involvement by biological systems than others, think here of the way anger may be accompanied by many physiological changes, while hope usually is not, or that some emotions are more closely associated with survival-related problems than others, this does not mean that these are any more "basic" than any other set of emotions one might choose. Averill's view of emotions as polythetic syndromes leads him to see the relationship between biology and emotion as a loose one. Because "any given emotion may be related to more than one biological system . . . [and] any given biological system may be related to more than one emotion" (Averill, 1980a, p. 328), it is difficult to decide which emotions are more basic than others simply in terms of their association with biological systems. Further, it is even difficult to decide which biological systems are more basic than others.

As Ortony and Turner (1990) note in their critique of the idea of basic emotions, what we choose to call basic emotions depends on which aspects of emotion we wish to emphasize over others. Averill, because his focus is on the social-cultural level of analysis, emphasizes the role of culture and not biology in the construction of emotions and so privileges the social functions of emotions (but see Kemper, 1987, for a sociocultural analysis that emphasizes biology). From the social constructivist perspective, it is much more interesting to examine what emotions are prescribed and proscribed in particular cultures—those emotions that the anthropologist Levy terms "hypercognized" and "hypocognized," respectively (Levy, 1984, p. 227)— and to attempt to reveal the social functions of emotions, for example, in the ways that emotions such as guilt or shame serve to maintain particular value systems (Armon-Jones, 1986a, 1986b) or how anger functions in the service of moral reproach (Sabini & Silver, 1982).

Can New Emotions Come into Being?

In Ted Mooney's novel *Easy Travel to Other Planets* (1981), people suddenly begin experiencing "new" emotions, emotions "that no one had ever felt before." If, as the social constructivists argue, emotions are products of culture, then it is possible that, given the right changes in society, people may indeed come to experience new emotions. Mooney implies as much in his book, as the appearance of new emotions parallels an epidemic of "information sickness" brought on by overexposure to the products of our information culture. The psychiatrist and historian Carol Stearns and the historian Peter Stearns, in their book on the history of anger in the United States (Stearns & Stearns, 1986), trace the evolution of American's current obsession with anger and its control from Colonial times to the present. They describe how Americans have become ever more uneasy about the unfettered expression of anger in public, especially in the workplace. They demonstrate not so much that new emotions came into being in the period they studied but that Americans came to experience one emotion, anger, in new ways as the "emotionology" of American culture changed. Stearns and Stearns coined the term *emotionology* to refer to, "the conventions and standards by which Americans evaluated anger, and the standards they developed to reflect and encourage these standards" (Stearns & Stearns, 1986, p. 14). In a similar manner, Demos (1988) explores the social context of shame and guilt in Puritan New England, and Modell (1988) examines the cultural models for parental love in the United States from the postwar period to the present.

These inquiries are important aspects of the social constructivist program for, in order to really demonstrate the validity of the social constructivist thesis, it is necessary to demonstrate, in the words of Stearns and Stearns (1986), "how a general worldview or a set of sociocultural assumptions may moderate emotional responses to the immediate environment" (p. 6). Presumably, changes in such assumptions would exert their influence

BOX 5.2

Learning to Touch But Not to Feel:
The Emotional Education of Medical Students

Consistent with his assertion that emotions are social and individual constructions, Averill argues that emotions may be transformed or even acquired anew at any time during our lives. In a fascinating illustration of the transformation of emotions in young adulthood, sociologists Allen Smith and Sherryl Kleinman (1989) examined how medical students learn new ways of responding to the intimate physical contacts they have daily with living and dead bodies (for a conceptually related account of the transformation of emotions for commercial purposes, see Hochschild, 1983). By means of 2.5 years of participant observation of medical students in their first 3 years of training, Smith and Kleinman were able to observe the way medical students' initial responses of disgust toward the cadavers they were required to dissect and the sexual arousal they feared they would feel during the physical examinations of patients they were required to do were systematically eliminated by a mostly implicit curriculum of emotional education carried out by their teachers and peers.

Even before they reached medical school, Smith and Kleinman argue, most of the medical-students-to-be knew they would have to change their accustomed ways of responding to intimate physical contact and contact with things they consider disgusting. In some sense, the students are able to prepare themselves somewhat for the emotional task they are about to undertake. Immediately upon entering medical school, however, the students are rudely confronted with the reality and enormity of the emotional re-education they must go through in the form of the cadavers they must dissect in gross anatomy class.

Students initially find it difficult not to respond to the cadaver as a person. As one student remarked, "they handled it like a butcher shop . . . Slice, move, pull, cut . . . I know it's absurd, but what if she's not really dead?," or as another remembered, "It felt tough when we had to turn the whole body over from time to time . . . It felt like real people" (Smith & Kleinman, 1989, p. 59). They quickly learn, however, that these are not considered appropriate ways to respond and that these are not even appropriate topics of conversation. Primarily by example, their teachers instruct them that the appropriate attitude toward the body is one of detachment: "Mentally, they transform the body and their contact with it into something entirely different from the contacts they have in their personal lives" (Smith & Kleinman, 1989, p. 60). This transformation

> sometimes involves changing the body into a nonhuman object. Students think of the body as a machine or as an animal specimen, and recall earlier, comfortable experiences in working on that

kind of object. The body is no longer provocative because it is no longer a body. (Smith & Kleinman, 1989, p. 61)

Students learn that this is an effective strategy for dealing with their accustomed ways of responding to living bodies as well.

I just told myself, "OK, doc, you're here to find out what's wrong, and that includes the axillae (armpits)." And I detach a little, reduce the person for a moment . . . Focus real hard on the detail at hand, the fact, or the procedure or the question. (Smith & Kleinman, 1989, p. 60)

Even though it shields them from a great deal of discomfort, adopting such a detached attitude has its costs, however. Sometimes students find it difficult to leave the attitude at the hospital or lab. "For some students, medical training creates a problem as new meanings for the body and for body contact go home with them at night" (Smith & Kleinman, 1989, p. 65). This is poignantly illustrated by the story told by one of the students Smith and Kleinman interviewed.

I have learned enough to find gross problems. And they taught us that breast cancer is one of the biggest threats to a woman's health. OK. So I can offer my expertise. But I found myself examining her, right in the middle of making love. Not cool! (Smith & Kleinman, 1989, p. 66)

Thus, the students encounter a second curriculum of emotional education, one that is perhaps even less explicit and more troubling than the first they have to endure.

on the individual through changes in socialization practices, as the research by Stearns and Stearns and other historians and that by Lutz (Lutz, 1985) and other anthropologists and psychologists (see, for example, Dorr, 1985) suggests. The emotions of infants and children are not the only ones to undergo change, however. As Averill argues, adults too may acquire new emotions, as when one falls in (or out of) love for the first time or experiences a life-changing religious conversion as an adult. This is not such a novel idea, as the recent spate of books (e.g., Lerner's, 1985, *Dance of Anger*) aimed at helping adult women experience anger attest (see also Thomas, 1993, for an examination of the normative context and everyday experience of women's anger).

Representative Research on Emotion
from the Social Constructivist Perspective

Laugh and the world laughs with you. Weep, and . . . I was recently at an outdoor production of Shakespeare's *Macbeth* during which two members of the audience laughed, or, I should say, guffawed, inappropriately through most of the play. Their continued cackling did not make me or anyone else in the audience experience the play as a light-hearted farce, but, in general, social constructivists maintain that our immediate context holds important information for us as to how we are to behave emotionally. The situations in which we find ourselves, including the other people present, the physical setting we are in, and so on, are seen by social constructivists as cueing us into what emotions are appropriate and how to display them. The sociologist Arlie Hochschild (1979) points out that because we are all familiar with what she calls the "feeling rules" of our culture, few of us laugh at funerals or when being interviewed by the IRS. In a recent empirical investigation of this notion, Susan Labott and her colleagues Randall Martin, Patricia Eason, and Elayne Berkey (1991) examined the influence of social context on people's emotional responses, specifically, weeping and laughing, to a film.

Placing their research within the social constructivist tradition, Labott et al. began with the assumption that, even though weeping is a relatively unexamined phenomenon, it is clear that, "adults weep to indicate that some important aspect of the self has been threatened or lost, and that they are no longer able to manage the situation themselves" (Labott et al., 1991, p. 398). Interestingly, when college students and young adults are asked to indicate the situations in which they often weep, "watching a film or television program" is one of the most frequent responses (Kraemer & Hastrup, 1986). There is good reason to believe, however, that weeping in public may result in embarrassment or other negative affect for either the weeper (see Hoover-Dempsey, Plas, & Strudler Wallston, 1986) or anyone witnessing the weeping. Like weeping, laughing is a little-studied phenomenon. However, unless the setting explicitly proscribes it, there seems to be no stigma attached to laughing in public. Thus, Labott et al. sought to contrast the reactions of subjects to the weeping or laughing of another person.

Labott et al. recruited a sample of undergraduate students and asked them to watch a short film along with another subject. The other subject was actually a confederate of the experimenters and responded in one of three predetermined ways to the film in the presence of each of the real subjects. In the *Control* condition, the confederate showed no emotion during or immediately after the film. In the *Crying* condition, the confederate sniffed, wiped his or her eyes with a tissue, and breathed in "short gasps." In the *Laughter* condition, the confederate chuckled out loud at four points during the film. After the film was over, the confederates in the *Crying* and *Laughter* conditions said "That was really something" and either sniffled or chuckled, respectively. The film, entitled *Peege*, which has often been used by researchers to elicit weeping from subjects, tells the story of a family's visit to their institutionalized grandmother. The film is not particularly funny, but there are points in the film where a little laughter would not be inappropriate.

After the film was over, the subjects completed a number of rating scales designed to ascertain what they thought of the film, how they felt during the film, whether or not they wept or laughed during the film, and so forth, as well as how they perceived and felt about the confederate. While the subjects viewed the film with the confederate, their behavior was observed by the experimenter, who noted the duration of any laughing or weeping by the subjects. The subjects' behavior was also recorded by means of a hidden videotape camera. The videotapes of the subjects were later coded for how much the subjects looked at the confederate and whether or not they laughed or wept during the film. The verbal behavior of the subjects for a 3-minute period immediately after the conclusion of the film was also coded for its general content.

Labott et al. first conducted a check to make sure that their subjects were in fact perceiving the behavior of the confederate they wanted them to perceive. Analysis of the subjects' perceptions of the confederate confirmed that the laughing confederate was in fact perceived as laughing and the weeping confederate was perceived as weeping. Labott et al. then examined what the subjects felt about the confederates and found that, regardless of the sex of the subject, male confederates who wept and female confederates who were nonemotional during the film were seen as the most likable by the subjects. Male confederates who showed no emotion and female confederates who laughed were liked the least by the subjects. Interestingly, again regardless of the sex of the subject, female confederates who laughed or were nonemotional were looked at the most by the real subjects.

To examine the effects of the different kinds of confederates on their subjects' mood, Labott et al. formed a global "mood disturbance" score from the subjects' ratings of the list of individual mood adjectives they asked them to complete. Analysis of this measure indicated that subjects in both the *Control* and *Crying* conditions had significant increases in mood disturbance during the film relative to subjects in the *Laughter* condition. Subjects in the *Control* and *Crying* conditions also reported that they laughed less during the film than did subjects in the *Laughter* condition. The subjects' behavior as observed by the experimenter during the film paralleled these results. Female subjects reported more tears than did male subjects, but their reports were not corroborated by the experimenter observation data. Finally, when Labott et al. analyzed the verbal behavior of the subjects after the film, they found that subjects seemed to be significantly less comfortable talking about personal topics when they had watched the film with a laughing or weeping confederate.

Labott et al. take these results to indicate that their subjects' emotional reactions during the film were indeed influenced by the emotional displays of the confederate. What is most interesting in their data in this regard is the finding that subjects who viewed the film with a confederate who laughed showed less mood disturbance or negative affect than did subjects who viewed the film with a weeping or nonemotional confederate. This finding is significant because the subjects' positive response to the confederate's laughter appears to have mitigated the otherwise negative mood-inducing effects of the film. Even more significant is the finding that male and female subjects were perceived differently according to what kind of affect they displayed. That men were more liked when they wept may have indicated that, because weeping is relatively rare in men, at least in public,

> subjects may believe that something truly important must have occurred for a man to engage in this behavior. Therefore, more significance is attached to [weeping] in men than in women. In addition, considering recent changes in gender expectations, individuals of both genders may find it more appropriate for men to weep, and may be more accepting of, and even attracted to this behavior (at least when it is not inappropriate or excessive). (Labott et al., 1991, p. 412)

(Men take note: the way to your beloved's heart may not be through an expensive meal. A tear or two shed appropriately during a sad movie may do just as well.)

Note Labott et al.'s reference to changes in gender expectations in the above quote. More research needs to be conducted into the expectations that people have of the emotional behavior of men and women, but such expectations are precisely where social constructivists would suggest we begin looking to reveal how the emotions of men and women are (differently) constructed in our culture. Let's take a look at a study that examined gender expectations for emotional behavior more directly.

Damned if you don't.   In order to explore the differences in the expectations that people have about the expression of positive emotions for males and females, Janet Stoppard and Carla Gunn Gruchy (1993) asked a sample of male and female undergraduate students to imagine themselves or another person winning a swimming competition or getting a high grade on an exam. The students were given written scenarios to read for which they were, "to imagine themselves as vividly as possible as the central character" (p. 146). Half of the scenarios described a situation in which the subject expressed happiness as the result of his or her achievement or the achievement of another person, and half of the scenarios described a situation in which the subject *did not* express happiness. Thus, the scenarios involved the expression of happiness for oneself or another person or the failure express happiness for oneself or another person.

Subjects who received the *Self* version of the swimming scenario read the following:

> You have been involved in swimming competitions for years. Today you competed in a varsity swim meet and won the gold metal. After the competition, you are surrounded by friends. The swimming coach walks up to you and says, "You must be so proud of yourself. This is a big accomplishment."

In the *Emotion Present* version, the scenario concluded with this description:

> You reply, "Yes, I'm very proud and happy. This has been a great day. I just knew I could win." As the coach wanders off to talk to some of the others, you think that this has been a very memorable day.

The *Emotion Absent* scenario concluded with this description:

> You reply, "Yeah, I'm happy." But as the tone of your voice indicates, that isn't really true. You do not feel happy— in fact you realize you are actually feeling a little down. (Stoppard & Gunn Gruchy, 1990, p. 147)

The *Other* version of the scenarios described the subject's "best friend" winning the competition and the subject either feeling happy and proud for his or her friend or not feeling happy and proud.

After reading a scenario, the subjects rated on a 22-item scale the rewards and costs of their imagined behavior in the scenario. The rewards and costs involved how others would respond to the subject and included "be polite to," "refuse to do favors for," "disapprove of," and "ignore socially." Stoppard and Gunn Gruchy manipulated the information they gave to their subjects to ascertain whether there would be differences in the perceived rewards and costs reported by males and females for either expressing or failing to express a positive emotion whose object was the self or another person. A preliminary study they conducted had indicated that when the gender of a person is unknown, individuals who are described as expressing positive emotion toward other people are seen by subjects as more likely to be female, while individuals who are described as expressing positive emotion toward themselves are perceived by subjects as more likely to be male. The aim of the main study was to examine whether or not males and females would see themselves as being differentially penalized for not expressing happiness in a situationally appropriate manner.

Upon analyzing their subjects' ratings of the rewards and costs of either expressing or not expressing happiness toward themselves or another person, Stoppard and Gunn Gruchy found a pronounced difference in the erceptions of male and female subjects. For males, there was essentially no difference in the perceived rewards and costs of expressing positive emotion toward oneself or another person. Males reported that greater rewards and fewer costs followed the presence than absence of happiness, but it did not seem to matter to them whether the happiness was expressed toward themselves or another person. Female subjects, on the other hand, clearly perceived there to be differences in the costs of not expressing happiness toward themselves or another person.

> [I]n a context in which self-directed expression of positive emotion would be appropriate, the social rewards/costs expected by females were uninfluenced by whether positive emotion was expressed. In contrast, in a context in which other-directed expression of positive emotion would be appropriate, women expected much more favorable social consequences when positive emotion was expressed than when it was not. (Stoppard & Gunn Gruchy, 1993, p. 148)

Thus, undergraduate women perceive there to be clear costs to not expressing happiness toward another person, while undergraduate men do not. These findings are interesting, according to Stoppard and Gunn Gruchy, because they indicate that, contrary to what many have reported about gender stereotypes (e.g., Broverman, Vogel, Broverman, Clarkson, & Rosenkrantz, 1972), "women are not *generally* required to be more expressive of positive emotion than [are] men" (Stoppard & Gunn Gruchy, 1993, p. 149). It remains to be seen, of course, whether or not these results will generalize to "real life." An indication that they may, however, comes from a study of gender differences in the behavior of retail sales clerks in which it was found that female clerks expressed more positive emotion toward customers than did male clerks (Rafaeli, 1989).

Findings such as these support the general constructivist notion that emotions arise out of the normative context of a culture. In American culture, there are clear differences in the prescriptions for the emotional behavior of women and men, as many feminist commentators have noted (see, for example, Bardwick, 1979, and Miller, 1991). Except for the suggestive evidence presented by Rafaeli (1989; see also the contributions to Stearns and Stearns, 1988), however, whether and how such prescriptions are translated into behavior remains unclear. The philosopher Claire Armon-Jones (1985) has presented a convincing argument as to how children acquire prescriptive knowledge about emotions, but detailed empirical studies of the relationship between prescription and behavior have yet to appear. In order for their program to be more than a promissory note, social constructivists, it would seem to me, will have to devote considerable energy in the near future demonstrating that how cultures and individuals talk about emotion is how individuals experience it.

Further Reading

AVERILL, J. R. (1980b). The emotions. In E. Staub (Ed.), *Personality. Basic aspects and current research* (pp. 134–199). Englewood Cliffs, NJ: Prentice-Hall.

HARRÉ, R. (Ed.). (1986a). *The social construction of emotions.* Oxford: Basil Blackwell.

LUTZ, C. A. (1988). *Unnatural emotions: Everyday sentiments on a Micronesian atoll and their challenge to Western theory.* Chicago: University of Chicago Press.

6

Of Elephants and Blind Men

◆

Comparing the Darwinian, Jamesian, Cognitive, and Social Constructivist Perspectives on Emotion

Have you ever had an argument with someone in which you realized that the other person would NEVER see your point of view? We've probably all had arguments with other people in which we "talked past" one another. This is something that happens in science as well. The philosopher of science Thomas Kuhn (1962) uses the term *incommensurate* to describe the way in which different explanatory paradigms and perspectives in science can also be said to talk past one another. An explanatory paradigm or perspective, you'll recall, is a set of assumptions about the way the world works and how to best study and explain the world (see Chapter 1). *Incommensurate* means, literally, "lacking a common measure," and some who have surveyed the landscape of competing explanatory paradigms in psychology have argued that it is impossible to compare the different paradigms meaningfully because they make such different assumptions about the way the world works. Now that we've examined the four perspectives that guide research on emotion in contemporary psychology, we need to ask whether the different perspectives, with their different assumptions about how to define and study emotions, are incommensurate as well, that is, whether or not they are so different that they have nothing to say to one another. If they are not incommensurate, then it should be possible not only to compare them meaningfully, but to synthesize the theories drawn from the different perspectives and begin to build a powerful, general theory of emotion. Given the success of Paul Ekman in developing a theory that links the ideas of Darwin with those of James, and of Richard Lazarus and others (e.g., Nico Frijda, Phoebe Ellsworth) in combining the ideas of Darwin, James, and Arnold, there is cause for some optimism that such a synthesis may be possible.

Before we can begin to talk about such an undertaking, however, we need to review briefly what the research carried out within each of the perspectives we have examined tells us about the nature of emotion and how each perspective accounts for common emotions such as anger, fear, love, and hope. In doing this, it is important to keep in mind that in science truth is not immutable. What is considered to be an established fact today may one day be viewed as an error as more is learned about a phenomenon or as changes in the way phenomena are interpreted take place (see Kuhn, 1962). Think here about how much ideas about differentiation of emotion in the autonomic nervous system have changed in the past 20 years (see Chapter 3). Scientific truths are provisional truths, and I've always thought that the best attitude a scientist can have toward the truth is something like the following: "This is what we know now and we're reasonably certain that we're right. However, as we gather more information or learn new ways to interpret these phenomena, things could change and so it's best not to become too attached to our theories." The difference between this kind of truth, truth with a lower-case *t*, and Truth, truth with a capital *t*, is the difference described by the historian and philosopher Jacob Bronowski (1973) between *knowledge,* which is the province of science, and *certainty,* which is the province of authoritarian dogma. Science provides us with a means to ask questions continually of the natural and social worlds in which we live, dogma forbids us to ask questions. With this distinction in mind, let's briefly review what we've learned about emotion from research in the four traditions, keeping in mind that what we understand about emotion today may change dramatically in the coming years.

What We've Learned About Emotion from the Four Perspectives

The Darwinian perspective.   Although research carried out within the evolutionary tradition has no shortage of critics, it is fair to say that our understanding of emotions has been furthered considerably by those students of emotion who have adopted an evolutionary perspective. I think it is reasonable to say that it has been established beyond any doubt that people in many different—often very different—cultures can recognize the facial expressions associated with a small number of emotions. The research of Ekman and his colleagues and that of Izard and his colleagues is, I think, convincing evidence that there are, indeed, "constants across cultures" in certain simple facial expressions of emotion, although one need not necessarily interpret these data as Ekman and Izard do (see Fridlund, 1992, 1994).

By implication, the research by Ekman and others on the universality of facial expressions of emotion can be taken as presenting a strong case for the proposition that human emotions are part of our evolutionary heritage. The face you make when you smell or taste something disagreeable, is similar to the face your dog makes when she smells or tastes something disagreeable because both are remnants of actions that once served important survival-related purposes and so have been selected for in the course of mammalian evolution. Likewise, the face you make when you are angry is similar to the faces other humans make when they are angry because such faces reliably communicated important information during our species' long prehistory. Seen from this perspective, the specific bodily changes that accompany certain emotions—this includes postures, facial expressions, and changes associated with sympathetic nervous system activation—are adaptive responses in that they represent our readiness to confront the kinds of environmental contingencies we've encountered throughout the evolutionary history of our species. The evidence in this regard is strongest for the Big Six (or Seven or Eight) emotions, namely, happiness, sadness, anger, fear, disgust, surprise (and perhaps interest and contempt).

The Jamesian perspective.   In spite of the lingering belief held by some psychologists who favor the cognitive approach that the physiological arousal that accompanies (some) emotions is undifferentiated, I think there is sufficient evidence to conclude that at least a small number of emotions show autonomic nervous system (ANS) specificity. The results of studies by Levenson and Ekman and their colleagues strongly suggest that fear, anger, sadness, and happiness may be distinguished by different patterns of autonomic activity. Ekman, for his part, evinces a belief in autonomic differentiation that is much stronger than the evidence warrants, I think, proposing that, "if there is no distinctive pattern of ANS activity we not call that state an emotion" (Ekman, 1984, p. 339). While the weight of the accumulated evidence clearly supports autonomic differentiation, the number of emotions that have been shown to display differentiation is not particularly great and the extent of the differentiation among them is not all that impressive. Given the evidence now in hand, love, hope, and many other phenomena that are commonly considered emotions would not qualify as such under Ekman's criterion. For these reasons, I don't find Ekman's argument very compelling.

Although the evidence consists more of theoretical assertions than empirical demonstrations, I think it is safe to say that the patterns of ANS activity associated with the Big Six emotions are related to the function of the emotions in question. The ANS changes that accompany some episodes of fear or anger, for example, do appear to be related to the vigorous activity sometimes required in defending oneself or challenging an interloper. That the ANS and other bodily changes associated with emotions have functional significance is also a prediction, of course, made by Darwinian theories of emotion.

Research carried out within the Jamesian tradition has also convincingly demonstrated, I think, that feedback from the ANS changes that accompany some emotions contributes something to the experience of the emotions in question. Although the evidence is not incontrovertible, the results of studies of people who have suffered spinal cord injuries suggest that ANS feedback helps to determine the intensity of the emotion experienced. Consistent with the proposal made many years ago by Allport (1924) and much more recently by advocates of the facial feedback hypothesis (see Izard, 1981), feedback from the face also appears to contribute to the intensity of emotion and may be involved in the physiological differentiation of emotion. Many questions about the role of facial feedback in the experience of emotion remain, however. For example, Levenson, Ekman, and their colleagues have shown that posed facial expressions appear to bring about the ANS changes associated with a small number of emotions (see Chapter 3), but the relationship between facial expressions and ANS change is far from clear.

The Cognitive perspective.   In spite of the objections raised by Zajonc about the extent of cognitive processing necessary for the generation of emotions, I think it has been clearly demonstrated that emotions depend in a crucial way on how events are appraised by a person. Emotions are responses to the *meaning* of events and are closely associated with a person's goals and motivations. More specifically, different emotions are associated with different patterns of appraisal. There is now a considerable body of research demonstrating that emotions may be predicted from the way a person appraises a situation, with different emotions associated with different patterns of appraisal (see, most recently, Roseman, Wiest, & Swartz, 1994). Change the way an event is appraised, and you change the particular emotion experienced. The findings of cognitively oriented students of emotion have theoretical importance, of course, but they are also significant for the practical implications they hold for psychotherapy.

The Social Constructivist perspective.   Congruent with the findings of cognitive emotion researchers that emotions are a function of appraisal, social constructivist students of emotion have shown that how we talk about emotions—the way we define emotions, the way emotions are differentiated in our language and social practices, and the metaphors and metonyms for emotion and emotional experience we use—helps to determine how we experience emotion. Central to the social constructivist approach to emotions is the idea that the experience and expression of emotions is dependent on learned conventions or rules and that, to the extent that cultures differ in the way they talk about and conceptualize emotions, how they are experienced and expressed will differ in different cultures as well. In line with this reasoning, social constructivist–oriented research has discovered important and interesting cross-cultural and historical differences in the way emotions are conceptualized and, presumably, experienced. Social constructivists have also shown that emotions such as anger, fear, and grief have important social functions over and above their individual functions.

It must be recognized that the evidence for cross-cultural variability in how emotions are conceptualized, let alone experienced, is quite controversial (but see Ellsworth's 1994 excellent attempt to integrate the data on cross-cultural similarities and differences in emotional appraisal). Those who take a more biologically grounded or evolutionary approach to the study of emotions question whether emotions indeed show the kind of cross-cultural variability claimed by social constructivists. Part of their critique of the social constructivist approach involves questioning the validity of the cross-cultural data presented by social constructivists, the claim being that the data are primarily anecdotal in nature (see Izard & Phillips, 1989).

While it is certainly true that social constructivist accounts of emotion have not yet been backed up with the kind of laboratory-based studies that characterize research in the Jamesian or cognitive traditions, or the more or less well-controlled field studies carried out from within the Darwinian tradition, there is considerable evidence to support the major claims of the constructivist program. Those outside of the social constructivist perspective sometimes denigrate the ethnographic and questionnaire-based methods of constructivists. Rigorously conducted ethnographic and questionnaire studies are, nevertheless, empirical studies too and, if well done, are every bit as informative as studies using experimental methodologies. The data such studies yield, however, is clearly different from those obtained from studies using other types of methodologies.[1]

---

[1]Following the personality psychologist George Kelly's dictum that if you want to know how someone thinks or feels about something you should ask him or her, I would argue that the methodologies social constructivists use to elicit emotional meanings from people are perfectly valid. It is another story altogether, of course, determining the socially constructed nature of such meanings. I see no reason, however, why the use of ethnographic techniques cannot be used to uncover the dependence of emotional meanings on local conventions. Given the very different way in which emotions are characterized by social·constructivists compared with, say, Jamesians, it is not surprising that the former employ methodologies that sometimes differ radically from those of the latter. Just because the methodologies are different, however, doesn't mean they are inferior.

Gnashing Teeth, Thumping Hearts, Dangerous Situations, and Perceived Transgressions: The Four Perspectives Confront Fear, Anger, Love, and Hope

Now that we've had the chance to review what research within each of the four theoretical traditions has contributed to our knowledge of emotion, let's examine what each of the perspectives has to say about fear, anger, love, and hope. Anger and fear are particularly good emotions to use in a comparison of the four perspectives because they are what most people would regard as prototypical emotions (Fehr & Russell, 1984; Shaver, Schwartz, Kirson, & O'Connor, 1987). Love is also considered by many to be a prototypical emotion (Fehr, 1988), but, as we shall see, it is clearly very different from anger and fear in many of its characteristics. Each of these is also a good emotion to use in our comparison because most of us have experienced them in our everyday lives. Hope is a good emotion to include in our comparison because, while it is certainly an emotion most of us have experienced, it is something of a problematic emotion as far as most theories of emotion are concerned. For one thing, most theories of emotion would not regard it as prototypic. It is also certainly not a "basic" or fundamental emotion, according to those theories that propose such things. For these reasons, and others discussed below, most emotion researchers have avoided any systematic treatment of hope. Indeed, they've treated it like the plague! (Actually, the plague gets much more attention.) The absence of any extensive investigations of hope, an emotion that we all nevertheless experience with some frequency, I think, makes it an excellent emotion to use in comparing the four perspectives.

While we are comparing the four perspectives, you should keep in mind how difficult it is to compare how well they each account for the various emotions, since any criteria we might use to compare them are themselves theoretically grounded in one or another of the perspectives. Nevertheless, I think it is possible to place explanations for each of the emotions from each of the four perspectives side by side to get a sense of what each perspective includes in its accounts and what each leaves out.

Fear. Theorists in both the Darwinian and Jamesian traditions regard fear as a so-called basic or fundamental emotion. For Darwinians like Izard and Ekman, fear is an innate response to conditions in one's internal or external environment that "signal danger" (Izard, 1977, p. 356). The English fear researcher Jeffrey Gray (1971) proposes that it is possible to categorize all of the causes of fear according to "four general principles: intensity, novelty, 'special evolutionary dangers' . . . , and stimuli arising from social interaction" (p. 20). Izard (1977) also identifies four classes of elicitors of fear, namely, environmental events, internal events such as pain, other emotions, and cognitive processes, and asserts that the causes of fear "within each of these classes may be primarily innate or primarily learned" (p. 357). Ekman (1984), on the other hand, has argued that there exist "universal, abstract, *prototypical* situations" that elicit basic emotions such as fear, so that even learned causes of fear such as that of an upcoming examination should display commonalties of meaning with unlearned causes of fear such as that of heights. This is a view also held by Shaver and his colleagues (see Shaver, Wu, & Schwartz, 1992).

Theorists within the Darwinian tradition place a great deal of emphasis on the finding that people in many different cultures reliably recognize the facial expression associated with fear. Ekman (1984, p. 330), has described the "distinctive, pan-cultural signal" for fear as a widening of the eyes, a raising of the upper eyelid, a tensing of the lower eyelid, and an opening of the mouth with the corners of the mouth drawn slightly back (see Ekman & Friesen, 1975, pp. 50–63). Although Darwinians recognize that this basic pattern may be modified by learning and cultural convention (see the discussion of "display rules" in Chapter 2), they argue that it is nevertheless possible to observe relatively pure examples of the expression, for example, in infants and young children. Moreover, since the facial expression for fear is a product of evolution, it is possible to observe it, and the facial expressions associated with other basic emotions, in our primate relatives (Chevalier-Skolnikoff, 1973; see also Hauser, 1993). Following Darwin's reasoning, we may assume that the facial expression for fear has the form that it does because, at one time in our evolutionary history, the movements that constitute it had some kind of functional significance. That the "fear face" in humans may now serve primarily as a signal to others in no way vitiates the argument that it, and the facial expressions associated with the other basic emotions, at one time served a purpose for the individual making the face and increased his or her chances of survival (see Fridlund, 1992, 1994).

Latter-day Jamesians like Ekman, who is also a latter-day Darwinian, of course, argue that all those phenomena that can properly be called emotions have a "distinctive pattern of ANS activity" (Ekman, 1984, p. 339). Although much research remains to be done by the Jamesians in their task of specifying the patterns of autonomic nervous system activity associated with each emotion, the preliminary research conducted by Ekman and his colleagues suggests that fear is characterized by an increase in heart rate and a decrease in skin temperature (see Ekman, 1984, p. 326). While Schwartz, Weinberger, and Singer (1981), in an earlier study of cardiovascular responses during emotional imagery, found that it was difficult to distinguish fear from sadness in terms of diastolic blood pressure and heart rate, they nevertheless speculated that the pattern of cardiovascular activity associated with fear was consistent with the notion that, in fear, the body is preparing itself to escape from danger. James would no doubt welcome these findings, believing as he did (see Chapter 3) that all animals, including humans, are "but a bundle of predispositions to react in particular ways upon the contact of particular features of the environment" (James, 1884, p. 190). Recall that, for James, the patterns of visceral activity and other bodily changes associated with emotions are useful adaptations to what we would now call our ancestral environment (see Tooby & Cosmides, 1990), and so one would expect to find that the ANS changes that accompany fear reflected the body's preparation to respond to the environment in a particular way.

Emotion theorists in the cognitive tradition regard the Darwinian and Jamesian accounts of emotion as incomplete because they fail to explain adequately how emotions are elicited by events in the environment or inside the person (but see Ellsworth, 1994b, for why we shouldn't fault James in this regard). For cognitive emotion theorists, of course, how events are appraised is of crucial importance, and this applies to fear as well as any other emotion. Merely specifying the various classes of stimuli that may elicit fear doesn't cut it according to the cognitivists, because different people may react differently to the same stimulus. One of the first modern emotion theorists to appreciate this fully, of course, was Magda Arnold.

While Arnold believed that fear had its own distinct pattern of physiological changes and that these were related to the behavior required of an organism in a fear-eliciting situation, she also believed that fear requires that the environment be appraised in a particular manner. At its most basic level, fear involves an appraisal that something in one's environment is liable and likely to harm one and that it is to be avoided (see Arnold, 1960a, p. 196). Later cognitive emotion theorists have elaborated on this basic notion. Roseman, for example, argues that fear involves an appraisal that an event in one's environment is "circumstance-caused," that its probability of occurrence is "uncertain," and that it is "motive-inconsistent" (see Roseman, 1984, p. 31), or, in other words, it is something that conflicts with one's goals and desires, that is outside of one's control, and that may or may not happen. Smith and Lazarus propose a similar decomposition of the appraisal involved in fear. For them, the "core relational theme" of fear is "danger/threat," whose component appraisals include the recognition that the event in question is "motivationally relevant" but "motivationally incongruent" and is one for which the person has low or uncertain "coping potential" (see Smith & Lazarus, 1993, p. 238).

From the perspective of social constructivism, fear is interesting for the sociocultural functions that it serves in maintaining particular social values by regulating behavior that is considered inappropriate or immoral. In her social constructivist analysis of the social functions of fear, Armon-Jones grants that there may exist "primitive 'fear' responses based on natural apprehensions of situations as menacing or dangerous" (Armon-Jones, 1986a, p. 62). She argues, however, that an analysis of fear should not end with an explication of the "natural" contexts within which fear occurs, for fear may occur in many other, purely socially determined contexts. Further, what are considered to be behavior and expressions indicative of fear in a particular culture may differ from the "natural" expression of the emotion.

Armon-Jones (1986a) points out that, among the Ifaluk, as described by Lutz (see Lutz, 1983), *metagu*, an emotion similar to what is called fear in English, "is prescribed for morally significant contexts" (p. 62) such as "'wandering away from the domestic area and visiting members of a higher rank without food'" (p. 63). For the Ifaluk, and for any other society for that matter, Armon-Jones argues, the situations in which fear is considered to be an appropriate response turn out to be situations that are also loaded with moral meaning. The Ifaluk, being a small society dependent on limited space and resources for their subsistence, value cooperation, nonaggression, and obedience. Children are taught to fear situations that threaten these values. *Metagu*, or fear, indeed, according to Lutz, "is at the very heart of the Ifaluk system of interpersonal interaction and social control and provides the motivational framework for the maintenance of the system of rank and the obedience and cooperation that accompany it" (Lutz, 1983, p. 250). Children's failure to show fear in a situation in which it is appropriate is a cause for some concern among the Ifaluk, and both rewards and punishments may be used to bring children's behavior into line with social expectations (although the Ifaluk prefer to socialize children by "lecturing"). In this way, the children's behavior—and this includes not only fear behaviors that Westerners would recognize, such as fleeing, but also "acting submissive and giving food," behaviors that Westerners might not immediately classify as denoting fear—serves to reinforce those values.

Lutz's account of the child-rearing practices of the Ifaluk provides many examples of how Ifaluk children are taught to recognize and respond appropriately with the socially prescribed emotion of fear to situations that involve important social values. Among the Ifaluk, fear is regarded as something children "should" experience and, while the Ifaluk recognize that fear is a naturally occurring emotion, they also recognize that considerable socialization is necessary before children experience the emotion in all of the situations in which it is socially required. According to Armon-Jones, this demonstrates the ways in which one can carry out an analysis of the social functions and, hence, socially constructed nature, of even an emotion as "natural" and basic as fear. Notice also how Averill's conception of emotions as "polythetic" is supported by Lutz ethnographic data. While there may indeed be a more or less primitive human response to dangerous situations, what counts as a dangerous situation and what counts as a fearful response are both subject to cultural conditioning.

Anger.   Like fear, anger is considered to be a basic emotion by students of emotion in both the Darwinian and Jamesian traditions. According to Izard, the anger we observe in people today is the expression of a more or less primitive response to "being either physically or psychologically restrained from doing what one intensely desires to do" (Izard, 1977, pp. 329–330). Anger, as such, provides us with the motivation and sometimes the means to remove whatever it is that is restraining us. Evolutionarily, the value of anger, "lay in its ability to mobilize one's energy and make one capable of defending oneself with great vigor and strength" (Izard, 1977, p. 333). According to Izard, as befits its status as a fundamental emotion with important survival functions, anger may be observed in very young infants and children (Izard, 1977), and though we may try to conceal our anger, "on the face of an angry person there is almost always one or more of the innate components of the natural expression which signals his or her internal state" (Izard, 1977, p. 330).

The facial expressions, bodily postures, and general bodily arousal associated with anger stand, according to the Darwinian way of thinking, as testimony to its distant phylogenetic origins. As Darwin himself noted, the human facial expressions associated with anger closely resemble the snarls of a dog about to attack (see Darwin, 1872/1965, pp. 117 and 243). Ekman and Friesen (1975) have noted, however, that there are actually two types of "anger mouths." According to Ekman and Friesen, anger in the human face is characterized by drawn-together eyebrows and tensed eyelids and *either* a closed "lip-pressed-against-lip" mouth or an open, "square" mouth (see Ekman & Friesen, 1975, Figure 34, p. 87). The former is often observed when a person is engaging in aggressive behavior of some kind and the latter is observed when a person is expressing anger verbally in some manner. As with the facial expression associated with fear, Ekman and his colleagues have demonstrated that people in many different cultures reliably recognize faces such as these as being associated with situations involving anger (see Ekman & Friesen, 1971; Ekman et al., 1987). A finding anticipated more than 100 years ago by Darwin (see Darwin, 1872/1965, p. 245).

Just as there appears to be a universal facial expression associated with anger, according to contemporary researchers in the Jamesian tradition, there also appears to be a more or less consistent pattern of bodily changes associated with the emotion. Consistent with the idea that anger serves to prepare the body to engage in the vigorous activity associated with fighting, research going all the way back to the 1950s (see Ax, 1953) has found that anger is characterized by large increases in heart rate and diastolic blood pressure, and higher skin surface temperatures when compared with fear (Ekman, 1984; Levenson, 1992; Schwartz et al., 1981). This pattern of physiological changes constitute what might be called a "'fight' motor program" in which "blood flow is redirected away from the periphery and toward large muscles of locomotion" (Levenson, 1992, p. 25). Evidence for this pattern comes from studies that actually sought to anger subjects more or less realistically (Ax, 1953), studies in which the emotion was elicited during a guided-imagery exercise (Schwartz et al., 1981; Levenson, Carstensen, Friesen, & Ekman, 1991), and studies in which subjects' facial musculature was manipulated into anger expressions (Levenson, Ekman, & Friesen, 1990). These findings are particularly compelling, I think, in that across a quite diverse set of methodologies, a consistent pattern of physiological changes associated with anger emerged (see Levenson, 1992, for a review).

For Jamesians, what it feels like to be angry is just as important as the bodily changes associated with the emotion, for, presumably, the experience of the emotion is a direct function of these changes (see Chapter 3). Clues as to the adaptive functions of anger may also be found in the characteristics of the experience of the emotion. According to Izard (1977) and others (see Lakoff & Kövecses, 1983, but your own experience will do just as well), when we are really angry our face becomes hot, our muscles tense up, and our heart may begin pounding. Often, we feel an impulse to strike out at another or simply to strike out at something, and we may have a feeling of loss of control (Averill, 1982). "Anger brings an urge to strike and tear, to use the muscles poised for action, to express the tension that threatens to smother us" (Arnold, 1960a, p. 178). Although he lived a hundred years ago in what was surely a very different culture from that of today, James would have no trouble recognizing these experiences, revealing as they do the role that anger plays in preparing our bodies for battles real and imagined. It should be recognized, of course, that not all episodes of anger feel this way. As Averill reminds us, being "cool, calm and collected" (as the deodorant ads put it) may be just as much a part of anger as being hopping mad.

According to researchers in the cognitive tradition, the bodily changes as impulses to action associated with anger don't tell us much about the emotion unless we know something about how the objects of anger are appraised. Arnold considered anger to be associated with appraising an event as something harmful that "frustrates and obstructs us," but which "can be overcome, though with difficulty" (Arnold, 1960a, pp. 196–197).[2] Although he considers himself to be a Darwinian, Izard (1977) acknowledges the importance of perceiving that one has been taken advantage of, "compelled to do something against one's wishes" (p. 330), or otherwise interrupted in some pleasant or positive activity as instigations to anger. Likewise, Ekman and Friesen (1975) describe the major provocation to anger as "[f]rustration resulting from interference with [one's] activity or the pursuit of [one's] goals" (p. 78). They go on to say that

> [y]our anger will be more likely and more intense if you believe that the agent of interference acted arbitrarily, unfairly, or spitefully. If a person

---

[2]Arnold differentiated emotions according to the strength of the impulse to action associated with them. She called emotions with weaker impulses to action "impulse" emotions and emotions with stronger impulses to action "contending" emotions (Arnold, 1960a).

wants to frustrate you, or frustrates you simply because he fails to consider how his actions might affect your activity, you are more likely to be angry than if you think he has no choice. (Ekman & Friesen, 1975, p. 78)

As we saw in Chapter 4, cognitive theorists proper like Roseman (1984) regard anger as an emotion that involves an appraisal that a "motive-inconsistent" state of affairs has been caused by another person in a situation in which one perceives oneself to be in a position of strength relative to the other person (compare this with Spellman's, 1989, analysis of anger and power). Similarly, for Smith and Lazarus (1993), the core relational theme of anger is "other-blame" and the appraisal components associated with the emotion are motivational relevance and incongruence and other-accountability. In a description of the instigation to anger that ironically echoes what Ekman says about the causes of anger, Averill (1982) contends that anger almost always involves an appraisal that one has been voluntarily wronged unjustifiably by another person. This is similar to the definition of anger offered by Aristotle (see Chapter 5).

In Chapter 5 we discussed Averill's social constructivist theory of anger in detail and so not much more needs to be said here. Social constructivists like Averill agree with cognitively oriented emotion theorists about the importance of appraisal but part company with the Darwinians and Jamesians and their insistence that anger is a basic emotion best understood from a biological perspective. While social constructivists acknowledge that there are biological components to the anger syndrome (notice the change in language here), they argue that to understand anger fully one must appreciate the ways in which the appraisals, behavior, experience, and functions of anger are shaped by social rules.

According to the social constructivist way of thinking, although it may be "natural" to want to remove an obstacle that is preventing one from obtaining a goal, the objects of anger appraisals are *social* objects—other people, possessions, abstract concepts and the like—whose meaning and value are learned. The appraisals involved in anger take their meaning from the moral order within which the angry person has been socialized. Moreover, the way that one's anger is played out in a particular situation is determined by learned regulative rules that guide the performance. Even while seemingly out of control, the angry person's behavior is nevertheless sensitive to its context (Averill, 1982). This is why not every episode of anger is alike. Further, the experience of oneself as an angry person or as the target of another's anger is, from a social constructivist perspective, the result of learning what it means to be angry from within a particular cultural context (compare your own experience with that of the Ifaluk or Inuit). Finally, all of the components of anger, the appraisals, experience, and behavior, must be seen for the ways in which they contribute to the social as well as the individual functions of anger. In the same way that gossip or ghost stories serve to reinforce moral values, anger may be seen to have a normative function. Every episode of anger involves a moral judgment and so helps to maintain particular systems of values (Armon-Jones, 1986a, 1986b).

Love. Darwin argued in his treatise on emotions that, even though love is one of the strongest emotions, "it can hardly be said to have any proper or peculiar means of expression; and this is intelligible, as it has not habitually led to any special line of action" (Darwin, 1872/1965, p. 213). He did, however, note that, because love is experienced as pleasurable, "it generally causes a gentle smile and some brightening of the eyes" (Darwin, 1872/1965, p. 213) and that, "when lovers meet, . . . their hearts beat quickly, their breathing is hurried, and their faces flush" (Darwin, 1872/1965, p. 79). Moreover, love is often accompanied by a strong desire to touch and be touched by one's beloved, a behavior that may be observed in other animals such as dogs and monkeys, which, Darwin argues, is most likely an "inherited habit, in association with the nursing and tending of our children, and with the mutual caresses of lovers" (Darwin, 1872/1965, p. 213).

Love is not included in Ekman's list of basic emotions (surprise, fear, disgust, anger, happiness, and sadness), and so it is not surprising that he has given scant attention to it in his research. Presumably, in spite of what Darwin had to say about the signs of love, because there is no "distinctive pan-cultural signal" (Ekman, 1984, pp. 330) associated with it, love simply does not qualify as an emotion for Ekman.[3] Love also does not appear on Izard's list of fundamental emotions (interest-excitement, joy, surprise, distress-anguish, anger, disgust, contempt, fear, shame, and guilt), although Izard, like Darwin, sees love as an especially powerful emotion. Love, for Izard, while not a fundamental emotion itself, is a combination of the fundamental emotions of interest and joy. *Romantic* love consists of these two emotions plus sexual arousal. Izard considers love to be not so much an emotion as "an aspect of a relationship," and describes love specifically as an "affective-cognitive orientation" (Izard, 1977, p. 95). According to Izard, affective-cognitive orientations result from the "frequent occurrence of two or more fundamental emotions that interact with a particular set of cognitions" (Izard, 1977, p. 50). Such orientations are not emotions themselves but consist of relatively long-lasting combinations of emotions and cognitions associated with particular situations or stimuli. From Izard's perspective, love is a particular way of interacting with another person that in-

---

[3]Although Ekman has not included love in any of his studies of the facial expressions of emotion, Antoinette Feleky did in hers. Feleky found that only 11% of the subjects in her facial-expression judgment study correctly identified her expression of romantic love (see Feleky, 1924). As I argued in Chapter 2, while there do seem to be characteristic facial expressions and bodily postures associated with love in our culture, they are probably best thought of as highly conventionalized rather than innately determined.

cludes the experience of the emotions of interest and joy and a number of characteristic cognitions, for example, idealizing or valuing one's beloved above all others.

Approaching love from an evolutionary but not specifically Darwinian perspective, Cindy Hazan and Phillip Shaver (1987) have argued that adult romantic love is a special case of *attachment*. Attachment is the "biosocial" process by which affective bonds between infants and their caregivers are formed (Bowlby, 1969). Hazan and Shaver base their approach on the work of John Bowlby (1907–1990), who might be called the "father of attachment theory" (or, more appropriate to his theory, the "primary caregiver of attachment theory"), and the considerable literature to which Bowlby's pioneering research gave birth (see Parkes & Stevenson-Hinde, 1982).

The function of attachment, according to Bowlby and his followers, is to ensure that helpless primate infants get cared for. They argue that, through the process of natural selection, there has evolved a system of reciprocal behavioral and affective responses on the part of infants and their caregivers during the early months of an infant's life that serve to keep caregivers in close proximity to their infants. According to attachment theory, infant crying has evolved into a powerful elicitor of parental nurturance (see Donovan & Leavett, 1985). Baby cries and mom or dad (but usually mom in American culture) attends to baby's needs. Research by Mary Ainsworth and her colleagues (Ainsworth, Blehar, Waters, & Wall, 1978) has demonstrated that consistent responding by mothers to the cries of their infants sets the stage for the development of strong affective bonds between infants and mothers. According to Hazan and Shaver (1987, 1994), the particular characteristics of the affective bonds that develop between adult partners in a romantic relationship are similar to the characteristics of the affective bonds between infants and their caregivers.

For example, according to Shaver, Hazan, and Bradshaw (1988), in adult relationships, feelings of love, "are related to an intense desire for the love object's (LO) (real or imagined) interest and reciprocation" (p. 73). In infant-caregiver relationships, "[f]ormation and quality of the attachment bond depends on the attachment object's (AO's) sensitivity and responsiveness" (p. 73). For adults, "LO's real or imagined reciprocation causes [the] person to feel confident, secure, safe, etc."; however, "[w]hen LO acts uninterested or rejecting, [the] person is anxious, preoccupied, unable to concentrate, etc." (p. 73). Likewise, for infants, "AO provides a secure base and infants feel competent and safe to explore"; however," [w]hen AO is not available, not sensitive, etc., [the] infant is anxious, preoccupied, unable to explore freely" (p. 73). Broadly speaking, the two kinds of relationships have the same end, namely, ensuring that the partners in each relationship remain near to one another. Given this basic similarity, it is not surprising, Hazan and Shaver (1987, 1994) argue, that romantic love and infant-caregiver attachment display remarkable behavioral similarities. In general, attachment behaviors consist of "proximity- and contact-seeking," "hold-ing, touching, caressing, kissing, rocking, smiling, crying, following, cling-ing, etc.," while romantic love is characterized by "wanting to spend time with LO; holding, touching, caressing, kissing, and making love with LO; smiling and laughing; crying; clinging; fearing separation, etc." (Shaver et al., 1988, p. 73).

Hazan and Shaver argue that such similarities between attachment and romantic love exist because both are part of the same biological, or, more properly, biosocial process: "The attachment-theory approach to ro-mantic love suggests that love is a biological as well as a social process, based in the nervous system and serving one or more important functions" (Hazan & Shaver, 1987, p. 523). Using attachment as a framework for their research, Hazan and Shaver and their colleagues have indeed accumulated an impressive amount of data showing that many of the characteristics of adult love relationships may be predicted from the kind of "internal work-ing model" a person has about the nature of relationships (see Hazan & Shaver, 1994, for an extensive review). Such working models, theoreti-cally, are a direct consequence of the quality of the attachment relationship between infants and their caregivers (see Bowlby, 1973). This work is im-portant for students of emotion who are trying to understand the nature of love because not only does it offer a general set of predictions about histori-cal and cross-cultural variations in the experience and expression of love—as Hazan and Shaver argue, "romantic love has always and everywhere ex-isted as a biological potential" (Hazan & Shaver, 1987, p. 523)—it also makes some very specific predictions about how love will be experienced differently by different people depending on their attachment histories. It also places romantic love, which is, as we have seen, regarded by some peo-ple as sacrosanct and not something amenable to scientific study (see Chap-ter 1), squarely within the framework of a powerful scientific theory. I should mention, by the way, that Bowlby's last book (Bowlby, 1990) was a biography of Darwin in which he claimed that the many illnesses Darwin suffered from throughout his life were psychosomatic and were due to bro-ken bonds of attachment Darwin had experienced as a child.

I should also mention that Hazan and Shaver's is not the only evolu-tionary theory of romantic love. Recent work by Buss and his colleagues (Buss, 1994; Buss & Schmitt, 1993) and Kenrick and his colleagues (Kenrick, Groth, Trost, & Sadella, 1993), as well as somewhat older work by Mellen (1981), Wilson (1983), and Hinde (1984), have also used the theory of evolu-tion by natural selection to explain behavior in romantic relationships. This work has focused specifically and primarily on how evolutionary theory may be used to account for sex differences in mate preferences, mating strategies, and specific behaviors in close, heterosexual relationships, with some very interesting and sometimes unsettling conclusions. According to Buss and Schmitt (1993), for example, evolution has favored the development of one kind of mating strategy in women and another in men, both "designed" to optimize the likelihood of their own genes being passed on. What results is a kind of sexual warfare in which women look for evidence of commitment in a potential romantic partner while men look for evidence of sexual receptivity.[4]

Love, romantic or otherwise, is an emotion that is largely absent from research on emotion from the Jamesian perspective. While common sense associates thumping hearts, hurried breaths, and flushed faces with the throes of romantic passion, the specific patterns of autonomic nervous system changes characteristic of love, if they indeed exist, have never been examined. James himself had a few things to say about love, of course (he had a few things to say about a great many things), but not in connection with his theory of emotion.

In particular, James included love in his discussion of instincts in *The Principles of Psychology* and concluded that both sexual and parental love are instinctual, that is, part of our evolutionary heritage (see James, 1890/1983, pp. 1053–1055). James repeats this opinion in his review of Henry T. Finck's (1887) *Romantic Love and Personal Beauty* (James, 1887; see also Averill, 1985). In the latter, James takes Finck to task for proposing that romantic love is of recent origin. Finck had concluded, after a detailed examination of literary and philosophical works on love, that romantic love as it was known in the late 1800s developed in the eleventh century (see also Averill, 1985), a conclusion with which James took great exception. Finck, James argued, "confounds men's feelings with their ideas about them . . . "

> So powerful and instinctive an emotion can never have been recently evolved. But our ideas *about* our emotions, and the esteem in which we hold them, differ very much from one generation to another; and literature (from which, of course, Mr. Finck's proofs have to be culled) is a record of ideas far more than of primordial psychologic facts. (James, 1887, p. 238)[5]

Just what the "primordial psychologic facts" of love are, especially with regard to the bodily changes associated with it, James is never clear. Nor have more recent researchers in the Jamesian tradition been able to precisely pin down the physiology of love, although Hatfield and Rapson

[4]This sounds like a legitimation for the old "double standard" doesn't it? One of the difficulties in trying to draw inferences about evolutionary processes from current social arrangements is that, sometimes, evolutionary and sociological theories make the same predictions. Feminists have long pointed to domination of women by men as the root cause of gender differences in behavior in close relationships (Ortner & Whitehead, 1981; see also Howard, Blumstein, & Schwartz, 1987). Currently, it's a matter of opinion—and politics—which theory, sociological or evolutionary, best accounts for the patterns of behavior in question.

[5]It is interesting to note in light of James' affection for Darwin's ideas that in his review he contended that Finck's book, "illustrates . . . the somewhat fatal effect of Darwinian ideas in letting loose the springs of irresponsible theorizing" (James, 1887, p. 238).

(1987) contend that passionate love is similar physiologically to sexual arousal. Romantic love and sexual arousal are indeed often closely associated with one another, and Hatfield and Rapson do make a good case for passionate love and sexual *desire* being similar (cynics, of course, have been saying this for some time). I think, however, that it is important to maintain a distinction between love and arousal.

Romantic love is an emotion and sexual arousal is a bodily state that may be instigated by romantic love; there is more to romantic love, presumably, than just sexual arousal (see Arnold, 1960a, p. 228 for a good discussion of how they are different), although it should be recognized that what one considers to be the components of love is a decision based on theory. We know a great deal about the physiology of sexual arousal (Rosen & Beck, 1988), but until more research is carried out on the specific patterns of bodily change associated with love, it is probably best to consider the two to be separate phenomena (Kelley & Byrne, 1983). We should not forget, however, that, occasionally, people, in their everyday lives, often do consider sexual arousal to be something akin to romantic love, a situation on which both Hatfield's theory of passionate love (Walster [Hatfield]1971) and Dutton and Aron's (1974) research on the misattribution of arousal capitalize (see Chapter 3).

Cognitively oriented students of emotion have had more to say about love than Jamesians, probably because love so obviously involves an appraisal of a particular person or object (see Frijda, 1986, p. 212). Indeed, the philosopher Robert Solomon, who sees emotions as primarily judgments about the world, defines love as one of the ways "we subjectively organize our experience" (Solomon, 1981, p. 40). Magda Arnold considered love to be a basic "impulse" emotion based on the simple appraisal of an object as beneficial (Arnold, 1960a, p. 196). However, because the object of the appraisal involved in love is likely to have "enduring value" to the person, Arnold distinguished love—along with hate—from more episodic emotions such as fear or anger and proposed that, sometimes, "[a] single emotional reaction may endure and develop into a sentiment, provided that the emotional object has enduring value beyond its immediate sensory appeal" (Arnold, 1960a, p. 199).

Sentiments, for Arnold, are more or less long-lasting emotional reactions to a particular object; in her words, they are, "enduring tendencies to react emotionally and overtly when the opportunity is given" (Arnold, 1960a, p. 199). Love, as a sentiment, may be expressed in an almost infinite number of ways and may give rise to a variety of other emotions, for example, jealousy and anger. However, "[t]he core of love . . . which is the sentiment remains identifiable throughout the various emotions and actions that grow out of it" (Arnold, 1960a, p. 199). At the center of all of the actions and emotions associated with love is an appraisal of the object of love as being valued over all others and, in most cases, we can say, an appraisal that the object of love reciprocates this appraisal (see Frijda, 1986, p. 343).

Within Lazarus' cognitive-motivational-relational theory of emotion, the core relational theme for love is

> *desiring or participating in affection, usually but not necessarily reciprocated.* In *romantic love* this consists of viewing the partner in a given moment in a highly positive way, probably but not necessarily with desire or passion, and the seeking of and yearning for sexual intimacy. (Lazarus, 1991a, p. 276)

The "primary appraisal components" upon which this core relational theme is based are "goal relevance" and "goal congruence," which together will produce any positive emotion, and "ego-involvement," which consists of a "desire for mutual appreciation." Given the appraisals of goal relevance and congruence, "[i]f the type of ego-involvement is desire for mutual appreciation, which is affirming to our ego-identity, then the emotion possibilities narrow to love (or at least liking); if to this is added sexual interest or passion, then love is romantic rather than companionate" (Lazarus, 1991a, p. 278).

Love, for Lazarus, being much more than a particular set of cognitive appraisals, also has a set of specific "action tendencies" associated with it. In romantic love, the action tendency is "the urge for both social intimacy and physical affection from the loved one," which includes "a strong impulse to approach, touch, and interact with the other and for mutual sexual gratification" (Lazarus, 1991a, p. 278). Joining ranks with attachment theorists such as Hazan and Shaver, Lazarus notes that the "desire for intimacy, commitment, and reciprocity" may be biologically determined. He nevertheless acknowledges that culture may play a considerable role in the experience of love when he avers that "[w]hat is attractive in the other is, of course, highly cultural and individual" (Lazarus, 1991a, p. 278). Unlike models of attraction that are based purely on reproductive strategies (e.g., Buss'), Lazarus' theory easily accounts for both heterosexual and homosexual romantic attraction.

Lazarus takes pains to emphasize that love, as an emotion, is "a process or a *momentary state,* a reaction that comes and goes" (Lazarus, 1991a, p. 274), just like any other emotion. He does this because we often confuse love-the-emotion with love-the-relationship. As a social relationship, love may, and often does, involve all kinds of other emotions such as anger and joy, to name just a few. Within a love relationship, of course, one expects that the partners involved do at least occasionally experience love for one another, and to develop "a disposition to feel love under appropriate conditions" (Lazarus, 1991a, p. 274). Nevertheless, while a love relationship is something that is more or less continuous during its existence, love itself, "is not necessarily constant" (Lazarus, 1991a, p. 274).

In spite of what Lazarus says, there is something artificial about his distinction between love-the-relationship and love-the-emotion, even if the distinction is intuitively pleasing. What is going on in love-the-emotion that is not going on in love-the-relationship? Wouldn't the basis of any love relationship, at least in American culture, be the exact same set of appraisals and action tendencies Lazarus identifies as being essential features of love-the-emotion? I think what Lazarus is trying to do by making the distinction is to preserve for love the *episodic* quality that is characteristic of emotions like anger or fear (see Ekman, 1984).

Although some episodes of anger may indeed last a long time (Averill, 1982), most of the time, our anger rises and falls rather quickly. Likewise with fear. Love, however, may be different. Comparing love with other emotions that *do* have an episodic quality, it is difficult to see how a person could have a brief, momentary experience of love. To be sure, we do say things like, "I'm feeling a lot of love for you right now," in the same way we say, "I'm feeling very angry at you right now!" I wonder, however, if in the former case we aren't so much describing our feelings as we are describing the state of our relationship with our beloved.[6] Averill uses this notion as the starting point for his social constructivist theory of romantic love.

In keeping with his conception of emotions as "socially constituted syndromes" (see Chapter 5), Averill considers love to consist of a number of component parts—idealization of the loved one, suddenness of onset, physiological arousal, and demonstrations of commitment—that together form a kind of cultural ideal for the experience of love (Averill, 1985). None of these component parts taken alone is sufficient for the experience of love to occur, but when all are present, a person's experience is not only more likely to be interpreted as love, but the experience is likely to be considered particularly intense or representative of what love should be.

Love, according to Averill, is an *interpretation* that we place on our behavior when it conforms to a socially constructed ideal. This ideal is a kind of blueprint or template that we use to make sense out of our experience ("If X is happening, then I must be in love") and, just as importantly, guide our behavior. "In its broadest sense," Averill says, "love refers to the principle(s) by which people organize their relationships with one another" (1985, pp. 90–91). When a person says "I love you" to another person, Averill argues, he or she is interpreting his or her experience and behavior in a

---

[6]Allison Nydick and I (Nydick & Cornelius, 1984) asked a similar question in a study of first-time confessions of love in the relationships of young adults. We concluded that, often, when young adults say "I love you" for the first time in a romantic relationship, they are not so much describing how they feel as they are asking for a reciprocal avowal from their partner.

particular manner and is entering into a certain kind of relationship with the person, a relationship that carries with it socially constituted expectations and obligations. "Paradigms of emotion, such as the romantic ideal, provide the individual with a model and rationale for behavior" (Averill, 1985, p. 93). When I say "I love you" to a person, there are certain things I'm *expected* to do and feel (idealize my beloved, display fidelity to him or her, feel tenderly toward him or her, etc.) by other people and by *myself.* When my experience and behavior match the template, I can say, without qualification, that I am indeed in love.

In a study of the extent to which people's experiences of love conform to the romantic ideal, Averill and Boothroyd had subjects rate how much their own experiences matched the following description of a rather extreme romantic encounter.

> On Monday, Cpl. Floyd Johnson, 23, and the then Ellen Skinner, 19, total strangers, boarded a train at San Francisco and sat down across the aisle from each other. Johnson didn't cross the aisle until Wednesday, but his bride said, "I'd already made up my mind to say yes if he asked me to marry him." "We did most of the talking with our eyes," Johnson explained. Thursday the couple got off the train in Omaha with plans to be married. (Averill & Boothroyd, 1977; originally cited in Burgess & Wallin, 1953, p. 151)

Averill and Boothroyd found that about 40% of their subjects said that their "most intense" experience of love did indeed resemble the description. About the same number of subjects, however, reported that their experience *did not* resemble it. What is interesting about these findings is that when Averill and Boothroyd examined their subjects' descriptions of their own relationships, they found that few of the descriptions of those subjects who said their experiences did resemble the ideal actually matched the ideal very closely.

Averill argues that what the subjects in the study were doing was reinterpreting their experiences in light of the romantic ideal. He concludes from this that, to the extent to which our experience of love includes idealization, suddenness of onset, some kind of commitment, and some sign of physiological arousal, we will interpret it as conforming to the romantic ideal and will use that ideal to guide and make sense of our behavior.

Averill, unlike Hazan and Shaver, does not view romantic love as something that has "always and everywhere existed as a biological potential" (Hazan & Shaver, 1987, p. 523). Rather, romantic love is a relatively recent social construction, the experience of which depends on the existence of certain social arraignments such as a separation of the individual from the collective and an extreme valuation of the individual and his or her rights. On an individual level, the function of love, like anger, is to provide a rationale for certain forms of behavior. Think here of what it means to say, "I couldn't help myself, I was in love." Professing our love for another allows us to violate some social norms (for example, the prohibition against premarital and extramarital sexual relations) and provides a legitimation for our behavior. Nydick and I (Nydick & Cornelius, 1984), for example, found that young adults quite often profess their love for a person the morning after sleeping with him or her for the first time. On a broader social level, romantic love serves as one way to ensure that heterosexual couples will form lasting, potentially procreative relationships in the absence of other social arraignments that might produce such couplings (see Greenfield, 1965).

If romantic love is a social construction, what about the biology of love? Averill would not disagree with the notion that most heterosexual relationships function to ensure that the human species gets reproduced and he probably would not disagree with the idea that our behavior in relationships is influenced by biological systems such as attachment (see Averill, 1990a). Averill does not deny that the attachment system is involved in romantic love. Romantic love, however, is more than just attachment. The supposed biological desire to be close to another person says nothing about how that desire is experienced, how it gets translated into actual behavior, what part it plays in a particular relationship, or what local social norms say about it. All of these, Averill would say, are just as much a part of love as is attachment, and they are aspects of love that are social constructions in a nontrivial sense. Attachment and other biological systems (e.g., sexual reproduction, but also vision, audition, gustation, olfaction, and perhaps even digestion) are surely important components of an emotion like romantic love, but love, for the social constructivist, cannot be reduced to attachment or any other biological system. Moreover, attachment itself is not immune to social influence and must be, moreover, expressed or *enacted* through some particularly complex, socially scripted behaviors (see Duck, 1994, pp. 170–171). As Averill says, "there is no hidden core to love, no component that represents love's true essence; and . . . when we examine love's components we do not find any that are not heavily and fundamentally influenced by social factors" (Averill, 1985, p. 107).

Hope.   Hope, as I said above, is a problematic emotion for many emotion theorists. Although most emotion theorists do not consider it to be a prototypical emotion (Averill, Catlin, & Chon, 1990), it nevertheless is something that people in the street regard as an emotion and report experiencing with some frequency in their everyday lives (Averill, 1975; Fehr & Russell, 1984; Shaver et al., 1987). Given its ubiquity, and the important role it plays in many people's lives (e.g., as the opposite of or antidote to despair), it is odd indeed that hope is not given the attention that it clearly deserves.

Darwin does not mention hope in his analysis of emotion and, like love, hope is not included in Ekman's list of basic emotions. As with love, hope has not found its way into Ekman's research because there is no easily distinguishable facial expression associated with hope, which for Ekman, of course, is a sine qua non of emotion (see Ekman, 1984). Hope was one of the emotions included in Antoinette Feleky's list of emotion names that her subjects were to match with her posed facial expressions (see Chapter 2). A small number of subjects identified the expressions she posed for "attention to an object" and "religious feeling" as hope (see Feleky, 1914, Table 1, p. 37), with the latter being the closest she came to posing hope directly—in her later, more extensive analysis of her data, she refers to this expression as "[p]osed for prayer that accident should not take place" (Feleky, 1924, p. 189).

Feleky's report that some of her subjects associated hope with the facial expression for attention to an object is interesting because Izard (1977) regards hope as a subspecies of the basic emotion of interest. Interest, according to Izard (1977), is, "the most prevalent motivational condition for the day-to-day functioning of normal human beings" (p. 211), and is, "the most frequently experienced positive emotion" (p. 212). It is a product of evolution in his view, and is behind all of our efforts to explore and learn about our environment. Befitting its status as an emotion so essential to human life, it is present from birth. And, even though the facial expression of interest is often difficult to identify, Izard argues that it nevertheless has a characteristic expression.

Izard has much to say about interest but he doesn't have all that much to say about hope. Hope, according to Izard (1977), following the learning-theory analysis of hope presented by Stotland (1969), occurs when one has some expectation of achieving a goal (cf. Snyder, 1994). When a goal is important to us and the probability of attaining it is high, we experience high levels of hope and positive affect such as joy or pleasure. When a goal is important to us and the probability of attaining it is low, however, we experience low levels of hope and high levels of negative emotions such as anxiety. Much like a cognitive emotion theorist, Izard thus defines hope in terms of the expectations we have about particular states of affair. Hope is important, according to Izard, because the basic emotion with which it is associated, interest, provides a level of stimulation during interaction with the environment that all organisms find reinforcing. Without this affective component, presumably, organisms wouldn't find exploring their environment very rewarding.

Notice that even though Izard sees hope as having an important role in the motivation of behavior, he doesn't say anything about the experience of hope as an emotion per se. Izard is not alone in this regard, as William James was silent on hope as an emotion and, to my knowledge, hope has never been included in any Jamesian-type research. Izard (1977) does argue that the emotion of interest has a characteristic feeling component, and so, by association, one would presume that hope would also. Izard, however, never describes what hope might feel like or what the pattern of physiological changes associated with hope might be. At this time, it is anybody's guess whether or not hope has a characteristic pattern of autonomic nervous system changes with which it is associated.

Hope gets somewhat better treatment from cognitively oriented emotion theorists. Arnold regarded hope as one of the basic emotions. Strong enough to be considered a "contending" emotion within her scheme of things, hope is elicited when a beneficial object that is currently not present is "judged attainable" (Arnold, 1960a, p. 196). Roseman (1984) classifies hope as a positive, circumstance-caused, motive-consistent emotion elicited when the occurrence of the appraised event is uncertain. Lazarus (1991a) also emphasizes the uncertainty of the appraised event in hope, but considers hope to be a *negative* emotion. Because hope at first appears to be a "goal-congruent" emotion, but in fact occurs in "goal-incongruent" situations, and because hope has no clear-cut action tendency with which it is associated, Lazarus describes hope as a "problematic emotion."

The core relational theme for hope, according to Lazarus (1991a) is, "yearning for amelioration of a dreaded outcome," or, *"fearing the worst but yearning for better"* (p. 282, his emphasis). The "primary appraisal components" of hope include "goal relevance" and "goal incongruence," which together may produce any negative emotion, as well as hope. These primary appraisal components, when combined with the secondary appraisal of uncertain "future expectations," produce hope (Lazarus, 1991a, p. 284). "Ego-involvement" is also an important aspect of the appraisal structure of hope to the extent to which the hoped for event involves our self-esteem, our loved ones and their well-being, or our life goals. In terms of ego-involvement, our hopes span a range from the very general or abstract, what I call "birthday candle hopes" (e.g., world peace, a cure for cancer), to the very specific (e.g., "I hope *she* doesn't start an argument again and prolong the faculty meeting another hour!").

Consistent with his classification of emotions as positive or negative depending on whether they are goal congruent or incongruent, Lazarus regards hope as a negative emotion because it involves a desire to avoid or escape from a negative situation. Hope may lead us to *feel* better, that is, more positive about an unpleasant state of affairs, but it is nevertheless an emotion that is based on a situation that is at odds with our goals and desires. Lazarus is also somewhat less than sanguine about the positive effects of hope. Hope is certainly preferable to despair, both as an experience and as a motivator; as Lazarus says, "hope sustains constructive efforts . . . [and] mitigates emotional distress and dysfunction" (Lazarus, 1991a, p. 283). Hope, however, may sometimes lead us to have unrealistic expectations and to remain committed to a course of action that we would be better off abandoning. In such situations, we "hope against hope" that what we don't want to happen probably will. The danger of this kind of hope, says Lazarus, is that it may leave us vulnerable to disappointment.

Similar in some respects to Lazarus' account of hope, Averill and his colleagues' social constructivist theory emphasizes the appraisal rules for hope and the open-ended nature of the behaviors associated with the emotion. After a historical survey of the some of the major teachings on hope in the Western intellectual tradition, Averill, Catlin, and Chon (1990) conclude that (1) hope is an important emotion to study given its prominence in the cultural traditions of the West, (2) hope is considered by many thinkers in the West (e.g., Aquinas, Hume, Kant) to be a basic emotion, and (3) conceptions of hope are historically and culturally relative. Averill et al. use these conclusions as the framework for a series of empirical studies of the everyday experience of hope in the United States and Korea.

On the basis of these studies, Averill et al. argue that hope may be described by means of three general principles or rules:

> The first principle emphasizes prudence—hope necessarily involves some uncertainty, but people should not hope for objects that are too improbable or unrealistic. The second principle concerns the importance of the object—people should not hope for trivial events . . . The third principle reflects moral values—people should not hope for objects that are socially unacceptable. (Averill et al., 1990, p. 13)

Averill et al. found that, within the limits specified by these rules, the kinds of events people hope for are greatly influenced by the degree of personal control they feel they have over the hoped-for events. The same is true for the affective experiences and behavioral responses associated with hope.

The affective experiences and behavioral responses that Averill et al. found to be associated with hope are particularly interesting because they appear to be so variable. Indeed, with regard to the former, Averill et al. were led to declare that, "[d]epending on the initiating circumstances, hope may be embedded in nearly opposite overall patterns of feeling" (Averill et al., 1990, p. 22). This makes sense when we think of all of the different kinds of situations that might elicit hope. While they all must include an element of uncertainty, one may experience hope in situations involving the whole gamut of common as well as uncommon emotions, from joy and love to resentment, sadness, and anxiety. Lazarus, thinking along similar lines, concluded that, "hope cannot be distinguished from what is hoped for any more than anger can be divorced from what one is angry about" (Lazarus, 1991a, p. 284).

Averill et al. found that when people felt a sense of control over the events they hoped for, they reported that they tended to "work harder" and be more "persistent" in their efforts to bring about those events. Hope, however, was not associated with any particular pattern of behavior. Hope appears to be similar to anger in this regard. Just as there is no single way to seek retribution from a person who has wronged you, so too, there is no single way to behave hopefully. The open-ended nature of hope in this regard fits well with Averill's conception of emotions as syndromes of behavior whose constituent parts are loosely bound together by means of social rules. What makes a particular experience or behavior "hopeful" is whether it conforms to the rules of hope; there appears to be no one set of feelings or behaviors that define the emotion. Significantly, Averill et al. found that the experience of hope is much like that of other emotions such as anger and love in that, given the appropriate instigating conditions, one "'can't help' but hope" (Averill et al., 1990, p. 46). Hope, in other words, is experienced as a "passion," just like other emotions (see Chapter 5).

Averill et al. found several differences between the ways Koreans and Americans experience hope. Koreans, for example, tended to report more achievement-related objects of hope than did Americans. The objects of the Korean subjects' altruistic hopes also tended to be broader and less specific than the American subjects': "I hoped to be the most humanistic person" vs. "I hoped my sister would have a healthy baby" (Averill et al., 1990, p. 83). Koreans also saw the objects of their hopes as more attainable and more under their control than did Americans. In addition, Koreans thought of hope more as a personality characteristic or disposition than as an emotion, and perhaps because of this, their experience of hope seemed to be less influenced by the amount of control they believed they had over the events they hoped for. Averill et al. relate the differences between the way Americans and Koreans experience hope to the influence of the Judeo-Christian intellectual and religious traditions on American culture and Confucian intellectual and religious traditions on Korean culture (see especially pp. 85–89). Given the very different emphases placed on hope in the two traditions, it is no surprise, they argue, that American and Korean conceptions of hope are so at variance with one another.

Having Your Cake and Eating It Too?
Integrating Research from the Four Perspectives

At the beginning of this chapter I asked whether or not it was possible to integrate research conducted from within each of the four perspectives on emotion into a kind of grand theory. I put off answering the question until we had had a chance to consider what research within each of the traditions had contributed to our general knowledge about emotion and had examined what each of the perspectives had to say about four specific emotions.

It's now time to face this most difficult and daunting question head-on. Is it indeed possible to combine research on emotion from the four perspectives meaningfully, or are the four perspectives truly incommensurate?

To a certain extent, the question may already have been answered in the work of Paul Ekman, Phoebe Ellsworth, Nico Frijda, Craig Smith, and others.[7] I've mentioned several times throughout the book that Ekman is both a Darwinian and a Jamesian. Carroll Izard and Ross Buck, about whose important research on the communication of emotions I have said far too little, may also be considered both Darwinians and Jamesians. Indeed, you may have noticed in the preceding section how comfortably the Darwinian, Jamesian, and cognitive perspectives fit together in Ekman's and Izard's accounts of anger and fear. In emphasizing the universality of the eliciting conditions and expressions of emotion and the role that autonomic arousal plays in the experience of emotion, Ekman's and Izard's work combines elements of both the Darwinian and Jamesian approaches to the study of emotions and presupposes, to some extent, the process of appraisal in the generation of emotion.

To get a sense of how cognitive Ekman and Izard are, compare what they have to say about the conditions that instigate anger and fear with what Lazarus says about such conditions. Lazarus, of course, is much more self-conscious about specifying the appraisals that elicit these two emotions, but what Ekman and Izard say does not differ appreciably from his analysis. Likewise, Lazarus, while he sees appraisal as being of central importance in understanding emotion, does not deny that universal action tendencies, facial expressions, or patterns of autonomic change might exist for some emotions (see Lazarus, 1991a, pp. 68–78). As he has recently said, "I believe that . . . facial and other forms of expression and neurophysiological changes bear a systematic relationship to each other and to the kinds and intensities of emotion that people experience" (Lazarus, 1991a, pp. 77–78). Similar conclusions may be found in Smith's (1989) attempt to link specific appraisals with specific patterns of physiological reactivity and facial expression. Smith's work combines elements of the Darwinian, Jamesian, and cognitive perspectives.

Thus, I think there is a real sense in which the Darwinian, Jamesian, and cognitive perspectives have already begun to be combined in the theories of Ekman, Izard, Lazarus, and Smith, as well as those of Buck (1985, 1984). There do not seem to be any aspects of the three perspectives that are entirely incommensurate. Even Ekman's contention that there are "universal, abstract, *prototypical* situations" (Ekman, 1984) that elicit what he considers to be the basic emotions would probably not get a rise out of Lazarus

---

[7] I had originally included only Ekman and Izard in this list. Craig Smith, however, pointed out how much the various perspectives were also integrated in the work of Ellsworth, Smith, and Frijda.

as long as Ekman acknowledged that *some* kind of appraisal process mediates the effects of such situations. The odd perspective out here, of course, is social constructivism. If any of the perspectives is at odds with the others, it is social constructivism. But is it really?

We have already seen how closely allied the cognitive and social constructivist perspectives are. As I said in Chapter 5, the social constructivist approach to emotions grew out of the cognitive approach and most social constructivist accounts of emotion place great emphasis on appraisal. That Averill assigns such a central role to appraisal in his social constructivist theory suggests that there may not be any basic incompatibility between these two approaches. Indeed, Ellsworth's (1994a) recent exploration of cross-cultural similarities and differences in the dimensions of appraisal is a bold attempt to bring a kind of evolutionary cognitive perspective and aspects of the constructivist perspective together. There does seem to be a considerable distance, however, between the Darwinian and Jamesian perspectives on the one hand and the social constructivist perspective on the other, at least as the latter is represented by theorists such as Averill, Harré, and Armon-Jones. Frijda's (see Frijda & Mesquita, 1994) recent account of his theory of emotion, however, combines elements of the Darwinian, Jamesian, and cognitive perspectives and, with his consideration of the role of culture in shaping emotions, his work draws upon constructivist thinking as well. Thus, the incompatibility between the constructivist and other three perspectives may be more apparent than real.

The basic assumption of the Darwinian perspective is that emotions are evolved phenomena and as such should show considerable uniformity within the human species. Jamesians hold that emotions are differentiated at the level of the autonomic nervous system and that feedback from the ANS or the face gives emotions their characteristic qualities. Together, Darwinians and Jamesians (I'm thinking here of Ekman and Izard, of course) believe that there are a small number of basic emotions that are constituted by specific patterns of ANS changes and characteristic expressions that can be seen on the face of humans living anywhere on the planet. Averill and Armon-Jones explicitly reject these assumptions. For both Averill and Armon-Jones and other social constructivists as well, emotions are not primarily biological phenomena; they are, rather, primarily social phenomena. How can such opposing views be reconciled?

The key to reconciling these apparently irreconcilable perspectives, I think, resides in the question of how one defines emotion or, more precisely, at what level of organization one places emotion. Darwinians and Jamesians and social constructivists may simply be calling different things emotions because each defines emotions in terms of different levels of organization. Let me illustrate what I mean by levels of organization by talking for a moment about eating. No one would deny that eating is a biological necessity, but eating, at least among humans, is much more than simply the process of providing the cells in one's body with the nutrients they need. A full understanding of eating would include reference to the neurophysiological mechanisms that control eating as well as to the physiology of taste, olfaction, and digestion. Attention to the neurophysiology of eating and digestion is, of course, attention to the biological aspects of eating, and so we could say these refer to the biological level of organization of the phenomenon. An understanding of eating in humans would also include, however, reference to a person's learning history and the idiosyncratic patterns of food choice and consumption that he or she has developed over a lifetime. Food is the source of the nutrients our bodies require, but food also has *meaning* (the label on the candy bar I'm eating right now, for example, says it's "Athletic Energy Food" and so I don't feel as guilty eating it as I would if it were labeled "Pure Sugar Rush"). A full understanding of eating requires that we pay attention to the habits and meanings associated with eating. We can think of this as the psychological level of organization of eating. Eating is also an organized social activity, and a full understanding of eating also requires us to attend to the ways in which eating is an important occasion of interaction among people and the reflection of and vehicle for the transmission of important cultural values. Important social "work" gets accomplished at mealtimes, from reaffirming affective bonds to planning joint activities, and we consume our food according to established social custom—such customs govern both how we eat and what we eat. Particular kinds of meals, the business lunch, the formal banquet, and the first-date dinner, for example, also have specific "interactional scripts" associated with them.[8] The levels of organization represented by the social aspects of eating are the social-psychological, the sociological, and the cultural.

Eating, then, may be studied in terms of any of its levels of organization. It is possible to study eating as a purely biological phenomenon, but, for most mammals at least, that is not all there is to eating. Eating as a coherent pattern of activity is organized biologically, psychologically, social-psychologically, and sociologically. Likewise, emotions may be seen as being organized on a variety of levels. Neurophysiologists are interested— almost by definition—in the neural organization of emotion, Darwinians are interested in the evolutionary organization of emotion, Jamesians are interested in the bodily organization of emotion (for want of a better term), cognitive-emotion theorists are interested in the psychological organization of emotion, and social constructivists are interested in the social-psychological and sociological organization of emotion. The difference between the Darwinians and Jamesians and the social constructivists is at least partly a matter of what level of organization each chooses to emphasize.

[8] I thank Craig Smith for pointing this out to me.

As we have seen, Averill does not deny that emotions may have component aspects that are entirely biologically determined (see also Averill, 1979b; Averill & Nunley, 1993). He does deny that emotions can be explained *entirely* by reference to biological principles, however. For someone like Averill, the most meaningful way to make sense out of the almost overwhelming number and complexity of emotional phenomena is to think of emotions as being organized into coherent wholes at the social or sociological level. Ekman, on the other hand, sees emotions as being organized at a much different level of organization, the biological. One might be tempted (I have been) to call the level of organization Averill emphasizes "higher" than the ones emphasized by Ekman since what Ekman calls emotions, that is, the facial expressions, patterns of visceral activity, and perhaps appraisals associated with emotion, Averill calls components of emotion. However, one could just as easily think of the *species* level of organization that Ekman emphasizes in his insistence that emotions are human universals as being higher than the cultural level that Averill emphasizes.

To a very great extent, I think, the major differences between Darwinians and Jamesians on the one hand and social constructivists on the other reside in what aspects of emotion each chooses to emphasize. Darwinians and Jamesians emphasize the continuity of emotional experience and expression across the human species, while social constructivists emphasize their discontinuity across individuals and cultures. Because of this, theorists within each perspective may be referring to somewhat different phenomena when they use the term emotion. The "polythetic" syndromes of Averill's theory and the genetically determined patterns of facial expression and physiological activation ("affect programs") of Ekman and Izard are clearly very different creatures. Averill casts a wide net and finds all kinds of phenomena in it that Ekman, Izard, and company don't consider to be emotional. This is not to say that there are no points of contact among the four perspectives. As we have seen, Averill includes reference to specieswide, biological aspects of emotion in his theory and Ekman acknowledges the importance of culture and learning on the expression, and, by implication, the experience of emotion (see Chapter 2 on "display rules"). Izard (1983) has even conceded that there may exist culturally specific "feeling rules" of the sort described by Arlie Hochschild (1979). Let us also not forget that the major point of contact of the Darwinian, Jamesian, and constructivist perspectives is the cognitive perspective. If an integration of the four perspectives is to take place, it will probably be through the way the cognitive perspective offers a way to talk meaningfully about both universals and cultural constructions in the generation of emotional experience as, for example, Ellsworth does (1994a).[9]

---

[9]I again thank Craig Smith for this insight.

I may be stretching things a bit, but I see no reason why future students of emotion (that's you) can't draw liberally from all four perspectives in developing a theory of emotion that takes seriously the full range and complexity of emotional phenomena. We are complex physiological systems with a long evolutionary history who exist in complex, socially constructed environments and whose emotional reactions to the world are determined both by built-in response mechanisms and less automatic, meaning-mediated mechanisms. In order to understand emotions, one must take into account their evolutionary history and functions, the ways in which they are embodied in patterns of physiological changes, the role that cognition plays in their elicitation and experience, *and* the ways in which they are products of individual learning and culture with important individual and social functions. Quite a tall order, of course, but psychology is a young science with much to learn and emotions have only recently come under the kind of intensive scrutiny they deserve.

Harmonic Convergence?

Several years ago a devotee of New Age religious ideas predicted the coming of a "harmonic convergence" in which the alignment of the planets would usher in a new era of spiritual transcendence and world peace (Barol & Abramson, 1987). The predicted convergence of all of the world's differences, alas, did not take place, but there are signs that a convergence of the four theoretical perspectives on emotions may already be happening. A recent introductory textbook by Neil Carlson (1990), a physiological psychologist, presents research by Darwinians, Jamesians, cognitivists, and social constructivists side-by-side without batting an eyelash. More substantively, the "new functionalism" proposed by Joseph Campos (see Campos & Barnett, 1984; Campos, 1994) holds the prospect of being a truly integrative theory of emotion to the extent to which it emphasizes the biological, psychological, and social functions of emotions and acknowledges the diverse biological and social influences on the development of emotions in infants and children. Frijda's (see Frijda & Mesquita, 1994) emotion theory is also broadly integrative and, for that reason, will probably have considerable influence on thinking about emotion in the near future. Ironically, LeDoux's (LeDoux, 1987, 1989) "dual pathway" neurophysiological model of emotional learning has the potential to provide a physiological basis for claims that emotions are both inherited, primitive, automatic reactions and learned, cognitively mediated responses. Perhaps there is hope for a harmonic convergence after all.

Further Reading

CAMPOS, J. J., & BARNETT, K. C. (1984). Toward a new understanding of emotions and their development. In C. E. Izard, J. Kagan, & R. B. Zajonc (Eds.), *Emotions, cognition, and behavior* (pp. 229–263). Cambridge: Cambridge University Press.

FRIJDA, N. H., & MESQUITA, B. (1994). The social roles and functions of emotions. In S. Kitayama & H. R. Markus (Eds.), *Emotion and culture. Empirical studies of mutual influence* (pp. 51–87). Washington, DC: American Psychological Association.

7

Concluding Unscientific Postscript

◆

Emotions and You

As I said in Chapter 1, I wanted to make this book more personal than the standard psychology textbook. I am a scientist, but I am also a human being, and I've always thought it was important not to separate these two parts of my life. Psychology speaks to me through the theoretical and empirical knowledge that I've gained about people from my own and other people's research as well as through the filter of my own experience. In this book, I've tried to let psychology speak to you in the same way. If I've been successful, then you've been able to glimpse a little bit of your own experience reflected in some of the examples I've used in presenting what we know about emotion from the four perspectives on emotion. This book is not intended to be one of those much-maligned self-help manuals, but I hope that you've found and will find at least some of what I've told you helpful and useful. Before concluding, I want to outline briefly some of the ways in which the research associated with the four perspectives might be of use to you in your everyday life.

The most general thing I hope you've learned from this book is that it is indeed possible to study emotions scientifically and that scientists who are students of emotion have learned a great deal about them. People who reject the idea that emotions are fitting objects of scientific scrutiny often back up their rejection of a science of emotion by describing emotions as purely personal, individual phenomena that can't be pinned down or precisely described in any way. If nothing else, I hope you've learned from this book that nothing could be further from what we now know about emotions. The practical side of knowing that emotions are not completely individual and unknowable is the recognition that other people's emotions are much like our own. If they weren't, most of the ways in which we make ourselves known to other people in everyday life would be impossible. Think about what life would be like if you had no idea what someone else meant when she or he said, "I really like you," or "I know how you feel." I'll have more to say about this notion shortly.

Moving from the most specific lessons to the most general, we can take from the research associated with the Jamesian perspective the idea that you may be able to alter your experience of certain emotions or moods by simply changing your posture. We've all had days when we are down-in-the-dumps, when we slouch around, and seem to wear a perpetual frown. According to James' original insight and the research we examined by Laird, Strack, and others, you can expect your mood to brighten somewhat if you are able to straighten up your posture and put a smile on your face (or simply hold a pencil in your mouth so that it doesn't touch your lips). As we've seen, there is more to emotion than just feedback from our bodies, of course, but such feedback does seem to add something important to our experience. We listen to our bodies all of the time when they tell us they are hungry or in pain, so why not turn the usual direction of influence around and use what we know of the relationship between feedback from the body and the experience of emotion to influence our emotions? What harm can there be from acting as if our bodies mattered? At the very least, you'll receive positive feedback from your friends and acquaintances about how self-confident and happy you look (or how silly you look if you haven't taken the pencil out of your mouth). And if the research on bodily feedback and emotional change has any validity, which it certainly seems to, then you'll also have a second source of influence helping you to get out from under the cloud that's been following you around.[1]

Missing from the advice we'd get from the Jamesians is the recognition that, in most episodes of emotion, our emotions depend in a crucial way on how we think about or appraise events in the world. According to the cognitive perspective, our goals and motivations, indeed, all of the things we believe about the world around us, are crucial components of our emotions. As my old teacher Seymour Epstein used to say, if you want to discover what's important to a person, look at the kinds of things over which he or she becomes emotional. This idea has at least two practical applications. First, you can use this idea to let your emotions teach you about

---

[1]Recent research suggests that certain kinds of repetitive, rhythmic activity may also alleviate depression (Jacobs, 1994), so get out your bongos and beat your blues away!

how you view the world. One way to do this is to keep a daily diary of your most intense positive and negative emotions (this is one of Epstein's research strategies, see Epstein, 1982). Write down what seemed to instigate each emotion and what you did while you were emotional. After a while you should notice a pattern emerging in the kinds of emotions you experience often, in what kinds of things you get emotional about, and in how you behave emotionally. Once you begin to recognize the patterns in your emotional life, you can work on changing them if you want, which is the second practical application of Epstein's idea. If our emotions are indeed dependent on our beliefs about the world, we can change how we respond emotionally to the world by changing our beliefs. This is a lot more difficult than it sounds, of course, but the basic idea is a sound one (as well as being the idea behind modern cognitive approaches to psychotherapy). Sometimes just finding out about some of the factors that influence our emotions, however, is enough.

Given their close association, it is no surprise that social constructivists would offer the same advice as their cognitively oriented colleagues with regard to changing our emotions: namely, if you want to change your emotions, you must first change your beliefs. For social constructivists, however, emotions are not merely a function of how we appraise the events in our lives, emotions also have important social functions. Because of this, the ways in which we appraise events, according to the social constructivist perspective, reflect what we, individually, and our culture, collectively, value. Exploring the kinds of things that make us emotional, then, is also a way to explore what our culture values. The idea that what our culture values is intimately connected with our emotions, coupled with the notion that emotions have important social functions, suggests that changing our emotions might not be as easy as it at first sounds because there is likely to be a certain degree of "cultural inertia" resisting any such changes, as women desiring to be assertive and men desiring to be more tender have discovered. Nevertheless, transforming one's typical emotional reactions or acquiring new emotions as an adult is not out of the question. Indeed, emotional transformation and growth supposedly happen all of the time in psychotherapy, as Averill's analysis of the acquisition of emotions in adulthood would predict.

The social constructivist perspective on emotions should also teach us to be more sensitive to cultural differences in the experience and expression of emotion. While certain forms of emotional expression may indeed be universal, it is likely that the full meaning of emotions is culturally determined. Even though weeping or a frown may connote sadness in almost every culture, knowing when such an expression and its associated emotion is appropriate and how one responds to such an expression, both in oneself and in others, may be largely a matter of social convention (see Averill, 1979, on the social functions and meanings of grief reactions). Paradoxically, while we should be sensitive to cultural differences in the experience and expression of emotion, we should also be sensitive to the *similarities* across cultures in the experience and expression of emotion.

The most valuable lesson we can learn from the Darwinian perspective is that, to use a phrase from the personality psychologist Harry Stack Sullivan, *"everyone is much more simply human than otherwise"* (Sullivan, 1953, p. 32). What Sullivan meant by this is that, despite all of our many differences, both within and across cultures, we are all intimately connected by our common humanity. The fact that you can go anywhere in the world and look into the eyes of another person and get at least a dim sense of what he or she is feeling is a powerful affirmation of the biological bonds that tie us all together as a species. Underneath all of the differences that appear to us to be so significant, we are all very much the same. To be sure, each of us is unique, the product of our individual genetic and learning histories and the families, societies, and cultures into which we were born, but we share much more with other humans than we think.

As I write this, various ethnic, political, and religious groups in the former Yugoslavia strive to exterminate not only their rivals but any trace of their rivals as a people. This is called genocide. I've followed the accounts of the horrors of the "ethnic cleansing" practiced in Bosnia with a sense of sad recognition. Genocide campaigns presuppose that those who must be exterminated are somehow less than human, and what is happening in Bosnia is no exception. The dehumanization of the victim allows one to destroy those who are innocent or in the way with a "clear conscience" (see Sabini & Silver, 1982, pp. 55–87). From the Holocaust of a half century ago to the ethnic cleansing of last week, the process is depressingly the same. Turning the "Other" into a monster or an animal or merely something faceless allows crimes of unspeakable cruelty and magnitude to be committed. Perhaps, in a small way, what Darwin and his followers have had to say about our shared humanity may help to stem our tendency to dehumanize those whom we don't like. The dream of the Enlightenment was the recognition of a common bond among all humans that surpassed religious, cultural, and political differences, and to these we now add racial, ethnic, and lifestyle differences. Darwin and his followers have taught us how strong and deep that bond is, it is up to us to recognize it.

Darwin and his followers have also taught us how strong and deep the bonds we have with other species are. As humans, we share a common ancestry with our fellow humans, as primates, we also share a common ancestry with other primates, and, as mammals, we share a common ancestry with other mammals, and so on. We are, indeed, part of a vast web of biological interconnections. Just as we can see ourselves in the face of any other human, so, Darwin taught us, we can see ourselves in the faces of other animals. Just as our failure to keep in mind our connectedness to other humans has led us to commit atrocious crimes against our fellow humans, our failure to recognize the connections we share with another animals has led us to commit atrocious crimes against our fellow animals. Our more general failure to recognize our place in the web of life has made it easy, I think, to treat nature as a thing to be used or gotten rid of when it suits us, with barely a thought given to the consequences (Merchant, 1979). The Darwinian view of life reminds us of the many ways in which we are inextricably a part of the natural world (Wilson, 1984) and it should help us to develop a sense of caring for that which is the mother of us all.

Emotions are central to our experience of the world and are crucial to our survival. Emotions and how they have been studied in psychology tell us important things about the world around us, about science, about psychology, and about ourselves. Just as emotions help us to avoid dangerous situations or stick up for ourselves, they can also help us to develop and sustain an approach to living with our fellow humans and the natural world based on the recognition of similarities as well as the appreciation of differences, on empathy instead of exploitation, on love instead of fear, on caring instead of hate.

Appendix
The Neurophysiology of Emotion

◆

Briefer Course

What follows is intended to provide you with a very brief overview of what are currently believed to be the neurophysiological mechanisms underlying most emotions. Without writing an entire book, there is no way that I can present a comprehensive account of what we know about the brain and emotion. Such an account would probably soon be outdated anyway, as our knowledge of the brain and nervous system grows daily. Indeed, the neurosciences are among the fastest growing areas of contemporary science. More comprehensive discussions of the neurophysiology of emotion are nevertheless available in LeDoux (1986) and Carlson (1994), among other sources (for example, McNaughton, 1989). For this appendix I have drawn heavily on LeDoux's 1986 excellent summary of the neurobiology of emotion and I recommend it, or any of his writings, to anyone who wishes to know more about the brain's role in emotion (see also LeDoux, 1995).

The Autonomic Nervous System

As we've seen, there is considerable controversy in psychology over what role feedback from the autonomic nervous system (ANS) plays in the experience of emotion. It is clear, however, that ANS changes are involved in a nontrivial way in at least *some* emotions. In light of this, it is important to know what the ANS is and what it does.

The nervous system is conventionally divided into two major divisions, the **central nervous system,** which includes the brain and spinal cord, and the **peripheral nervous system.** The peripheral nervous system is further divided into the **somatic system,** which consists of nerve fibers that carry impulses from the brain to the muscles, and the **autonomic nervous system,** which consists of nerve fibers that carry impulses from the brain to the various organs that make up the viscera in which students of emotion have been so interested, for example, the heart, lungs, stomach, adrenal glands, and so forth. Peripheral nerves also carry information from the sense organs, muscles, organs, and glands *back* to the central nervous system.

The autonomic nervous system gets its name because its various components control the automatic functions of those glands and organs that are necessary for survival. Fortunately, we do not have to consciously command our hearts to beat or our lungs to fill with air, the neural activity of the ANS does these things for us. In general, it can be said that the ANS maintains our bodies in a state of equilibrium, or *homeostasis* (a term coined by Walter Cannon), and constantly adjusts the activity level of our "life support systems" in response to the demands of our environment. As we run or climb up a tree to flee from a rabid woodchuck, for example, the ANS sees to it that our heart rate increases so that more blood is available to the muscles in our legs and arms.

The autonomic nervous system is functionally and anatomically divided into two subsystems, the **sympathetic nervous system** and the **parasympathetic nervous system.** Conventionally, the sympathetic nervous system is seen as serving to excite the various organs under its control. During heavy exercise or in a situation in which you have been suddenly surprised by a loud noise or fear-inducing stimulus, it is the sympathetic branch of the ANS that leads your heart to begin beating faster. The sympathetic nervous system typically "responds as a whole," so that, "all or most of the tissue innervated by sympathetic nerves [is] simultaneously influenced" (LeDoux, 1986, p. 309).

The parasympathetic nervous system, on the other hand, is usually thought of as exerting a modulating or inhibitory influence on the organs excited by the sympathetic nervous system. It is parasympathetic nervous system activity that brings your heart rate back to normal after you've been frightened, for example. Strictly speaking, however, it is not correct to say that the sympathetic and parasympathetic systems always have opposite effects (LeDoux, 1986). Some organs, such as the sweat glands, are under the control of only the sympathetic system, while other organs, such as the lachrymal glands, are more under the control of the parasympathetic system (Milder, 1975). Sympathetic and parasympathetic activation of organs that are innervated by both systems may have very different, but not necessarily

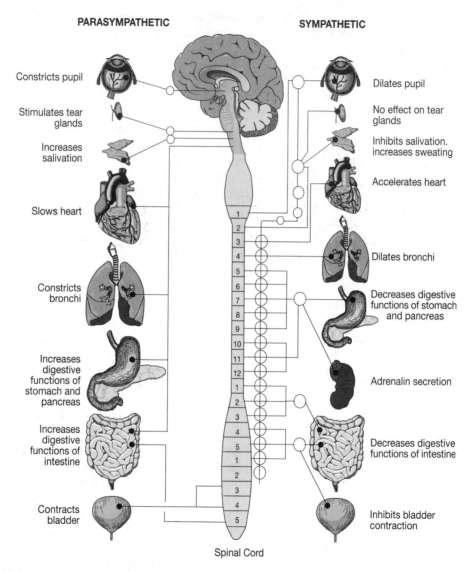

PARASYMPATHETIC

Constricts pupil

Stimulates tear glands

Increases salivation

Slows heart

Constricts bronchi

Increases digestive functions of stomach and pancreas

Increases digestive functions of intestine

Contracts bladder

SYMPATHETIC

Dilates pupil

No effect on tear glands

Inhibits salivation. increases sweating

Accelerates heart

Dilates bronchi

Decreases digestive functions of stomach and pancreas

Adrenalin secretion

Decreases digestive functions of intestine

Inhibits bladder contraction

Spinal Cord

FIGURE A.1. *The sympathetic and parasympathetic divisions of the autonomic nervous system.*

opposite, effects (see Figure A.1). In contrast to the sympathetic system, the parasympathetic system typically exerts its influence on its target organs individually.

The sympathetic and parasympathetic nervous systems are further distinguished by their different anatomical configurations. Nerve fibers for both originate in the central nervous system (CNS) and "synapse," or connect, with the cell bodies of bundles of neurons outside of the CNS. These are called **ganglion cells**—the cell bodies of neurons within the CNS are called **nuclei**. The ganglion cells for the sympathetic system are located in a kind of chain along the spinal cord between the spinal cord and the target organs innervated by the sympathetic nervous system. Ganglion cells for the parasympathetic system, on the other hand, are located on or near the target organs themselves (Carlson, 1994) (see Figure A.1). This anatomy makes sense given the differences in the specificity of the influence of the two systems on their target organs.

The **neurotransmitters** released at the target organs by neurons of the sympathetic and parasympathetic systems are also different in ways that correspond to their different effects on the organs they innervate. The **terminal buttons** or business end of neurons in the sympathetic system release **norepinephrine,** which has excitatory postsynaptic effects (that is, it stimulates the activity of the target organ). The terminal buttons of the parasympathetic system, on the other hand, release **acetylcholine,** a neurotransmitter that may have excitatory or inhibitory effects, with its effects on heart muscle, for example, being inhibitory (Carlson, 1994).

The sympathetic and parasympathetic systems are the "hardware" that makes possible the kinds of bodily changes Jamesians see as essential components of emotion. Since the time of Walter Cannon, it has been known that the ANS, particularly the sympathetic branch, and thus the viscera, respond as a whole during situations involving acute stress or danger. This has been called the emergency or "fight or flight" response (LeDoux, 1986). It has also been discovered, as we have seen, that different emotions may be accompanied by somewhat different patterns of bodily response that probably correspond to the specific needs of the body while it is in the particular emotion-eliciting situation. Such patterns occur against the backdrop of the more "diffuse sympathetic activation" that accompanies the body's response to many different kinds of situations calling for action of some kind (LeDoux, 1986).

Visceral Feedback to the Brain

Nerve impulses traveling out from the brain are called "efferent" impulses, while those traveling to the brain are called "afferent" impulses. Students of emotion are interested in the ANS as an efferent system because it is the mechanism by which the patterns of bodily change associated with some emotions takes place. Students of emotion who view the body as the source of the particular experiential qualities associated with different emotions are interested in the neural pathways that send information back from the peripheral organs to the brain. According to LeDoux (1986), the brain may receive feedback from the body in two ways. The **visceral afferent system** consists of receptors that originate on the various organs of the viscera and send sensory impulses back to the brain. The various glands of the **endocrine system** release hormones into the bloodstream that have effects on specific sites in the brain, including those involved in emotion (see later discussion). Hormones may also have an indirect influence on the brain through their effects on the various organs of the viscera (LeDoux, 1986).

As we have seen in Chapter 3, feedback from the body does seem to play some role in the experience of emotion. Studies of the neurophysiology of emotion support this conclusion but not necessarily the strong form of the James-Lange theory. LeDoux (1986), after reviewing studies of the consequences of disrupting feedback from the periphery to the brain concludes that

> attenuation of interactions between the peripheral nervous system and the brain reduces the intensity of emotional reactions but does not alter the appropriateness of emotional reactions and felt experiences to the emotional situation. (LeDoux, 1986, pp. 325–326)

He goes on the say that, while Cannon's critique of the James-Lange theory "was not wholly justified," "there is little positive evidence to support the James-Lange notion that visceral and other bodily changes actually determine emotional feelings" (LeDoux, 1986, p. 327). For LeDoux, emotional feelings are more profitably viewed as a consequence of neural activity in the brain. This is a conclusion with which Davidson (1993), in a recent review of the neurophysiology and psychophysiology of emotion, largely concurs (see especially pp. 467–468; see also Halgren & Marinkovic, 1995).

The Brain

Given the complexity of the brain and fast-moving nature of neurophysiological research, it is always a little dangerous to refer to this or that part of the brain as being the "emotional brain." It is almost certainly the case that some emotions involve more or different brain areas than other emotions. Nevertheless, several relatively well-studied areas of the brain appear to be vitally important for the evaluation of emotional stimuli and the experience and expression of emotion. Chief among these are the **Papez loop,** the **limbic system,** and various areas of the **cerebral cortex.**

The Papez loop.   Deep in the middle of the brain at the top and somewhat forward of the **brainstem** is a region of the brain called the **thalamus.**

The thalamus is a kind of central relay station for sensory information coming into the brain. In 1937, James Papez (1883–1958) proposed that such information coming into the thalamus is split into three different "streams," a "stream of thought," a "stream of movement," and a "stream of feeling" (Papez, 1937). In what has come to be called the Papez loop or Papez circuit, nerve fibers from the third "stream" have been found to project to an area of the brain called the **hypothalamus,** which in turn project back to the front of the thalamus to the **anterior thalamus.** From there, the circuit connects the anterior thalamus with the **cingulate cortex,** areas of **association cortex,** and a structure called the **hippocampus.** The circuit is completed by connections between the hippocampus and the hypothalamus (see Figure A.2).

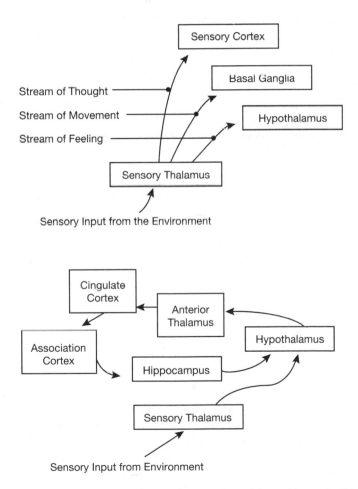

FIGURE A.2. *The Papez loop. (From LeDoux, "The Neurobiology of Emotion," in Le Doux, J. E. & Hirst, W., eds.,* Mind and Brain, *1986, Fig. 15.7, p. 329. © Copyright Cambridge University Press 1986. Reprinted with the permission of Cambridge University Press and of the author.)*

The importance of the Papez loop is that it identified a possible circuit by which emotional meaning gets added to the analysis of incoming stimulus information. The cingulate cortex, for Papez, is the area in the cortex that first receives emotional information from "lower," subcortical areas of the brain. Meanings and memories stored in association cortex get "tagged" with emotion by way of the cingulate cortex. By means of their connection with the hypothalamus via the hippocampus, these "higher" areas of the brain may influence the expression of emotion in the connections between the latter two brain areas and the ANS (LeDoux, 1986). Modern neurophysiological research, however, has shifted interest away from the Papez loop to the structures of the limbic system, particularly, the **amygdala** (LeDoux, 1987).

The limbic system.   The amygdala is a small but very important collection of nuclei found on both sides of the brain on the inside of the anterior **temporal lobe** (Isaacson, 1974) (see Figure A.3). In humans, this places the amygdala beneath the cerebral cortex, just behind the ears. The name of the amygdala, from the Latin word for "almond," describes the shape of the structure; it is shaped roughly like an almond but is somewhat larger. The amygdala is a part of the so-called limbic system. The limbic system consists of a number of interconnected brain structures located around the inside of the cerebral hemispheres, atop and around the thalamus (see Figure A.4). The cerebral cortex is mapped out in terms of four lobes and two hemispheres. The **temporal lobe** is located on the sides of the brain, beneath and behind the ears. The **occipital lobe** is located at the back of the brain, at the back of the head. The **parietal lobe** is located above the temporal lobe and in front of the occipital lobe. It spans an area from the front of the occipital lobe to a fissure, the **central fissure,** that runs roughly from ear to ear. The **frontal lobe** is located at the front of the brain, in front of the parietal lobe, and above and in front of the temporal lobe. The cerebral cortex is divided into **left** and **right hemispheres,** so there are temporal, parietal, occipital, and frontal lobes on each side of the brain. The limbic system is comprised of both cortical and subcortical components. Two of the most important parts of the limbic system are the hippocampus and the amygdala.

Both the hippocampus and amygdala are complexly interconnected with inputs from both the sensory organs and the viscera. They also serve as the origin of projections that connect them with the ANS as well as higher cortical areas. They, and perhaps other structures of the limbic system, appear to integrate sensory information with information from the various organs of the viscera as well as feedback from the ANS to control the "output" of emotional expression in the ANS and other parts of the nervous system (LeDoux, 1986). The limbic system as a whole was once thought of as the emotional brain because of its role in the experience and expression of emotion. Recently, however, as LeDoux (1995) notes, the idea that the limbic

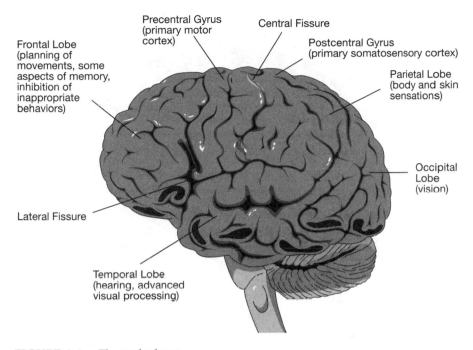

FIGURE A.3.   *The cerebral cortex.*

system is THE site of emotions has fallen into disfavor, as has the concept of the limbic system as a discrete anatomical structure. Nevertheless, evidence continues to mount that the amygdala is centrally involved in the generation of emotion, especially fear.

The amygdala appears to play an important role in the interpretation of the emotional significance of stimuli and in the control of emotional expression and experience (LeDoux, 1987). According to LeDoux, the amygdala serves "a general homeostatic function, evaluating the significance of inputs from exteroceptive and interoceptive sources [sensory input from outside of and inside of the body, respectively] and initiating behavioral and visceral responses accordingly" (LeDoux, 1987, pp. 437–438). The amygdala appears to be a crucial component of the neural circuitry of fear. Damage to its various parts leads to an inability to learn to avoid aversive stimuli and to various changes in the autonomic responses associated with fear (LeDoux, 1995). Although much of the work on the role that the amygdala plays in fear has been conducted on rats, studies of those rare cases in which humans have suffered damage to one or both amygdalae indicate that such damage results in often quite severe emotional impairment (Aggleton, 1992; see also Damasio, 1994, pp. 69–70).

It is now known that the hippocampus plays a major role in the estab-

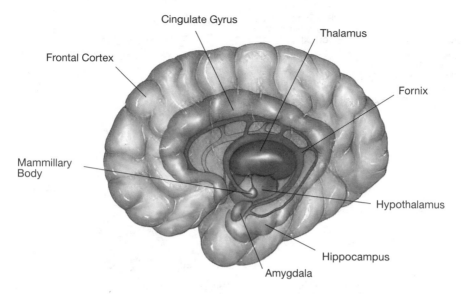

FIGURE A.4.   *The limbic system. Adapted from Carlson,* Psychology: The Science of Behavior *(4th ed.), Figure 3.21, p. 70. Copyright © 1993 by Allyn and Bacon. Adapted by permission.*

lishment of new memories, but its contribution to the control of emotional experience and expression is not entirely clear. There is evidence that the hippocampus is involved in the experience of anxiety (Gray, 1982), but some consider it to be equivocal (see LeDoux, 1987, p. 433). Given the clear role that the hippocampus plays in cognitive functions and its possible role in assigning meaning to emotional stimuli, LeDoux avers that "[p]erhaps the hippocampus participates in emotional processing by transmitting cognitive information to the amygdala" (LeDoux, 1987, p. 433). Studies in rats using a classical conditioning paradigm in which a shock is paired with an auditory stimulus indicate that lesions of the hippocampus have no effect on the rats' learning an association between the shock and the auditory stimulus. Such lesions, however, disrupt the development of an association between the shock and the chamber in which the shock is delivered, so-called contextual conditioning (LeDoux, 1995). Thus, the hippocampus may be involved in the integration of contextual or "higher order" information with information about the feared stimulus, as are various areas of the cerebral cortex, particularly association cortex (see Halgren & Marinkovic, 1995).

Dual pathways.   Explorations of the role of the amygdala and other structures of the limbic system in emotion have revealed some neuroanatomical support for the contention by Zajonc that emotional reactions may precede the cognitive analysis of stimuli from the environment *as well as* the contention by Lazarus that all emotional reactions are based on appraisal (see Chapter 4). LeDoux and his colleagues have found evidence that sensory projections from the thalamus terminate in both the cortex, where the higher cognitive functions are supposedly housed and, hence, where appraisal would presumably take place, and in the amygdala and hypothalamus, where an emotional reaction could be initiated in the absence of cortical input (see LeDoux, 1986; or LeDoux, 1987, especially pp. 435–438). Sensory information of possible emotional significance may thus be acted upon at subcortical levels before much of any cognitive analysis of the stimulus has taken place. What is most interesting about the "dual pathways" LeDoux and his colleagues have identified is that the pathways reconverge at the subcortical level (in areas below the cortex). That is, the pathway that routes sensory information to the cortex routes it back again to the structures of the limbic system. The pathway from the thalamus to the limbic system, however, is much shorter than that from the thalamus to the limbic system via the cortex. This means, as LeDoux argues, that, "[i]nput reaching target areas such as the amygdala may therefore prime the area to receive the better analyzed neocortical inputs" (LeDoux, 1986, p. 346). It also means, of course, that emotional responses may be based on only a relatively "crude" but nevertheless faster analysis of the emotional significance of a stimulus.

Cerebral cortex. There is still much to be learned about the role of the cerebral cortex in emotion. It is clear, of course, that the various areas of the cortex, in particular, association cortex (basically areas of the cortex not involved in sensorimotor functions), are intimately involved in the integration of information from the senses and memory with information from the amygdala and other sources to generate the conscious experience of emotion (LeDoux, 1995; Halgren & Marinkovic, 1995). Many emotions in humans, episodes of anger, for example, that involve issues of long-standing tension between partners in a close relationship, obviously require the use of complex information that must be processed in sensory cortex with the aid of material stored in association cortex. It is also clear that the higher-order meanings of emotional stimuli, especially those associated with the facial expressions of other humans, depend critically on cortical processes (Magnussen, Sunde, & Dyrnes, 1994). However, the devil, as they say, is in the details.

Some details about cortical involvement in emotions are relatively clear, although they are not necessarily without controversy. Electroencephalographic studies of normal subjects under a variety of conditions strongly suggest a right-hemisphere dominance for negative emotion (Davidson & Tomarken, 1989) in that the right side of the brain is more active during the experience and expression of negative emotions. The right hemisphere also displays a clear superiority in the processing of emotional stimulus information. Studies of the emotional impairments of subjects with right-hemisphere brain damage largely corroborate such findings (see Robinson, Kubos, Starr, Rao, & Price, 1984). Richard Davidson has argued, however, that, more specifically, the anterior right hemisphere is specialized for *withdrawal-related* emotional behavior and the anterior left hemisphere is specialized for *approach-related* emotional behavior (Davidson, Ekman, Saron, Senulis, & Friesen, 1990; Davidson, 1993). This means that negative emotions such as fear and disgust that clearly involve withdrawal should show more right hemisphere activation, while positive, approach-related emotions such as happiness should display more left hemisphere activation. Negative emotions such as anger may show either greater right or left activation, depending on whether the anger involves withdrawal or approach tendencies. Davidson argues that the relevant data show precisely this pattern (Davidson, 1993). Interestingly, given our earlier discussion of gender differences in the use of information from visceral feedback (Chapter 3), there is some indication that men and women differ in the extent to which they show such cerebral asymmetry. A recent study (Harrison, Gorelczenko, & Cook, 1990) found that men displayed a very clear right-hemisphere bias for the processing of information about emotional faces, while women showed a less pronounced asymmetry.

Findings about cerebral hemispheric specialization for emotion are paralleled by the results of research on lateral asymmetries in the *production* of emotion faces. In an early and much-cited study in which subjects were asked to judge the emotionality of composite photographs of the left and right sides of human faces as well as the original faces, Sackeim, Gur, and Saucy (1978) found that emotions appeared to be expressed much more intensely by the left side of the face (the so-called left hemiface). Motor control of the lower part of the face, particularly the mouth, is **contralaterial.** This means that the left hemiface is controlled primarily by the right hemisphere and the right hemiface is controlled by the left hemisphere.[1] A recent review by Jean Borod (1993) of the research conducted since Sackeim et al.'s original study found strong support for the conclusion that the left hemiface moves more extensively and expresses emotion more intensely than does the right hemiface. From these studies Borod concluded that, "the right hemisphere (because of its greater connectivity to the left hemisphere) appears to be dominant for facial emotional expression" (Borod, 1993, p. 458). She also found clear evidence for right-hemispheric specialization for emotion in the deficits in the linguistic features associated with emotion of sub-

---

[1]There may be differences between spontaneous and posed emotional expressions in this regard. While it is clear that posed emotional expressions are controlled contralaterially, involuntary expressions may be controlled bilaterally. Much less is known about the neuroanatomy of involuntary than of voluntary emotional facial expressions, however (see Borod & Koff, 1990).

jects with right-hemisphere brain damage, although the evidence for right-hemisphere superiority for the production of emotional expressions was not as strong among these subjects. Davidson (1993) has argued, however, that the latter may reflect methodological problems that obscure the role of the right hemisphere in emotional facial expression.

We know much more about the neural circuitry of the "emotional brain" than this brief review suggests, of course. There is also obviously still much to be learned about the neural mechanisms that underlie emotional experience and expression, particularly of the more complex emotions. The role that the amygdala plays in fear is perhaps the most understood, and it may turn out that the amygdala is involved in most, if not all, emotions (Aggleton & Miskin, 1986). However, many other areas of the brain are also undoubtedly involved in the control of emotional experience, expression, and evaluation. One of the major tasks for the psychology of the twenty-first century is to identify these areas and, hence, to construct a more complete map of the emotional brain.

Further Reading

GRAY, J. A. (1982). *The neuropsychology of anxiety.* New York: Oxford University Press.

LEDOUX, J. E. (1987). Emotion. In F. Plum & V. B. Mountcastle (Eds.), *Handbook of physiology. The nervous system: Vol. 5. Higher function* (pp. 419–459). Washington, DC: American Physiological Society.

LEDOUX, J. E. (1995). In search of an emotional system in the brain: Leaping from fear to emotion and consciousness. In M. S. Gazzaniga (Ed.), *The cognitive neurosciences* (pp. 1049–1061). Cambridge: MIT Press.

MCNAUGHTON, N. (1989). *Biology and emotion.* Cambridge: Cambridge University Press.

References

ABU-LUGHOD, L., & LUTZ, C. (1990). Introduction: Emotion, discourse, and the politics of everyday life. In C. Lutz & L. Abu-Lughod (Eds.), *Language and the politics of emotion* (pp. 1–23). Cambridge: Cambridge University Press.

ADELMANN, P. K., & ZAJONC, R. (1989). Facial efference and the experience of emotion. *Annual Review of Psychology, 40,* 249–280.

AGGLETON, J. P. (1992). The functional effects of amygdala lesions in humans: A comparison with findings from monkeys. In J. P. Aggleton (Eds.), *The amygdala: Neurobiological aspects of emotion, memory, and mental dysfunction* (pp. 485–503). New York: Wiley.

AGGLETON, J. P., & MISKIN, M. (1986). The amygdala: Sensory gateway to the emotions. In R. Plutchik & H. Kellerman (Eds.), *Emotion: Theory, research and experience,* Vol. 3 (pp. 281–299). Orlando, FL: Academic Press.

AGNEW, N. M., & PYKE, S. W. (1994). *The science game: An introduction to research in the social sciences.* Englewood Cliffs, NJ: Prentice-Hall.

AINSWORTH, M. D. S., BLEHAR, M. C., WATERS, E., & WALL, S. (1978). *Patterns of attachment: A psychological study of the strange situation.* Hillsdale, NJ: Erlbaum.

ALLEN, J. B., KENRICK, D. T., LINDER, D. E., & McCALL, M. A. (1989). Arousal and attraction: A response-facilitation alternative to misattribution and negative-reinforcement models. *Journal of Personality and Social Psychology, 57,* 261–270.

ALLPORT, F. H. (1924). *Social psychology.* Boston: Houghton Mifflin.

ANDREW, R. J. (1963). Evolution of facial expression. *Science, 142,* 1034–1041.

ANDREW, R. J. (1965). The origins of facial expressions. *Scientific American, 213,* 88–94.

ARISTOTLE (1954). *The Rhetoric and the Poetics of Aristotle* (W. R. Roberts, Trans.). New York: Modern Library.

ARMON-JONES, C. (1985). Prescription, explication and the social construction of emotion. *Journal for the Theory of Social Behaviour, 15,* 1–22.

ARMON-JONES, C. (1986a). The social functions of emotion. In R. Harré (Ed.), *The social construction of emotions* (pp. 57–82). Oxford: Basil Blackwell.

ARMON-JONES, C. (1986b). The thesis of constructionism. In R. Harré (Ed.), *The social construction of emotions* (pp. 32–56). New York: Blackwell.

ARNOLD, M. B. (1960a). *Emotion and personality: Vol. 1. Psychological aspects.* New York: Columbia University Press.

ARNOLD, M. B. (1960b). *Emotion and personality: Vol. 2. Physiological aspects.* New York: Columbia University Press.

ARNOLD, M. B. (1969). Human emotion and action. In T. Mischel (Ed.), *Human action: Conceptual and Empirical Issues* (pp. 167–197). New York: Academic Press.

AVERILL, J. R. (1969). Autonomic response patterning in sadness and mirth. *Psychophysiology, 5,* 399–414.

AVERILL, J. R. (1974). An analysis of psychophysiological symbolism and its influence on theories of emotion. *Journal for the Theory of Social Behaviour, 4,* 147–190.

AVERILL, J. R. (1975). A semantic atlas of emotional concepts. *JSAS Catalog of Selected Documents in Psychology, 5*(330) (Ms. No. 421).

AVERILL, J. R. (1979a). Anger. In R. A. Dienstbier (Ed.), *Nebraska symposium of motivation, 1978: Human emotion* (pp. 1–80). Lincoln: University of Nebraska Press.

AVERILL, J. R. (1979b). The functions of grief. In C. E. Izard (Ed.), *Emotions in personality and psychopathology* (pp. 339–368). New York: Plenum.

AVERILL, J. R. (1980a). A constructivist view of emotion. In R. Plutchik & H. Kellerman (Eds.), *Emotion: Theory, research and experience,* Vol. 1 (pp. 305–339). New York: Academic Press.

AVERILL, J. R. (1980b). The emotions. In E. Staub (Ed.), *Personality: Basic aspects and current research* (pp. 134–199). Englewood Cliffs, NJ: Prentice-Hall.

AVERILL, J. R. (1982). *Anger and aggression: An essay on emotion.* New York: Springer.

AVERILL, J. R. (1983). Studies in anger and aggression: Implications for theories of emotion. *American Psychologist, 38,* 1145–1180.

AVERILL, J. R. (1984). The acquisition of emotions during adulthood. In C. Z. Malatesta & C. E. Izard (Eds.), *Emotion in adult development* (pp. 23–43). Beverly Hills, CA: Sage.

AVERILL, J. R. (1985). The social construction of emotion: With special reference to love. In K. J. Gergen & K. E. Davis (Eds.), *The social construction of the person* (pp. 89–109). New York: Springer-Verlag.

AVERILL, J. R. (1990a). Emotions in relation to systems of behavior. In N. L. Stein, B. Leventhal, & T. Trabasso (Eds.), *Psychological and biological approaches to emotion* (pp. 385–404). Hillsdale, NJ: Erlbaum.

AVERILL, J. R. (1990b). Inner feelings, works of the flesh, the beast within, diseases of the mind, driving force, and putting on a show: Six metaphors of emotion and their theoretical extensions. In D. E. Leary (Ed.), *Metaphors in the history of psychology* (pp. 104–132). Cambridge: Cambridge University Press.

AVERILL, J. R. (1994). Aristotle meets the computer and becomes conflicted. *Cognition and Emotion, 8,* 73–91.

AVERILL, J. R., & BOOTHROYD, P. (1977). On falling in love in conformance with the romantic ideal. *Motivation and Emotion, 1,* 235–247.

AVERILL, J. R., CATLIN, G., & CHON, K. K. (1990). *The rules of hope.* New York: Springer-Verlag.

AVERILL, J. R., & NUNLEY, E. P. (1993). Grief as an emotion and as a disease: A social-constructionist perspective. In M. S. Stroebe, W. Stroebe, & R. O. Hansson (Eds.), *Handbook of bereavement: Theory, research, and intervention* (pp. 77–90). Cambridge: Cambridge University Press.

AX, A. F. (1953). The physiological differentiation between fear and anger in humans. *Psychosomatic Medicine, 15,* 433–442.

BAARS, B. J. (1986). *The cognitive revolution in psychology.* New York: Guilford Press.

BARDWICK, J. M. (1979). *In transition: How feminism, sexual liberation, and the search for self-fulfillment have altered our lives.* New York: Holt, Rinehart and Winston.

BAROL, B., & ABRAMSON, P. (1987, August 17). The end of the world (again). *Newsweek,* p. 70–71.

BARON, R. A. (1987). Effects of negative ions on interpersonal attraction: Evidence for intensification. *Journal of Personality and Social Psychology, 52,* 547–553.

BARON, R. A., RUSSELL, G. W., & ARMS, R. L. (1985). Negative ions and behavior: Impact on mood, memory and aggression among Type A and Type B persons. *Journal of Personality and Social Psychology, 48,* 746–754.

BELL, C. (1840/1877). *The anatomy and philosophy of expression as connected with the fine arts.* London: George Bell.

BENISON, S., BARGER, A. C. &., & WOLFE, E. L. (1987). *Walter B. Cannon: The life and times of a young scientist.* Cambridge: Harvard University Press.

BIRDWHISTELL, R. L. (1970). *Kinesics and context.* Philadelphia: University of Pennsylvania Press.

BLASCOVICH, J. (1990). Individual differences in physiological arousal and perception of arousal: Missing links in Jamesian notions of arousal-based behaviors. *Personality and Social Psychology Bulletin, 16,* 665–675.

BLASCOVICH, J. (1992). A biopsychosocial approach to arousal regulation. *Journal of Social and Clinical Psychology, 11,* 213–237.

BLASCOVICH, J., & KATKIN, E. S. (1983). Visceral perception and social behavior. In J. T. Cacioppo & R. E. Petty (Eds.), *Social psychophysiology: A sourcebook* (pp. 493–509). New York: Guilford.

BOOTZIN, R. R., HERMAN, C. R., & NICASSIO, P. (1976). The power of suggestion: Another examination of misattribution and insomnia. *Journal of Personality and Social Psychology, 34,* 673–679.

BOROD, J. C. (1993). Cerebral mechanisms underlying facial, prosodic, and lexical emotional expression: A review of neuropsychological studies and methodological issues. *Neuropsychology, 7,* 445–463.

BOROD, J. C., & KOFF, E. (1990). Lateralization for facial emotional behavior: A methodological perspective. *International Journal of Psychology, 25,* 157–177.

BOWLBY, J. (1969). *Attachment and loss. Vol. 1: Attachment.* New York: Basic Books.

BOWLBY, J. (1973). *Attachment and loss. Vol. 2: Separation: Anxiety and anger.* New York: Basic Books.

BOWLBY, J. (1990). *Charles Darwin: A new life.* New York: W. W. Norton.

BRIGGS, J. L. (1970). *Never in Anger: Portrait of an Eskimo family.* Cambridge: Harvard University Press.

BRIGHTMAN, V. J., SEGAL, A. L., WERTHER, P., & STEINER, J. (1977). Facial expression and hedonic response to taste stimuli. *Journal of Dental Research, 56,* B161 (Abstract).

BRONOWSKI, J. (1973). *The ascent of man.* Boston: Little, Brown.

BROVERMAN, I. K., VOGEL, S. R., BROVERMAN, D. M., CLARKSON, F. E., & ROSENKRANTZ, P. S. (1972). Sex-role stereotypes: A current appraisal. *Journal of Social Issues, 28,* 59–78.

BUCK, R. (1980). Nonverbal behavior and the theory of emotion: The facial feedback hypothesis. *Journal of Personality and Social Psychology, 38,* 811–824.

BUCK, R. (1984). *The communication of emotion.* New York: Guilford Press.

BUCK, R. (1985). Prime theory: An integrated view of emotion and motivation. *Psychological Review, 92,* 389–413.

BURGESS, E. W., & WALLIN, P. (1953). *Engagement and marriage.* Philadelphia: Lippincott.

BUSS, D., & SCHMITT, D. P. (1993). Sexual strategies theory: An evolutionary perspective on human mating. *Psychological Review, 100,* 204–232.

BUSS, D. M. (1994). *The evolution of desire: Strategies of human mating.* New York: Basic Books.

CALHOUN, C., & SOLOMON, R. C. (1984). *What is an emotion? Classic readings in philosophical psychology.* New York: Oxford University Press.

CALVERT-BOYANOWSKY, J., & LEVENTHAL, H. (1975). The role of information in attenuating behavioral responses to stress: A reinterpretation of the misattribution phenomenon. *Journal of Personality and Social Psychology, 32,* 214–221.

CAMPOS, J. J. (1994, Spring). The new functionalism in emotion. *SRCD Newsletter,* p. 1, 7, 9–11, 14.

CAMPOS, J. J., & BARNETT, K. C. (1984). Toward a new understanding of emotions and their development. In C. E. Izard, J. Kagan, & R. B. Zajonc (Eds.), *Emotions, cognition, and behavior* (pp. 229–263). Cambridge: Cambridge University Press.

CAMPOS, J. J., & STENBERG, C. R. (1981). Perception, appraisal and emotion: The onset of social referencing. In M. Lamb & L. Sherrod (Eds.), *Infant social perception.* Hillsdale, NJ: Erlbaum.

CANNON, W. B. (1914). The interrelations of emotions as suggested by recent physiological researchers. *American Journal of Psychology, 25,* 252–282.

CANNON, W. B. (1927). The James-Lange theory of emotions: A critical examination and an alternative theory. *American Journal of Psychology, 39,* 106–124.

CANNON, W. B. (1931). Again the James-Lange and the thalamic theories of emotion. *Psychological Review, 38,* 281–295.

CANNON, W. B. (1945). *The way of an investigator: A scientist's experiences in medical research.* New York: W. W. Norton.

CANTOR, J. R., ZILLMANN, D., & BRYANT, J. (1975). Enhancement of experienced sexual arousal through misattribution of unrelated residual excitation. *Journal of Personality and Social Psychology, 32,* 69–75.

CANTRIL, H., & HUNT, W. A. (1932). Emotional effects produced by injection of adrenalin. *American Journal of Psychology, 44,* 300–307.

CARLSON, N. (1990). *Psychology: The Science of behavior.* Boston: Allyn and Bacon.

CARLSON, N. (1993). *Psychology: The Science of behavior.* (4th ed.) Boston: Allyn and Bacon.

CARLSON, N. R. (1994). *Physiology of behavior.* Boston: Allyn and Bacon.

CHEVALIER-SKOLNIKOFF, S. (1973). Facial expressions of emotion in nonhuman primates. In P. Ekman (Ed.), *Darwin and facial expression: A century of research in review* (pp. 11–89). New York: Academic Press.

CHURCHLAND, P. (1988). *Matter and consciousness.* Cambridge: MIT Press.

CHWALISZ, K., DIENER, E., & GALLAGHER, D. (1988). Autonomic arousal feedback and emotional experience: Evidence from the spinal cord injured. *Journal of Personality and Social Psychology, 54,* 820–828.

CHWELOS, G., & OATLEY, K. (1994). Appraisal, computational models, and Scherer's expert system. *Cognition and Emotion, 8,* 245–257.

CONNOLLY, W. E. (1974). Theoretical self-consciousness. In W. E. Connolly & G. Gordon (Eds.), *Social structure and political theory* (pp. 40–66). Lexington, MA: D. C. Heath.

CORNELIUS, R. R. (1984). A rule model of adult emotional expression. In C. Z. Malatesta & C. E. Izard (Eds.), *C. E. Izard* (pp. 213–233). Beverly Hills, CA: Sage.

CORNELIUS, R. R. (1991). Gregorio Marañon's two-factor theory of emotion. *Personality and Social Psychology Bulletin, 17,* 65–69.

CORNELIUS, R. R., & AVERILL, J. R. (1980). The influence of various types of control on psychophysiological stress reactions. *Journal of Research in Personality, 14,* 503–517.

CORNELIUS, R. R., & AVERILL, J. R. (1983). Sex differences in fear of spiders. *Journal of Personality and Social Psychology, 45,* 377–383.

COTTON, J. L. (1981). A review of research on Schachter's theory of emotion and the misattribution of arousal. *European Journal of Social Psychology, 11,* 365–397.

COULTER, J. (1989). *Mind in action.* Atlantic Highlands, NJ: Humanities Press International.

CUTTER, S. L., TIEFENBACHER, J., & SOLECKI, W. D. (1992). En-gendered fears: Femininity and technological risk perception. *Industrial Crisis Quarterly, 6,* 5–22.

DAMASIO, A. R. (1994). *Descartes' error: Emotion, reason, and the human brain.* New York: Grosset/Putnam.

DARWIN, C. (1871). *The Descent of man and selection in relation to sex.* London: J. Murphy.

DARWIN, C. (1872/1965). *The expression of the emotions in man and animals.* Chicago: University of Chicago Press.

DARWIN, C. (1877). A biographical sketch of an infant. *Mind, 2,* 285–294.

DARWIN, F. (1904). *The life and letters of Charles Darwin.* New York: Appleton.

DAVIDSON, R. J. (1993). Parsing affective space: Perspectives from neuropsychology and psychophysiology. *Neuropsychology, 7,* 464–475.

DAVIDSON, R. J., EKMAN, P., SARON, C. D., SENULIS, J. A., & FRIESEN, W. V. (1990). Approach-withdrawal and cerebral asymmetry: Emotional expression and brain physiology I. *Journal of Personality and Social Psychology, 58,* 330–341.

DAVIDSON, R. J., & TOMARKEN, A. J. (1989). Laterality and emotion: An electrophysiological approach. In F. Boller & J. Grafman (Eds.), *Handbook of neurophysiology,* Vol. 3 (pp. 419–441). Amsterdam: Elsevier.

DAVIS, M. R., LANGER, A. W., SUTTERER, G., P. D., & MARLIN, M. (1986). Relative discriminability of heartbeat-contingent stimuli under three procedures for assessing cardiac perception. *Psychophysiology, 23,* 76–81.

DE RIVERA, J. (1977). *A structural theory of the emotions.* New York: International Universities Press.

DEBORD, J.-F. (1990). The Duchenne de Boulogne Collection in the Department of Morphology, L'Ecole Nationale Supérieure des Beaux Arts. In A. Cuthbertson (Ed.), *The mechanism of human facial expression by G.-B. Duchenne de Boulogne* (pp. 242–256). Cambridge: Cambridge University Press.

DEMOS, J. (1988). Shame and guilt in early New England. In C. Z. Stearns & P. N. Stearns (Eds.), *Emotion and social change: Toward a new psychohistory* (pp. 69–85). New York: Holmes and Meier.

DESCARTES, R. (1637/1911). Passions de l'âme. In E. L. Haldane & G. R. Ross (Eds.), *The philosophical works of Descartes* (pp. 329–427). Cambridge: Cambridge University Press.

DOI, T. (1973). *The anatomy of dependence.* Tokyo: Kodansha International.

DONOVAN, W. L., & LEAVETT, L. A. (1985). Physiology and behavior: Parents' response to the infant cry. In B. M. Lester & C. F. Z. Boukydis (Eds.), *Infant crying: Theoretical and research perspectives* (pp. 241–261). New York: Plenum.

DORR, A. (1985). Contexts for experience with emotion, with special attention to television. In M. Lewis & C. Saarni (Eds.), *The socialization of emotions* (pp. 55–85). New York: Plenum.

DUCHENNE, G.-B. (1862/1990). *The mechanism of human facial expression* (Cuthbertson, R. A., Trans.). Cambridge: Cambridge University Press.

DUCK, S. (1994). *Meaningful relationships: Talking, sense, and relating.* Thousand Oaks, CA: Sage.

DUCLOS, S. E., LAIRD, J. D., SCHNEIDER, E., SEXTER, M., STERN, L., & VAN LIGHTEN, O. (1989). Emotion-specific effects of facial expressions and postures on emotional experience. *Journal of Personality and Social Psychology, 57,* 100–108.

DURKHEIM, E. (1897/1966). *Suicide.* New York: Free Press.

DUTTON, D., & ARON, A. (1974). Some evidence for heightened sexual attraction under conditions of high anxiety. *Journal of Personality and Social Psychology, 30,* 510–517.

EKMAN, P. (1972). Universals and cultural differences in facial expressions of emotion. In J. K. Cole (Ed.), *Nebraska symposium on motivation* (pp. 207–282). Lincoln: University of Nebraska Press.

EKMAN, P. (Ed.). (1973). *Darwin and facial expression: A century of research in review.* New York: Academic Press.

EKMAN, P. (1984). Expression and the nature of emotion. In K. Scherer & P. Ekman (Eds.), *Approaches to emotion* (pp. 319–343). Hillsdale, NJ: Erlbaum.

EKMAN, P. (1992a). Are there basic emotions? *Psychological Review, 99,* 550–553.

EKMAN, P. (1992b). Facial expressions of emotion. *Psychological Science, 3,* 34–38.

EKMAN, P. (1994). Strong evidence for universals in facial expressions: A reply to Russell's mistaken critique. *Psychological Bulletin, 115,* 268–287.

EKMAN, P., DAVIDSON, R. J., & FRIESEN, W. V. (1990). The Duchenne smile: Emotional expression and brain physiology, II. *Journal of Personality and Social Psychology, 58,* 342–353.

EKMAN, P., & FRIESEN, W. V. (1971). Constants across cultures in the face and emotion. *Journal of Personality and Social Psychology, 17,* 124–129.

EKMAN, P., & FRIESEN, W. V. (1975). *Unmasking the face: A guide to recognizing emotions from facial cues.* Englewood Cliffs, NJ: Prentice-Hall.

EKMAN, P., & FRIESEN, W. V. (1978). *Facial Action Coding System: A technique for the measurement of facial movement.* Palo Alto, CA: Consulting Psychologists Press.

EKMAN, P., & FRIESEN, W. V. (1986). A new pan-cultural facial expression of emotion. *Motivation and Emotion, 10,* 159–168.

EKMAN, P., & FRIESEN, W. V. (1988). Who knows what about contempt: A reply to Izard and Haynes. *Motivation and Emotion, 12,* 17–22.

EKMAN, P., FRIESEN, W. V., & ELLSWORTH, P. (1972). *Emotion in the human face.* New York: Pergamon Press.

EKMAN, P., FRIESEN, W. V., O'SULLIVAN, M., CHAN, A., DIACOYANNI-TARLATZIS, I., HEIDER, K., KRAUSE, R., LECOMPTE, W. A., PITCAIRN, T., RICCI-BITTI, P. E., SCHERER, K. R., TOMITA, M., & TZAVARAS, A. (1987). Universals and cultural differences in the judgments of facial expressions of emotion. *Journal of Personality and Social Psychology, 53*(4), 712–717.

EKMAN, P., & HEIDER, K. G. (1988). The universality of a contempt expression: A replication. *Motivation and Emotion, 12,* 303–308.

EKMAN, P., LEVENSON, R. W., & FRIESEN, W. V. (1983). Autonomic nervous system activity distinguishes between emotions. *Science, 221,* 1208–1210.

EKMAN, P., & O'SULLIVAN, M. (1987). The role of context in interpreting facial expression: Comment on Russell and Fehr. *Journal of Experimental Psychology, General, 117,* 86–88.

EKMAN, P., O'SULLIVAN, M., & MATSUMOTO, D. (1991). Confusions about context in the judgment of facial expression: A reply to "The contempt expression and the relativity thesis." *Motivation and Emotion, 15,* 169–176.

ELLSWORTH, P. C. (1994a). Sense, culture, and sensibility. In S. Kitayama & H. R. Markus (Eds.), *Emotion and culture: Empirical studies of mutual influence* (pp. 23–50). Washington, DC: American Psychological Association.

ELLSWORTH, P. C. (1994b). William James and emotion: Is a century of fame worth a century of misunderstanding? *Psychological Review, 101,* 222–229.

ELLSWORTH, P. C., & TOURANGEAU, R. (1981). On our failure to disconfirm what nobody ever said. *Journal of Personality and Social Psychology, 40,* 363–369.

EPSTEIN, S. (1982). A research paradigm for the study of personality and emotions. In M. M. Page (Ed.), *Nebraska Symposium on Motivation 1982. Personality: Current theory and research* (pp. 91–154). Lincoln: University of Nebraska Press.

ERDMANN, G., & JANKE, W. (1978). Interaction between physiological and cognitive determinants of emotions: Experimental studies on Schachter's theory of emotions. *Biological Psychology, 6,* 61–74.

FEHR, B. (1988). Prototype analysis of the concepts of love and commitment. *Journal of Personality and Social Psychology, 55,* 557–579.

FEHR, B. (1994). Prototype-based assessment of laypeople's views of love. *Personal Relationships, 1,* 309–331.

FEHR, B., & RUSSELL, J. A. (1984). Concept of emotion viewed from a prototype perspective. *Journal of Experimental Psychology: General, 113,* 464–486.

FEHR, F. S., & STERN, J. A. (1970). Peripheral physiological variables and emotion: The James-Lange theory revisited. *Psychological Bulletin, 74,* 411–424.

FEIST, G. J., BODNER, T. E., JACOBS, J. F., MILES, M., & TAN, V. (1995). Integrating top-down and bottom-up structural models of subjective well-being: A longitudinal investigation. *Journal of Personality and Social Psychology, 68,* 138–150.

FELEKY, A. (1914). The expression of the emotions. *Psychological Review, 21,* 33–41.

FELEKY, A. (1924). *Feelings and emotions.* New York: Pioneer.

FIELD, T. M., WOODSON, R., GREENBERG, R., & COHEN, D. (1982). Discrimination and imitation of facial expressions by neonates. *Science, 218*, 179–181.

FINCK, H. T. (1887). *Romantic love and personal beauty*. London: Macmillan.

FOLKMAN, S., & LAZARUS, R. S. (1985). If it changes it must be a process: Study of emotion and coping during three stages of a college examination. *Journal of Personality and Social Psychology, 48*, 150–170.

FREY, W. H., & LANGSETH, M. (1985). *Crying: The mystery of tears*. Minneapolis: Winston Press.

FRIDLUND, A. J. (1991). Evolution and facial action in reflex, social motive, and paralanguage. In P. K. Ackles, J. R. Jennings, & M. G. H. Coles (Eds.), *Advances in psychophysiology*. London: Jessica Kingsley.

FRIDLUND, A. J. (1992). The behavioral ecology and sociality of human faces. In M. S. Clark (Ed.), *Emotion: Review of Personality and Social Psychology*, Vol. 13 (pp. 90–121). Newbury Park, CA: Sage.

FRIDLUND, A. J. (1994). *Human facial expression: An evolutionary view*. San Diego: Academic Press.

FRIDLUND, A. J., & GILBERT, A. N. (1985). Emotions and facial expression. *Science, 230*, 607–608.

FRIEDMAN, H. S., & MILLER-HERRINGER, T. (1991). Nonverbal display of emotion in public and private: Self-monitoring, personality, and expressive cues. *Journal of Personality and Social Psychology, 61*, 766–775.

FRIESEN, W. V. (1972). *Cultural differences in facial expressions in a social situation: An experimental test of the concept of display rules*. Unpublished dissertation, University of California, San Francisco.

FRIJDA, N. H. (1986). *The emotions*. Cambridge: Cambridge University Press.

FRIJDA, N. H. (1988). The laws of emotion. *American Psychologist, 43*, 349–358.

FRIJDA, N. H., KUIPERS, P., & TER SCHURE, E. (1989). Relations among emotion, appraisal, and emotional action readiness. *Journal of Personality and Social Psychology, 57*, 212–228.

FRIJDA, N. H., & MESQUITA, B. (1994). The social roles and functions of emotions. In S. Kitayama & H. R. Markus (Eds.), *Emotion and culture. Empirical studies of mutual influence* (pp. 51–87). Washington, DC: American Psychological Association.

FRIJDA, N. H., & SWAGERMAN, J. (1987). Can computers feel? Theory and design of an emotional system. *Cognition and Emotion, 1*, 235–258.

FUNKENSTEIN, D. H., KING, S. H., & DROLETTE, M. (1954). The direction of answer during a laboratory stress-inducing situation. *Psychosomatic Medicine, 16*, 404–413.

GARDNER, H. (1985). *The mind's new science*. New York: Basic Books.

GARRY, A., & PEARSALL, M. (Eds.). (1989). *Women, knowledge, and reality: Explorations in feminist philosophy*. Boston: Unwin Hyman.

GAZZANIGA, M. S. (Ed.). (1995). *The cognitive neurosciences*. Cambridge: MIT Press.

GERGEN, K. J. (1985). The social constructionist movement in modern psychology. *American Psychologist, 40*, 266–275.

GERGEN, K. J., & DAVIS, K. E. (1985). *The social construction of the person*. New York: Springer-Verlag.

GERRARDS-HESSE, A., SPIES, K., & HESSE, F. W. (1994). Experimental inductions of emotional states and their effects: A review. *British Journal of Psychology, 85,* 55–78.

GILBERT, A. N., FRIDLUND, A. J., & SABINI, J. (1987). Hedonic and social determinants of facial displays to odors. *Chemical Senses, 12,* 355–363.

GIRODO, M. (1973). Film-induced arousal, information search, and the attribution process. *Journal of Personality and Social Psychology, 25,* 357–360.

GRAY, J. (1971). *The psychology of fear and stress.* New York: McGraw-Hill.

GRAY, J. A. (1982). *The neuropsychology of anxiety.* New York: Oxford University Press.

GREENFIELD, S. M. (1965). Love and marriage in modern America: A functional analysis. *Sociological Quarterly, 6,* 361–377.

GRINGS, W. W., & DAWSON, M. E. (1978). *Emotions and bodily responses: A psychophysiological approach.* New York: Academic Press.

HAGAR, J. C., & EKMAN, P. (1981). Methodological problems in Tourangeau and Ellsworth's study of facial expression and experience of emotion. *Journal of Personality and Social Psychology, 40,* 358–362.

HALL, J. A. (1984). *Nonverbal sex differences.* Baltimore, MD: Johns-Hopkins University Press.

HALGREN, E., & MARINKOVIC, K. (1995). Neurophysiological networks integrating human emotions. In M. S. Gazzaniga (Ed.), *The cognitive neurosciences* (pp. 1137–1151). Cambridge: MIT Press.

HARRÉ, R. (1979). *Social being.* Oxford: Basil Blackwell.

HARRÉ, R. (1981). *Great scientific experiments: 20 experiments that changed our view of the world.* Oxford: Phaidon.

HARRÉ, R. (Ed.). (1986a). *The social construction of emotions.* Oxford: Basil Blackwell.

HARRÉ, R. (1986b). An outline of the social constructionist viewpoint. In R. Harré (Ed.), *The social construction of emotions* (pp. 1–14). Oxford: Basil Blackwell.

HARRÉ, R. (1994). *The discursive mind.* Thousand Oaks, CA: Sage.

HARRISON, D. W., GORELCZENKO, P. M., & COOK, J. (1990). Sex differences in the functional asymmetry for facial affect perception. *International Journal of Neuroscience, 52,* 11–16.

HATFIELD, E., & RAPSON, R. L. (1987). Passionate love/sexual desire: Can the same paradigm explain both. *Archives of Sexual Behavior, 16,* 259–278.

HAUSER, M. D. (1993). Right hemisphere dominance for the production of facial expression in monkeys. *Science, 261,* 475–478.

HAZAN, C., & SHAVER, P. (1987). Romantic love conceptualized as an attachment process. *Journal of Personality and Social Psychology, 52,* 511–524.

HAZAN, C., & SHAVER, P. R. (1994). Attachment as an organizational framework for research on close relationships. *Psychological Inquiry, 5,* 1–22.

HEELAS, P. (1986). Emotion talk across cultures. In R. Harré (Ed.), *The social construction of emotions* (pp. 234–266). Oxford: Basil Blackwell.

HEIDEGGER, M. (1927/1962). *Being and time* (Macquarrie, J., & Robinson, E., Trans.). New York: Harper.

HINDE, R. A. (1984). Why do the sexes behave differently in close relationships? *Journal of Social and Personal Relationships, 1,* 471–501.

HOCHSCHILD, A. R. (1979). Emotion work, feeling rules, and social structure. *American Journal of Sociology, 85,* 551–575.

HOCHSCHILD, A. R. (1983). *The managed heart: The commercialization of human feeling.* Berkeley: University of California Press.

HOHMANN, G. W. (1966). Some effects of spinal cord lesions on experienced emotional feelings. *Psychophysiology, 3,* 143–156.

HOOVER-DEMPSEY, K. V., PLAS, J. M., & STRUDLER WALLSTON, B. (1986). Tears and weeping among professional women: In search of new understanding. *Psychology of Women Quarterly, 10,* 19–34.

HORN, M. (Ed.). (1976). *The world encyclopedia of comics.* New York: Chelsea House.

HOWARD, J. A., BLUMSTEIN, P., & SCHWARTZ, P. (1987). Social or evolutionary theories? Some observations on preferences in human mate selection. *Journal of Personality and Social Psychology, 53,* 194–200.

HULL, C. L. (1943). *Principles of behavior.* New York: Appleton-Century.

ISAACSON, R. L. (1974). *The limbic system.* New York: Plenum.

IZARD, C. (1971). *The face of emotion.* New York: Appleton-Century-Crofts.

IZARD, C. (1977). *Human emotions.* New York: Plenum.

IZARD, C. (1979). *The maximally discriminative facial movement coding system (Max).* Newark: University of Delaware, Instructional Resources Center.

IZARD, C. E. (1981). Differential emotions theory and the facial feedback hypothesis of emotion activation: Comments on Tourangeau and Ellsworth's "The role of facial response in the experience of emotion." *Journal of Personality and Social Psychology, 40,* 350–354.

IZARD, C. E. (1983). Emotions in personality and culture. *Ethos, 11,* 305 312.

IZARD, C. E. (1990). "The substrates and functions of emotion feelings." William James and current emotion theory. *Personality and Social Psychology Bulletin, 16,* 626–635.

IZARD, C. E. (1992). Basic emotions, relations among emotions, and emotion-cognition relations. *Psychological Review, 99,* 561–565.

IZARD, C. E. (1994). Innate and universal facial expressions: Evidence from developmental and cross-cultural research. *Psychological Bulletin, 115,* 288 299.

IZARD, C. E., & HAYNES, O. M. (1987). On the form and universality of the contempt expression: A challenge to Ekman and Friesen's claim of discovery. *Motivation and Emotion, 11,* 1–15.

IZARD, C. E., & PHILLIPS, R. D. (1989). Emotions from a different perspective (Review of Rom Harré's "The social construction of emotion"). *Contemporary Psychology, 34,* 362.

JACOBS, B. L. (1994). Serotonin, motor activity and depression-related disorders. *American Scientist, 82,* 456–463.

JAMES, W. (1884). What is an emotion? *Mind, 19,* 188–205.

JAMES, W. (1887). Review of *Romantic love and personal beauty* by Henry T. Finck. *The Nation, 45,* 237–238.

JAMES, W. (1890/1983). *The principles of psychology.* Cambridge: Harvard University Press.

JAMES, W. (1894). The physical basis of emotion. *Psychological Review, 1,* 516–529.

JAMES, W. (1899/1912). *Talks to teachers on psychology: And to students on some of life's ideals.* New York: Henry Holt.

KATKIN, E. S. (1985). Blood, sweat, and tears: Individual differences in autonomic self-perception. *Psychophysiology, 22,* 125–137.

KATKIN, E. S., BLASCOVICH, J., & GOLDBAND, S. (1981). Empirical assessment of visceral self-perception: Individual and sex differences in the acquisition of heartbeat discrimination. *Journal of Personality and Social Psychology, 40,* 1095–1101.

KELLEY, K., & BYRNE, D. (1983). Assessment of sexual responding: Arousal, affect, and behavior. In J. T. Cacioppo & R. E. Petty (Eds.), *Social psychophysiology: A sourcebook* (pp. 467–490). New York: Guilford Press.

KELLOGG, R., & BARON, R. S. (1975). Attribution theory, insomnia, and the reverse placebo effect: A reversal of Storms' and Nisbett's findings. *Journal of Personality and Social Psychology, 32,* 231–236.

KELTNER, D. (1995). Signs of appeasement: Evidence for the distinct displays of embarrassment, amusement, and shame. *Journal of Personality and Social Psychology, 68,* 441–454.

KEMPER, T. (1987). How many emotions are there? Wedding the social and the autonomic components. *American Journal of Sociology, 93,* 263–289.

KENRICK, D. T., GROTH, G. E., TROST, M. R., & SADELLA, E. K. (1993). Integrating evolutionary and social exchange perspectives on relationships: Effects of gender, self-appraisal, and involvement level on mate selection criteria. *Journal of Personality and Social Psychology, 64,* 951–969.

KITAYAMA, S., & MARKUS, H. R. (Eds.). (1994a). *Emotion and culture: Empirical studies of mutual influence.* Washington, DC: American Psychological Association.

KITAYAMA, S., & MARKUS, H. R. (1994b). Introduction to cultural psychology and emotion research. In S. Kitayama & H. R. Markus (Eds.), *Emotion and culture: Empirical studies of mutual influence* (pp. 1–19). Washington, DC: American Psychological Association.

KLINEBERG, O. (1938). Emotional expression in Chinese literature. *Journal of Abnormal and Social Psychology, 33,* 517–520.

KÖVECSES, Z. (1990). *Emotion concepts.* New York: Springer-Verlag.

KRAEMER, D. L., & HASTRUP, J. L. (1986). Crying in natural settings: Global estimates, self-monitored frequencies, depression and sex differences in an undergraduate population. *Behaviour, Research and Therapy, 24,* 371–373.

KRAUT, R. E., & JOHNSON, R. E. (1979). Social and emotional messages of smiling: An ethological approach. *Journal of Personality and Social Psychology, 37,* 1539–1553.

KUHN, T. S. (1962). *The structure of scientific revolutions.* Chicago: University of Chicago Press.

LABARRE, W. (1947). The cultural basis of emotions and gestures. *Journal of Personality, 16,* 49–68.

LABOTT, S. M., MARTIN, R. B., EASON, P. S., & BERKEY, E. Y. (1991). Social reactions to the expression of emotion. *Cognition and Emotion, 5,* 397–417.

LAIRD, J. D. (1974). Self-attribution of emotion: The effects of expressive behavior on the quality of emotional experience. *Journal of Personality and Social Psychology, 29,* 475–486.

LAIRD, J. D. (1984). The real role of facial response in the experience of emotion: A reply to Tourangeau and Ellsworth and others. *Journal of Personality and Social Psychology, 47,* 909–917.

LAIRD, J. D., & BRESLER, C. (1990). William James and the mechanisms of emotional experience. *Personality and Social Psychology Bulletin, 16,* 636–651.

LAKOFF, G., & KÖVECSES, Z. (1983). The cognitive model of anger inherent in American English. *Berkeley Cognitive Science Report No. 10.*

LANDIS, C., & HUNT, W. A. (1932). Adrenalin and emotion. *Psychological Review, 39,* 467–485.

LANG, P. J. (1979). A bio-informational theory of emotional imagery. *Psychophysiology, 16,* 495–512.

LANGE, C. G. (1885/1922). The emotions: A psychophysiological study. In C. G. Lange & W. James, *The emotions* (pp. 33–90). Baltimore: Williams and Wilkins.

LANGE, C. G., & JAMES, W. (1922). *The emotions.* Baltimore: Williams and Wilkins.

LANZETTA, J. T., CARTWRIGHT-SMITH, J., & KLECK, R. E. (1976). Effects of nonverbal dissimulation on emotional experience and autonomic arousal. *Journal of Personality and Social Psychology, 33,* 354–370.

LAZARUS, R. S. (1982). Thoughts on the relations between emotion and cognition. *American Psychologist, 37,* 1019–1024.

LAZARUS, R. S. (1991a). *Emotion and adaptation.* New York: Oxford University Press.

LAZARUS, R. S. (1991b). Progress on a cognitive-motivational-relational theory of emotion. *American Psychologist, 46,* 819–834.

LAZARUS, R. S. (1993). From psychological stress to the emotions: A history of changing outlooks. *Annual Review of Psychology, 44,* 1–21.

LAZARUS, R. S., & ALFERT, E. (1964). Short-circuiting of threat by experimentally altering cognitive appraisal. *Journal of Abnormal and Social Psychology, 69,* 195–205.

LAZARUS, R. S., & AVERILL, J. R. (1972). Emotion and cognition: With special reference to anxiety. In C. D. Spielberger (Ed.), *Anxiety: Current trends in theory and research,* Vol. 2 (pp. 242–282). San Diego: Academic Press.

LAZARUS, R. S., AVERILL, J. R., & OPTON, E. M., JR. (1970). Toward a cognitive theory of emotions. In M. B. Arnold (Ed.), *Feelings and emotions* (pp. 207–232). New York: Academic Press.

LEDOUX, J. E. (1986). The neurobiology of emotion. In J. E. LeDoux & W. Hirst (Eds.), *Mind and brain: Dialogues in cognitive neuroscience* (pp. 301–354). Cambridge: Cambridge University Press.

LEDOUX, J. E. (1987). Emotion. In F. Plum & V. B. Mountcastle (Eds.), *Handbook of physiology. The nervous system: Vol. 5. Higher function* (pp. 419–459). Washington, DC: American Physiological Society.

LEDOUX, J. E. (1989). Cognitive-emotional interactions in the brain. *Cognition and Emotion, 3,* 267–289.

LEDOUX, J. E. (1995). In search of an emotional system in the brain: Leaping from fear to emotion and consciousness. In M. S. Gazzaniga (Ed.), *The cognitive neurosciences* (pp. 1049–1061). Cambridge: MIT Press.

LERNER, H. G. (1985). *The dance of anger: A woman's guide to changing the patterns of intimate relationships.* New York: Harper and Row.

LEVENSON, R. W. (1992). Autonomic nervous system differences among emotions. *Psychological Science, 3,* 23–27.

LEVENSON, R. W., CARSTENSEN, L. L., FRIESEN, W. V., & EKMAN, P. (1991). Emotion, physiology, and expression in old age. *Psychology and Aging, 6,* 28–35.

LEVENSON, R. W., EKMAN, P., & FRIESEN, W. V. (1990). Voluntary facial action generates emotion-specific autonomic nervous system activity. *Psychophysiology, 27,* 363–384.

LEVY, R. I. (1984). Emotion, knowing, and culture. In R. Shweder & R. LeVine (Eds.),

Culture theory: Essays on mind, self, and emotion (pp. 214–237). Cambridge: Cambridge University Press.

LEWIS, M., & SAARNI, C. (1985). Culture and emotions. In M. Lewis & C. Saarni (Eds.), *The socialization of emotions* (pp. 1–17). New York: Plenum.

LEWIS, R. W. B. (1991). *The Jameses: A family narrative.* New York: Farrar, Straus and Giroux.

LOFTUS, E. F., & LOFTUS, G. R. (1980). On the permanence of stored information in the human brain. *American Psychologist, 35,* 409–420.

LUTZ, C. (1983). Parental goals, ethnopsychology, and the development of emotional meaning. *Ethos, 11,* 246–262.

LUTZ, C. (1985). Cultural patterns and individual differences in the child's emotional meaning system. In M. Lewis & C. Saarni (Eds.), *The socialization of emotions* (pp. 37–53). New York: Plenum.

LUTZ, C. (1986). The domain of emotion words on Ifaluk. In R. Harré (Ed.), *The social construction of emotions* (pp. 267–288). Oxford: Basil Blackwell.

LUTZ, C., & WHITE, G. M. (1986). The anthropology of emotions. *Annual Review of Anthropology, 15,* 405–436.

LUTZ, C. A. (1988). *Unnatural emotions: Everyday sentiments on a Micronesian atoll and their challenge to Western theory.* Chicago: University of Chicago Press.

LUTZ, C. A., & ABU-LUGHOD, L. (Eds.). (1990). *Language and the politics of emotion.* Cambridge: Cambridge University Press.

MACDOWELL, K. A., & MANDLER, G. (1989). Construction of emotion: Discrepancy, arousal, and mood. *Motivation and Emotion, 13,* 105–124.

MAGNUSSEN, S., SUNDE, B., & DYRNES, S. (1994). Patterns of perceptual asymmetry in processing facial expression. *Cortex, 30,* 215–229.

MALATESTA, C. Z., FIORE, M. J., & MESSINA, J. J. (1987). Affect, personality, and facial expressive characteristics of older people. *Psychology and Aging, 2,* 64–69.

MANDLER, G. (1975). *Mind and emotion.* New York: Wiley.

MANDLER, G. (1990). William James and the construction of emotion. *Psychological Science, 1,* 179–180.

MANDLER, G., MANDLER, J. M., & UVILLER, E. T. (1958). Autonomic feedback: The perception of autonomic activity. *Journal of Abnormal and Social Psychology, 56,* 367–373.

MANSTEAD, A. S. R., & TETLOCK, P. E. (1989). Cognitive appraisals and emotional experience: Further evidence. *Cognition and Emotion, 3,* 225–240.

MARAÑON, G. (1924). Contribution à l'étude de l'action émotive de l'adrénaline. *Revue Française d'Endocrinologie, 2,* 301–325.

MARSHALL, G. D., & ZIMBARDO, P. G. (1979). Affective consequences of inadequately explained physiological arousal. *Journal of Personality and Social Psychology, 37,* 970–988.

MARX, K. (1897/1977). *Das Kapital.* New York: Vintage Books.

MASLACH, C. (1979). Negative emotional biasing of unexplained arousal. *Journal of Personality and Social Psychology, 37,* 953–969.

MATSUMOTO, D. (1987). The role of facial response in the experience of emotion: More methodological problems and a meta-analysis. *Journal of Personality and Social Psychology, 52,* 769–774.

MATSUMOTO, D. (1990). Cultural similarities and differences in display rules. *Motivation and Emotion, 14,* 195–214.

McGUIRE, W. J. (1983). A contextualist theory of knowledge: Its implications for innovation and reform in psychological research. In L. Berkowitz (Ed.), *Advances in experimental social psychology*, Vol. 16 (pp. 1–47). Orlando, FL: Academic Press.

McHUGH, P. (1968). *Defining the situation: The organization of meaning in social interaction*. Indianapolis: Bobbs-Merrill.

McKELLIGOTT, J. W. (1959). Autonomic functions and affective states in spinal cord injury. Unpublished doctoral dissertation, University of California, Los Angeles.

McMULLIN, E. (Ed.). (1988). *Construction and constraints: The shaping of scientific rationality*. South Bend, IN: University of Notre Dame Press.

McNAUGHTON, N. (1989). *Biology and emotion*. Cambridge: Cambridge University Press.

MELLEN, S. L. W. (1981). *The evolution of love*. San Francisco: Freeman.

MERCHANT, C. (1979). *The death of nature. Women, ecology, and the scientific revolution: A feminist reappraisal of the scientific revolution*. San Francisco: Harper and Row.

MESQUITA, B., & FRIJDA, N. H. (1992). Cultural variations in emotions: A review. *Psychological Bulletin, 112*, 179–204.

MIDDLETON, D. R. (1986). The production and management of fear in urban contexts. In D. L. Scruton (Ed.), *Sociophobics: The anthropology of fear* (pp. 122–141). Boulder, CO: Westview Press.

MILDER, B. (1975). The lacrimal apparatus. In R. A. Moses (Ed.), *Adler's physiology of the eye: Clinical application* (pp. 18–37). St. Louis: C. V. Mosby.

MILLER, J. B. (1991). The construction of anger in women and men. In J. Jordon, A. Kaplan, J. B. Miller, I. Stiver, & J. Surrey (Eds.), *Women's growth in connection: Writings from the Stone Center* (pp. 181–196). New York: Guilford Press.

MILLS, T., & KLEINMAN, S. (1988). Emotions, reflexivity, and action: An interactionist analysis. *Social Forces, 66*, 1009–1027.

MINSKY, M. (1986). *The society of mind*. New York: Simon and Schuster.

MODELL, J. (1988). Meanings of love: Adoption literature and Dr. Spock, 1946–1985. In C. Z. Stearns & P. N. Stearns (Eds.), *Emotion and social change: Toward a new psychohistory* (pp. 151–191). New York: Holmes and Meier.

MOONEY, T. (1981). *Easy travel to other planets*. New York: Farrar, Strauss and Giroux.

MOORE, M. S. (1987). The moral worth of retribution. In F. Schoeman (Ed.), *Responsibility, character, and the emotions: New essays in moral psychology* (pp. 179–219). Cambridge: Cambridge University Press.

MORELAND, R. L., & ZAJONC, R. B. (1977). Is stimulus recognition a necessary condition for the occurrence of exposure effects? *Journal of Personality and Social Psychology, 35*, 191–199.

MORELAND, R. L., & ZAJONC, R. B. (1979). Exposure effects may not depend on stimulus recognition. *Journal of Personality and Social Psychology, 37*, 1085–1089.

MORRIS, C. G. (1993). *Psychology: An introduction* (8th ed.). Englewood Cliffs, NJ: Prentice-Hall.

MORROW, J., & NOLEN-HOEKSEMA, S. (1990). Effects of responses to depression on the remediation of depressive affect. *Journal of Personality and Social Psychology, 58*, 519–527.

MORSHBACH, H., & TYLER, W. J. (1986). A Japanese emotion: Amae. In R. Harré (Ed.), *The social construction of emotions* (pp. 289–307). Oxford: Basil Blackwell.

MOTLEY, M. T., & CAMDEN, C. T. (1988). Facial expression of emotion: A comparison of posed expressions versus spontaneous expressions in an interpersonal communication setting. *Western Journal of Speech Communication, 52,* 1–22.

MYERS, G. E. (1986). *William James: His life and thought.* New Haven: Yale University Press.

NAKAMURA, M., BUCK, R., & KENNY, D. A. (1990). Relative contribution of expressive behavior and contextual information to the judgment of the emotional state of another. *Journal of Personality and Social Psychology, 59,* 1032–1039.

NEISSER, U. (1967). *Cognitive psychology.* New York: Appleton-Century-Crofts.

NISBETT, R. E., & SCHACHTER, S. (1966). Cognitive manipulations of pain. *Journal of Experimental Social Psychology, 2,* 227–236.

NISBETT, R. E., & WILSON, T. D. (1977). Telling more than we can know: Verbal reports on mental processes. *Psychological Review, 87,* 231–259.

NYDICK, A., & CORNELIUS, R. R. (1984). *What we talk about when we talk about love.* In Second International Conference on Personal Relationships. Madison, WI.

OATLEY, K. (1992). *Best laid schemes: The psychology of emotions.* Cambridge: Cambridge University Press.

OATLEY, K., & DUNCAN, E. (1994). The experience of emotions in everyday life. *Cognition and Emotion, 8,* 369–381.

OATLEY, K., & JOHNSON-LAIRD, P. N. (1987). Towards a cognitive theory of emotions. *Cognition and Emotion, 1,* 29–50.

OCHS, E., & SCHIEFFELIN, B. (1989). Language has a heart. *Text, 9,* 7–25.

OLSON, J. M. (1988). Misattribution, preparatory information and speech anxiety. *Journal of Personality and Social Psychology, 54,* 758–767.

ORNE, M. T. (1962). On the social psychology of the psychology experiment: With particular reference to demand characteristics and their implications. *American Psychologist, 17,* 776–783.

ORTNER, S. B., & WHITEHEAD, H. (1981). *Sexual Meanings: The cultural construction of gender and sexuality.* New York: Cambridge University Press.

ORTONY, A., CLORE, G. L., & COLLINS, A. (1988). *The cognitive structure of emotions.* Cambridge: Cambridge University Press.

ORTONY, A., & TURNER, T. J. (1990). What's basic about basic emotions? *Psychological Review, 97,* 315–331.

OSGOOD, C., MAY, W. H., & MIRON, M. S. (1975). *Cross-cultural universals of affective meaning.* Urbana: University of Illinois Press.

OSTER, H., HEGLEY, D., & NAGEL, L. (1992). Adult judgments and fine-grained analysis of infant facial expressions: Testing the validity of a priori coding formulas. *Developmental Psychology, 28,* 1115–1131.

PAPEZ, J. (1937). A proposed mechanism of emotion. *Archives of Neurology and Psychiatry, 38,* 725–743.

PARKES, C. M., & STEVENSON-HINDE, J. (Eds.). (1982). *The place of attachment in human behavior.* New York: Basic Books.

PENNEBAKER, J. (1982). *The psychology of physical symptoms.* New York: Springer-Verlag.

PENNEBAKER, J. W., & ROBERTS, T. A. (1992). Toward a his and hers theory of emotion: Gender differences in visceral perception. *Journal of Social and Clinical Psychology, 11,* 199–212.

PETERS, R. S. (1970). The education of the emotions. In M. B. Arnold (Ed.), *Feeling and emotions: The Loyola symposium* (pp. 187–203). New York: Academic Press.

PLUTCHIK, R. (1962). *The emotions: Facts, theories and a new model.* New York: Random House.

PLUTCHIK, R. (1980). *Emotion: A psychoevolutionary synthesis.* New York: Harper and Row.

PLUTCHIK, R. (1984). Emotions: A general psychoevolutionary theory. In K. R. Scherer & P. Ekman (Eds.), *Approaches to emotion* (pp. 197–219). Hillsdale, NJ: Erlbaum.

PLUTCHIK, R., & AX, A. F. (1967). A critique of "Determinants of emotional state" (by Schachter and Singer, 1962). *Psychophysiology, 4,* 79–82.

POPE, L. K., & SMITH, C. A. (1994). On the distinct meanings of smiles and frowns. *Cognition and Emotion, 8,* 65–72.

POSNER, M. I., & SNYDER, C. R. R. (1975). Facilitation and inhibition in the processing of signals. In P. M. A. Rabbitt & S. Dornic (Eds.), *Attention and performance.* New York: Academic Press.

PROXMIRE, W. (1980). *The fleecing of America.* Boston: Houghton Mifflin.

PRYOR, J. B., REEDER, G. D., & MCMANUS, J. A. (1991). Fear and loathing in the workplace: Reactions to AIDS-infected co-workers. *Personality and Social Psychology Bulletin, 17,* 133–139.

RAFAELI, A. (1989). When clerks meet customers. A test of variables related to emotion expressions on the job. *Journal of Applied Psychology, 74,* 385–393.

REISENZEIN, R. (1983). The Schachter theory of emotion: Two decades later. *Psychological Bulletin, 94,* 239–264.

REISENZEIN, R., & SCHÖNPFLUG, W. (1992). Stumpf's cognitive-evaluative theory of emotion. *American Psychologist, 47,* 34–45.

RISKIND, J. H., & GOTAY, C. C. (1982). Physical posture: Could it have regulatory or feedback effects on motivation and emotion? *Motivation and Emotion, 6,* 273–298.

ROBERTS, T. A., & PENNEBAKER, J. W. (1995). Gender differences in perceiving internal state: Toward a his-and-hers model of perceptual cue use. In M. P. Zanna (Eds.), *Advances in experimental social psychology,* Vol. 27 (pp. 143–175). Orlando, FL: Academic Press.

ROBINSON, R. G., KUBOS, K. L., STARR, L. B., RAO, K., & PRICE, T. R. (1984). Mood disorders in stroke patients: Importance of location of lesion. *Brain, 107,* 81–93.

ROSALDO, M. Z. (1980). *Knowledge and passion: Ilongot notions of self and social life.* Cambridge: Cambridge University Press.

ROSALDO, R. (1989). *Culture and truth: The remaking of social analysis.* Boston: Beacon Press.

ROSEMAN, I. J. (1984). Cognitive determinants of emotion. In P. Shaver (Ed.), *Review of personality and social psychology:* Vol. 5. *Emotions, relationships and health* (pp. 11–36). Beverly Hills, CA: Sage.

ROSEMAN, I. J. (1991). Appraisal determinants of discrete emotions. *Cognition and Emotion, 5,* 161–200.

ROSEMAN, I. J., SPINDEL, M. S., & JOSE, P. E. (1990). Appraisals of emotion-eliciting events: Testing a theory of discrete emotions. *Journal of Personality and Social Psychology, 59,* 899–915.

ROSEMAN, I. J., WIEST, C., & SWARTZ, T. S. (1994). Phenomenology, behaviors, and goals differentiate discrete emotions. *Journal of Personality and Social Psychology, 67,* 206–221.

ROSEN, R. C., & BECK, J. G. (1988). *Patterns of sexual arousal: Psychophysiological processes and clinical applications*. New York: Guilford Press.

ROZIN, P., & FALLON, A. E. (1987). A perspective on disgust. *Psychological Review, 94*, 23–41.

RUSSELL, J. A. (1991a). The contempt expression and the relativity thesis. *Motivation and Emotion, 15*, 149–168.

RUSSELL, J. A. (1991b). Culture and the categorization of emotions. *Psychological Bulletin, 110*, 426–450.

RUSSELL, J. A. (1994). Is there universal recognition of emotion from facial expression? A review of the cross-cultural studies. *Psychological Bulletin, 115*, 102–141.

RUSSELL, J. A., & FEHR, B. (1987). Relativity in the perception of emotion in facial expressions. *Journal of Experimental Psychology: General, 117*, 89–90.

SABINI, J., & SILVER, M. (1982). *Moralities of everyday life*. Oxford: Oxford University Press.

SACKEIM, H. A., GUR, R. C., & SAUCY, M. C. (1978). Emotions are expressed more intensely on the left side of the face. *Science, 202*, 434–436.

SCHACHTER, S. (1959). *The psychology of affiliation*. Palo Alto, CA: Stanford University Press.

SCHACHTER, S. (1964). The interaction of cognitive and physiological determinants of emotional state. In L. Berkowitz (Ed.), *Advances in experimental social psychology* (pp. 49–80). New York: Academic Press.

SCHACHTER, S. (1967). Cognitive effects on bodily functioning: Studies of obesity and eating. In D. C. Glass (Ed.), *Neurophysiology and emotion*. New York: Rockefeller University Press and Russell Sage Foundation.

SCHACHTER, S. (1980). Non-psychological explanations of behavior. In L. Festinger (Ed.), *Retrospections on social psychology* (pp. 131–157). New York: Oxford University Press.

SCHACHTER, S., & SINGER, J. E. (1962). Cognitive, social, and physiological determinants of emotional state. *Psychological Review, 69*, 379–399.

SCHACHTER, S., & WHEELER, L. (1962). Epinephrine, Chlorpromazine, and amusement. *Journal of Abnormal and Social Psychology, 65*, 121–128.

SCHERER, K. R. (1988). Criteria for emotion-antecedent appraisal: A review. In V. Hamilton, G. H. Bower, & N. H. Frijda (Eds.), *Cognitive perspectives on emotion and motivation* (pp. 89–126). Dordrecht: Nijhoff.

SCHERER, K. R. (1993). Studying the emotion-antecedent appraisal process: An expert system approach. *Cognition and Emotion, 7*, 325–355.

SCHOEMAN, F. (Ed.). (1987). *Responsibility, character, and the emotions: New essays in moral psychology*. Cambridge: Cambridge University Press.

SCHWARTZ, G. E., WEINBERGER, D. A., & SINGER, J. A. (1981). Cardiovasular differentiation of happiness, sadness, anger, and fear following imagery and exercise. *Psychosomatic Medicine, 43*, 343–364.

SCOTT, J. P. (1958). *Animal behavior*. Chicago: University of Chicago Press.

SCOTT, J. P. (1980). The functions of emotions in behavioral systems: A systems theory analysis. In R. Plutchik & H. Kellerman (Eds.), *Emotion: Theory, research and experience*, Vol. 1 (pp. 35–56). New York: Academic Press.

SCRUTON, D. L. (1986). The anthropology of an emotion. In D. L. Scruton (Ed.), *Sociophobics* (pp. 7–49). Boulder, CO: Westview Press.

SHAUGHNESSY, J. J., & ZECHMEISTER, E. B. (1994). *Research methods in psychology*. New York: McGraw-Hill.

SHAVER, P., SCHWARTZ, J., KIRSON, D., & O'CONNOR, C. (1987). Emotion knowledge: Further exploration of a prototype approach. *Journal of Personality and Social Psychology, 52*, 1061–1086.

SHAVER, P. R., HAZAN, C., & BRADSHAW, D. (1988). Love as attachment: The integration of three behavioral systems. In R. J. Sternberg & M. L. Barnes (Eds.), *The psychology of love* (pp. 68–99). New Haven: Yale University Press.

SHAVER, P. R., WU, S., & SCHWARTZ, J. C. (1992). Cross-cultural similarities and differences in emotion and its representation: A prototype approach. In M. S. Clark (Ed.), *Emotion* (pp. 175–212). Newbury Park, CA: Sage.

SHIELDS, S. A. &. SHIELDS, R. M. (1979). Emotion: The perception of bodily change. In P. Pliner, K. R. Blankstein, & I. M. Spigel (Eds.), *Perception of emotion in self and others: Advances in the study of communication and affect,* Vol. 5 (pp. 85–106). New York: Plenum.

SMITH, A. C., & KLEINMAN, S. (1989). Managing emotions in medical school: Students' contacts with the living and the dead. *Social Psychology Quarterly, 52,* 56–69.

SMITH, C. A. (1989). Dimensions of appraisal and physiological response to emotion. *Journal of Personality and Social Psychology, 56,* 339–353.

SMITH, C. A., & ELLSWORTH, P. C. (1985). Patterns of cognitive appraisal in emotion. *Journal of Personality and Social Psychology, 48,* 813–838.

SMITH, C. A., & ELLSWORTH, P. C. (1987). Patterns of appraisal and emotions related to taking an exam. *Journal of Personality and Social Psychology, 52,* 475–488.

SMITH, C. A., & LAZARUS, R. S. (1993). Appraisal components, core relational themes, and the emotions. *Cognition and Emotion, 7,* 233–269.

SMITH, C. A., & POPE, L. K. (1992). Appraisal and emotion: The interactional contributions of dispositional and situational factors. In M. S. Clark (Ed.), *Emotion and social behavior: Review of personality and social psychology,* Vol. 14 (pp. 32–62). Newbury Park, CA: Sage.

SNYDER, C. R. (1994). *The psychology of hope*. New York: Free Press.

SNYDER, M. (1974). Self-monitoring of expressive behavior. *Journal of Personality and Social Psychology, 30,* 526–537.

SOLLIER, P. (1894). Recherches sur les rapports de la sensibilité et de l'émotion. *Revue Philosophique, 37,* 241–266.

SOLOMON, R. C. (1976). *The passions*. Berkeley: University of California Press.

SOLOMON, R. C. (1981). *Love: Emotion, myth and metaphor*. Garden City, NY: Anchor Press/Doubleday.

SPEISMAN, J. C., LAZARUS, R. S., MORDKOFF, A., & DAVISON, L. (1964). Experimental reduction of stress based on ego-defense theory. *Journal of Abnormal and Social Psychology, 68,* 367–380.

SPELLMAN, E. V. (1989). Anger and insubordination. In A. Garry & M. Pearsail (Eds.), *Women, knowledge and reality: Explorations in feminist philosophy* (pp. 263–273). Boston: Unwin Hyman.

SPERRY, R. W. (1993). The impact and promise of the cognitive revolution. *American Psychologist, 48,* 878–885.

STEARNS, C. Z., & STEARNS, P. N. (1986). *Anger: The struggle for emotional control in America's history*. Chicago: University of Chicago Press.

STEARNS, C. Z., & STEARNS, P. N. (Eds.). (1988). *Emotion and social change: Toward a new psychohistory.* New York: Holmes and Meier.

STEINKE, P., & SHIELDS, S. A. (1992). *Self-report as a research methodology: Innovation from "limitations."* Unpublished manuscript, University of California, Davis.

STEPPER, S., & STRACK, F. (1993). Proprioceptive determinants of emotional and non-emotional feelings. *Journal of Personality and Social Psychology, 64,* 211–220.

STOPPARD, J. M., & GUNN GRUCHY, C. D. (1993). Gender, context, and the expression of positive emotion. *Personality and Social Psychology Bulletin, 19,* 143–150.

STORMS, M. D., & NISBETT, R. E. (1970). Insomnia and the attribution process. *Journal of Personality and Social Psychology, 16,* 319–328.

STOTLAND, E. (1969). *The psychology of hope.* San Francisco: Josey-Bass.

STRACK, F., STEPPER, S., & MARTIN, L. L. (1988). Inhibiting and facilitating conditions of the human smile: A nonobtrusive test of the facial feedback hypothesis. *Journal of Personality and Social Psychology, 54,* 768–777.

STRONGMAN, K. T. (1973). *The psychology of emotion.* Chichester: Wiley.

SULLIVAN, H. S. (1953). *The interpersonal theory of psychiatry.* New York: W. W. Norton.

TAYLOR, E. (1990). William James on Darwin: An evolutionary theory of consciousness. *Annals of the New York Academy of Sciences, 602,* 7–33.

THOMAS, S. P. (Ed.). (1993). *Women and anger.* New York: Springer.

TINBERGEN, N. (1952). "Derived" activities; their causation, biological significance, origin and emancipation during evolution. *Quarterly Review of Biology, 27,* 1–32.

TITCHENER, E. B. (1914). An historical note on the James-Lange theory of emotion. *American Journal of Psychology, 25,* 425–447.

TOMKINS, S. S. (1962). *Affect, imagery, and consciousness: Vol. 1. The positive affects.* New York: Springer.

TOMKINS, S. S. (1975). The phantasy behind the face. *Journal of Personality Assessment, 39,* 550–562.

TOMKINS, S. S. (1981). The role of facial response in the experience of emotion: A reply to Tourangeau and Ellsworth. *Journal of Personality and Social Psychology, 40,* 355–357.

TOOBY, J., & COSMIDES, L. (1990). The past explains the present: Emotional adaptations and the structure of ancestral environments. *Ethology and Sociobiology, 11,* 375–424.

TOURANGEAU, R., & ELLSWORTH, P. C. (1979). The role of facial response in the experience of emotion. *Journal of Personality and Social Psychology, 37,* 1519–1531.

TURKLE, S. (1984). *The second self: Computers and the human spirit.* New York: Simon and Schuster.

VALENTINE, G. (1989). The geography of women's fear. *Area, 21,* 385–390.

WAGNER, H. (1988). The theory and application of social psychophysiology. In H. L. Wagner (Ed.), *Social psychophysiology and emotion: Theory and clinical applications* (pp. 1–15). Chichester: Wiley.

WALSTER [HATFIELD], E. (1971). Passionate love. In B. I. Murstein (Ed.), *Theories of attraction and love* (pp. 85–99). New York: Springer.

WATTERSON, B. (1988). *The essential Calvin and Hobbes.* Kansas City, MO: Andrews and McMeel.

WEINER, J. (1994). *The beak of the finch: A story of evolution in our time.* New York: Knopf.

WIERZBICKA, A. (1986). Human emotions: Universal or culture-specific? *American Anthropologist, 88,* 584–594.

WIERZBICKA, A. (1994). Emotion, language, and cultural scripts. In S. Kitayama & H. R. Markus (Eds.), *Emotion and culture: Empirical studies of mutual influence* (pp. 133–196). Washington, DC: American Psychological Association.

WILSON, E. O. (1984). *Biophilia.* Cambridge: Harvard University Press.

WILSON, G. (1983). *Love and instinct.* New York: Quill.

WILSON, T. D. (1985). Strangers to ourselves: The origins and accuracy of beliefs about one's own mental states. In J. H. Harvey & G. Weary (Eds.), *Attribution: Basic issues and applications* (pp. 9–36). New York: Academic Press.

WINTON, W. M. (1990). Jamesian aspects of misattribution research. *Personality and Social Psychology Bulletin, 16,* 652–664.

WORCHEL, S., & YOHAI, S. M. L. (1979). The role of attribution in the experience of crowding. *Journal of Experimental Social Psychology, 15,* 91–104.

YOUNG, R. K., GALLAHER, P., BELASCO, J., BARR, A., & WEBBER, A. W. (1991). Changes in fear of AIDS and homophobia in a university population. *Journal of Applied Social Psychology, 21,* 1848–1858.

ZAJONC, R. (1980). Feeling and thinking: Preferences need no inferences. *American Psychologist, 35,* 151–175.

ZAJONC, R. (1984). On the primacy of affect. *American Psychologist, 39,* 117–123.

ZAJONC, R. (1985). Emotion and facial efference: A theory reclaimed. *Science, 228,* 15–21.

ZAJONC, R., MURPHY, S. T., & INGLEHART, M. (1989). Feeling and facial efference: Implications of the vascular theory of emotion. *Psychological Bulletin, 96,* 395–416.

ZILLMANN, D. (1978). Attribution and misattribution of excitatory reactions. In J. H. Harvey, W. J. Ickes, & R. F. Kidd (Eds.), *New directions in attribution research* (pp. 335–368). Hillsdale, NJ: Erlbaum.

ZILLMANN, D., & BRYANT, J. (1974). Effect of residual excitation on the emotional response to provocation and delayed aggressive behavior. *Journal of Personality and Social Psychology, 30,* 782–791.

ZILLMANN, D., JOHNSON, R. C., & DAY, K. D. (1974). Attribution of apparent arousal and proficiency of recovery from sympathetic activation affecting excitation transfer to aggressive behavior. *Journal of Experimental Social Psychology, 10,* 503–515.

Index

Markus, H. R., 165
Marlin, M., 99
Marshall, G. D., 88–89
Martin, L. L., 105
Martin, R. B., 178
Marx, K., 151
Maslach, C., 86, 88, 89
Matsumoto, D., 37, 38, 44, 105
Max, 36
May, W. H., 169
McCaffrey, A., 58
McCall, M. A., 91
McGuire, W. J., 6
McHugh, P., 148
McKelligott, J. W., 77
McManus, J. A., 163
McMullin, E., 151
McNaughton, N., 220
Mekons, xiv
Mellen, S. L. W., 198
Merchant, C., 219
Mere exposure effect, 129
Mesquita, B., 154, 158, 164, 166, 210, 213
Messina, J. J., 55
Metagu, 192
Miami Vice, 92
Middlemarch, 138
Middleton, D. R., 164
Milder, B., 221
Miles, M., 13
Miller, J. B., 182
Miller-Herringer, T., 15, 37, 38
Mills, T., 157
Minsky, M., 137
Miron, M. S., 169
Misattribution, 81, 87, 89–91, 93
Miskin, M., 231
Modell, J., 175
Mooney, T., 175
Moore, M. S., 162
Mordkoff, A., 121
Moreland, R. L., 129
Morrow, J., 13
Morshbach, H., 171, 172
Motley, M. T., 45
Multidimensional scaling, 199, 169–70
Multiple regression analysis, 146
Murphy, S. T., 42
Myers, G. E., 71

Nakamura, M., 45
National Science Foundation, 8
Neisser, Ulrich
    Cognitive Psychology, 131
Nervous system, divisions of, 221
Neurotransmitters, 223
Nicassio, P., 90
Nisbett, R. E., 14, 81, 82, 90
Nolen-Hoeksema, S., 13
Norepinephrine, 223
Norm of conciliation. *See* Averill, James
Norm of retribution. *See* Averill, James
Nuclei, 223

Nunley, E. P., 212
Nydick, A., 202, 204

O'Connor, C., 49, 173, 189
O'Lucky Man (Anderson), 100
O'Sullivan, M., 44
Oatley, K., 3, 134–38, 155, 174
Occipital lobe, 226
Ochs, E., 166
Olson, J. M., 90
Operational definitions, 5, 54–55
Orne, M. T., 14
Ortner, S. B., 199
Ortony, A., 141, 165, 174, 199
Osgood, C., 169
Oster, H., 45
Ovid, 92, 93–94

Pak, 171
Papez loop, 224, 225–26
Papez, J., 225
Parasympathetic nervous system, 221–23
Parietal lobe, 226
Parkes, C. M., 197
Passion, 156–58
Passions of the Soul (Descartes), 156
Pearsall, M., 151
Peege, 179
Pennebaker, J. W., 98, 99
Pentagon Papers, 150
Peripheral nervous system, 221
Phillips, R. D., 151, 188
Plas, J. M., 178
Plutchik, R., 11, 13, 41, 46–47, 50, 87–88,
    101, 173
Pope, L. K., 14, 146
Posner, M. I., 129
Potency, in multidimensional scaling of
    emotion terms, 170
Price, T. R., 230
Pride, 144
Proxmire, W., 8
Pryor, J. B., 163
Psychophysiology, defined, 14
Puritanism, 175
Pyke, S. W., 5

Radical behaviorism, 114
Rafaeli, A., 182
Rao, K., 230
Rapson, R. L., 199–200
Reeder, G. D., 163
Regret, appraisals associated with, 143, 144
Reisenzein, R., 73, 79, 81, 87, 90, 94
Relief, appraisals associated with, 141, 142,
    143, 144
Resentment, 110, 207
Riskind, J. H., 105
Roberts, T.-A., 99
Robinson, R. G., 230
Rosaldo, M., 171
Rosaldo, R., 151